The Myanmar Economy

Konosuke Odaka
Editor

The Myanmar Economy

Its Past, Present and Prospects

Springer

Editor
Konosuke Odaka
Hitotsubashi University
Tokyo, Japan

ISBN 978-4-431-55734-0 ISBN 978-4-431-55735-7 (eBook)
DOI 10.1007/978-4-431-55735-7

Library of Congress Control Number: 2015951620

Springer Tokyo Heidelberg New York Dordrecht London

Printed on acid-free paper

Springer Japan KK is part of Springer Science+Business Media (www.springer.com)

Foreword

I welcome the publication of this book, which fills a huge void in the knowledge on Myanmar. With its potentials and challenges, this populous Southeast Asian country has attracted a lot of attention and activity, particularly from foreign investors and international development agencies. There has also been an increase in information about the country. However, comprehensive analysis of the fundamental structure of this hitherto-isolated country's economy and its historical background is still very scarce.

Myanmar (Burma) under the British Administration in the early twentieth century was one of the wealthiest in Southeast Asia. However, decades of political turmoil, misguided policies, and the seclusion from the rest of the world have together turned the country into one of the most impoverished in the ASEAN, with the lowest per capita income in the region and deplorable social indicators.

Since its policy change in 2011, the country has embarked on a new journey—a journey towards political reform and economic development. Hopes are high, given its abundant resources including agriculture, forestry, and fisheries and a highly educated labour force and its potential as a market with a population of about 80 million. Many challenges, however, continue to confront Myanmar: poverty, lack of administrative and institutional capacity, poor business environment, and the list goes on.

I am sure that this book will be useful to the leaders and people of Myanmar as well as to those who are supporting them. To grow into a country of abundance—which it deserves to be—Myanmar needs to be led wisely with strategic and realistic development plans with support from international partners; such collective efforts should in turn be based on an accurate, comprehensive, and systematic understanding of the country's economy. I am convinced that this book can be one of the important sources of such a body of knowledge.

I also rejoice at this publication because my agency [Japan International Cooperation Agency (JICA)] has been involved in the process leading up to it. Even during the period of international sanction, Japan continued its cooperation with the country, largely out of humanitarian considerations. One such activity was an intellectual partnership project conducted through JICA from 2000 to 2003. Entitled

"Myanmar–Japan Cooperation Programme for Economic Structural Adjustment of Myanmar", this policy dialogue exercise involved members of academia and high-ranking government officials of the two countries, just like other similar projects for Vietnam (1995–2000) and Laos (2000–2004). Following the submission of the programme's final report to Myanmar's prime minister in 2004, its objective was judged worthwhile to be pursued further, and a small research group was organised at the JICA Research Institute from 2008 to 2010 to follow up the subject. This volume represents a report of this intellectual endeavour, and I am very pleased that it is now available worldwide in book form.

Japan International Cooperation Agency (JICA) Akihiko Tanaka
Tokyo, Japan

Preface

A new light is emerging in the Myanmar economy. Whether or not the economy will progress towards sustained growth greatly depends on how its past structure is transformed and adapted to the new international economic environment. For this purpose, a new road map for market development needs to be drawn and executed, with support both from inside and outside of the country.

As the country has shied away from open contact with the outside world for most of the second half of the twentieth century, neither the international community nor the citizens of Myanmar themselves have been sufficiently informed about the reality of the country's economic conditions. It is essential, under the circumstances, that the public be given accurate information as to the basic tasks required of the economy, where difficulties may lie, and how to overcome them in order to achieve the objective of sustained improvement in economic welfare. This volume aims to fill the gap in understanding these issues with the hope of assisting concerned citizens to formulate a basic policy agenda for the nation. The book's originality, if any, lies in its analyses of Myanmar's economic structures, which seek to identify the socio-economic and historical reasons that have yielded the current conditions in the Myanmar economy. Moreover, these analyses were carried out with the conviction that such knowledge is essential to formulating a policy road map for raising the economic welfare of the nation.

The book is composed of eight chapters and consists essentially of three parts: (1) two chapters (Chaps. 1 and 2) that review past literature; (2) five empirical studies that utilise information collected and analysed by the authors since the end of the twentieth century, which is the result of field surveys and innumerable dialogues with Myanmar citizens, both public and private, in addition to intensive desk studies; and (3) a brief summary and conclusion. Throughout the volume an effort has been made to interpret the outcomes of the studies in light of the nation's economic history, as historical experiences constitute an important socio-political condition in which market development occurs.

The second part of the book, mentioned above, lays out the essential ingredients for drawing a road map for realising the above-mentioned objective. Specifically, it focuses on the issues of financial development, physical social capital, agrarian development, indigenous modern manufactures, and economic relations with China. A brief explanation may be in order here to explain why the five topics have been selected.

When modern economic development began in Myanmar (then called Burma) after its independence, the basic guiding economic principle was chosen to be that of state planning and was later renamed "the Burmese way to socialism". The country's political leaders at the time chose this as a natural testament of their exposure to anti-capitalist ideologies (such as Fabian socialism) in their youth, when they earnestly sought ways and means to assert their country's post-colonial independence.

The planned way of managing the economy through the late 1980s, however, did not quite fulfil original expectations. First of all, its quantity-oriented mindset weighed the role of prices too lightly, leading it to ignore the importance of monetary policy. It is almost imperative to rectify the lingering memory of follies committed by past macro monetary policies (e.g. demonetisation, slow and inadequate action at the time of bank crush, etc.), which may have abetted distrust in the government's economic policies. Furthermore, although in its colonial days Myanmar had earned the title of the top rice exporter in the world, the government's agrarian policy-making, with little concern for proper pricing, failed to improve the efficiency of the country's rice production. On the industrialisation side, its production enterprises, which were in principle state-controlled, tended to be excessively capital-intensive and inefficient due partly to overcapacity and underutilisation and did not create large enough employment opportunities. In addition, as the regime's inward-looking economic policies resulted in a chronic shortage of foreign exchange, the country faced difficulties importing the materials, parts, and components highly essential to manufacturing. These economic policies also made it hard to construct and/or to maintain the sufficient number of electricity-generating stations required for industrialisation.

In 1988, the ruling military junta, who had taken over the socialistic regime, replaced planning with the market principle. However, when the junta was determined to stay in power despite having lost the 1990 general election, international sanctions were imposed on the country and were further strengthened after 2004. These sanctions had the effect of limiting Myanmar's international transactions to a minimum and led the country to seek to establish closer ties with China.

Following the 2010 general election, a new administration was duly established in 2011. The social and international environment of the country changed drastically, as international sanctions were gradually lifted and the market principle could finally be put into practice. It would still take some time, however, before the remnants of the planned economy disappear and the rules of the market assume the full extent of their effects.

Economic development purports to achieve and maintain a reasonable rate of improvement in the standard of living or national income per capita, with little or low rates of inflation. In the early phases of industrialisation, the most important areas for policy consideration are the proper provision of (a) physical social overhead capital and the building of social frameworks for market development, particularly in areas of rulemaking and regulatory devices, and of (b) financial development. It is also essential to mobilise national savings for capital formation and to supply a healthy, motivated labour force (entrepreneurs, administrators, engineers, and production workers). In addition, the choice of industry, as well as that of technology, should be in line with the medium- and long-term comparative advantages of the nation, with due consideration being paid to environmentally friendly resource endowment. Concurrently, there should be a place for public policy to play its role, such as assisting the private sector to overcome information asymmetry, to improve its productive efficiency, and to protect against unforeseeable business risks.

In carrying out this grand task in the age of globalised economic transactions, Myanmar should be able to weave a unique growth strategy. This could best be achieved by taking note of past incidents of failures in economic growth throughout the world and by skilfully inviting the now plentiful international financial sources to assist the national economy to stand on its own feet without resorting to an overly aggressive strategy for industrialisation—as was once adopted by some latecomers to development, such as Japan.

Tokyo, Japan
December 2014

Konosuke Odaka

Acknowledgements

At one time or another since the end of the twentieth century, the authors of this volume have been directly or indirectly involved in intellectual partnership programmes between the governments of Myanmar and Japan. Perhaps for this reason the writing style of the volume is characterised by a sense of identification with the country and with its people.

The origin of the research, on the basis of which this volume is formed, goes back to 1999 and is closely related to the above-mentioned partnerships. The project has continued more or less without interruption since then, always in close association with the Japan International Cooperation Agency (JICA). However, the project to write this book would not have begun without the strong push from Mr. Takahiro Sasaki, who was director of the JICA Myanmar Office in the years 2003–2005. In keeping with Mr. Sasaki's vision to fulfil this project, the JICA Research Institute provided financial assistance during the fiscal years 2008–2011, while Dr. Haruyuki Shimada acted as its coordinator. A report of the project, entitled as "Issues and Challenges for Economic Development in Myanmar", was published in Japanese in 2012 with the title *Myanmar keizai no atarashii hikari* (New Lights of the Myanmar Economy) by Keiso Shobo Publishing Co., Ltd., Tokyo. This volume is a wholly revised, new version of the report, the contents having been updated and rewritten with the exception of the introductory chapter. In executing this study, the authors were guided and assisted by an innumerable number of generously minded persons—too many to list here. I would merely confine myself to expressing the authors' special thanks for the heartfelt encouragement offered from time to time by Retired General David Abel, Dr. Khin San Yee, Professor Myat Thein, U Than Lwin, and U Tin Htut Oo.

The members of the JICA Myanmar Office have repeatedly gone out of their way to arrange research trips, factory visits, professional interviews, discussion meetings with government officers and/or the members of business communities, and much more. Without their efficient and effective assistance, the execution of the research would simply not have been possible. Special thanks go to Professor Hal Hill of the Australian National University for making helpful suggestions and encouraging me to proceed with editing this volume. I also thank Ms. Aiko Aikawa and Mr. Yasuhiko Sato of the JICA Research Institute, who have been instrumental in carrying out the highly complicated process of preparing, editing, and formatting the manuscript and getting in touch with the publisher. Last, but by no means least, I express my appreciation for the favourable comments given by the reviewers on the final version of our manuscripts. These manuscripts are now ready to go to press and to become part of social science volumes from a great publisher.

All the authors of this volume join me in sending our best wishes to the citizens of Myanmar, who are engaged in the highly promising and honourable task of building a unique welfare economy.

May I close this note by stating that the views and interpretations expressed in this volume are those of the authors and do not necessarily represent those of the organisations or the persons mentioned above.

Contents

Contributors

Koichi Fujita Division of Economic and Political Dynamics, Center for Southeast Asian Studies, Kyoto University, Kyoto, Japan

Koji Kubo Bangkok Research Center, Institute of Developing Economies-Japan External Trade Organization (IDE-JETRO), Bangkok, Thailand

Toshihiro Kudo National Graduate Institute for Policy Studies (GRIPS), Tokyo, Japan

Masahiko Matsuda College of International Relations, Ritsumeikan University, Kyoto, Japan

Fumiharu Mieno Division of Economic and Political Dynamics, Center for Southeast Asian Studies, Kyoto University, Kyoto, Japan

Asuka Mizuno Faculty of Economics, Asia University, Tokyo, Japan

Atsuko Mizuno Department of International Economy and Business, Faculty of Economics, Kyushu University, Fukuoka, Japan

Konosuke Odaka Institute of Economic Research, Hitotsubashi University, Tokyo, Japan

Hosei University, Tokyo, Japan

Professional association is as of January 2015.

Chapter 1
A New Light to Shine? Historical Legacies and Prospects for Myanmar's Economy

Konosuke Odaka

1 Introduction: Preconditions for Economic Development

Market development is an essential precondition for economic development, that is, an increase in material welfare for each and every member of society.[1] In turn, political stability and mutual trust among members of a society (citizens) are prerequisites for the development of markets.

In Western economies up to the early twentieth century, these initial conditions were commonly brought about through national unification by way of the formation of nations or, in some cases, city states.[2] Japan's experience was similar. However, in Burma's case,[3] the modern dynasty of the nineteenth century was directly replaced by British colonial rule without the establishment of a nation state. Under dynastic rule, regional markets based on rice agriculture had developed. Each of these markets had its own system of commerce and of artisans. While the Burmese capital

---

The present chapter summarises the author's thoughts based on the sources listed in the conclusion of this chapter. The author is indebted to Dr. Asuka Mizuno for having introduced him to these studies. However, he alone is responsible for the views expressed herein.

[1] The theoretical rationale for interpreting market development and economic development as being closely interrelated processes comes from Ishikawa (1990).

[2] Iwasaki (1998: 119). The theoretical rationale for national unification being a prerequisite for economic development is not self-evident. The case of Canada, a multicultural federation of states, presents a contrast to the industrial development under a centralised government, such as Japan's (see, e.g. Katô 2009 and Japanese Association for Canadian Studies 2009).

[3] Burma (*Bamar*) is the former name for Myanmar. In this chapter, for the sake of convenience, the old name (Burma) will be retained when discussing events in the country prior to 18 June 1989. After this time the name was changed to 'Myanmar', which is the written expression of the term 'Burma' (Ino 1996: 5–8).

K. Odaka (✉)
Institute of Economic Research, Hitotsubashi University, Tokyo, Japan

Hosei University, Tokyo, Japan
e-mail: k-odaka@ier.hit-u.ac.jp

K. Odaka (ed.), *The Myanmar Economy*, DOI 10.1007/978-4-431-55735-7_1

had been established in the city where the king was situated, its social and political institutions were not taken up by the British colonial government.

Traditionally, Burmese society was not based on the concept of the extended family. Little value was placed on the accumulation of material wealth, but rather the emphasis was on compassion and tolerance towards others. Monks and the elderly were respected, and with the exception of public sphere, men and women were treated equally. Although the use and understanding of the written word was not essential for daily life, at the beginning of the nineteenth century, literacy levels among the Burmese were said to have exceeded those of Western countries (Hagen 1956: 7–10).[4]

In Burma, where peace and tolerance were valued above all, neither a legal system nor the concept of contracts was developed. As villages were highly autonomous, there were few common standards shared among the different communities. The monarch did not possess a standing army, nor did it have systems for maintaining public order or settling legal disputes. Essentially it kept no diplomatic relations with foreign powers and, accordingly, rarely entered into external negotiations. Thus, the Burmese society prior to the nineteenth century was static and lacked the preconditions necessary for industrialisation (ibid.: 11–13).

The succession of chiefs was a matter of inheritance. They were 'leaders' but not necessarily 'rulers' and were sometimes murdered if they failed to rule effectively (ibid.: 9). In addition, the order of succession was not predetermined and was frequently a cause of conflict. Hagen argues that if the royal household had been able to predetermine the order of succession, Burma may have averted British occupation (ibid.: 14). In any case, the Burmese dynasties of the nineteenth century did not exercise a strong, self-independent sovereignty over Burma.

2 Contact with the British Empire

Despite its weaknesses of the Burmese dynastic system, the Konbaung Dynasty was a formidable regional power from the end of the eighteenth century up to the beginning of the nineteenth century.[5] During this period, the dynasty succeeded in overtaking Ayutthaya in 1767, repelling invasions by Qing China in 1766–1770,

[4] According to Hagen, the early modern Burmese society lacked the following three social values, which are motivating factors for economic development: respect for strangers, the dignity of business and respect for the opinions of younger generations. While Buddhism does not discourage technological development, it does not promote savings, which are necessary for the accumulation of capital. The reason why Burmese citizens did not value business may be related to the fact that King Mindon ('Mindon Min') did not encourage existing businesses. In addition, it is argued that the lack of interest in science among the Burmese led them, in part, to an indifference to vocational education and training (Hagen 1956: 61–65).

[5] The last six kings of the Konbaung Dynasty were Bodawpaya (1782–1819), Bagyidaw (1819–1837), Tharrawaddy (1837–1846), Pagan (1846–1853), Mindon (1853–1878) and Thibaw (1878–1885). Details of the rule of each of these kings can be found in Cœdès (1962/1980: Pt. 5, Ch. 3).

conquering the Kingdom of Arkan in 1795 and occupying Manipur and Assam in 1814 and 1817, respectively. Its expansionary doctrine, which amounted to the taking over of other sovereignties, also served as the basis for legitimacy of its rule.

However, as a result of its expansionary policies, the Konbaung Dynasty repeatedly came into confrontation with British troops, particularly when it pursued refugees who had fled into British protected territories. This ultimately led to its defeat in the First Anglo-Burmese War (1824–1826). It is said that the cause of the military conflict lay in 'differences in European and Asian concepts of diplomacy and national borders' (Watanabe 2001: 132–133).[6] Subsequent to the War, disputes continued between the two governing rulers over such issues as each side's territorial borders, diplomatic protocols, commercial treaties, tariff negotiations and the treatment of British merchants. Britain was seen by Burma as an obstacle to its management of national affairs, and Burma was viewed by Britain as a hindrance to the pursuit of its commercial interests (ibid.: 132, 136).

In 1852, Britain seized Lower Burma and unilaterally declared its annexation (the Second Anglo-Burmese War).[7] As Burma had lost its open port and access to supplies such as rice, King Mindon (Mindon Min) attempted to consolidate national power and assert political independence by adopting policies to improve the productive potential of domestic industries (much like the Tokugawa shogunate near the end of the Edo era). Specifically, Mindon Min introduced a standardised national tax system (*Thathameda*),[8] attempted to centralise government administration[9] and moved towards 'modernisation' by adopting Western science and technology.[10] However,

> the attempt to centralise government was met with fierce resistance from various domestic factions that stood to lose power, throwing the country into a state of chaos. Due to the influx of cheap imports, the majority of state-owned factories, which attempted to increase the nation's productivity, ended up being a sinkhole for national funds (ibid.: 136).

---

[6] According to Watanabe (2001), in premodern Burma, 'the periphery (of the territory) depended on the central, core region. The nation took the name of the capital. The extent of [center's] influence changed with the brightness of the central core' (p.139). As a result, 'the outer boundaries were not well-defined, and were, by nature, ambiguous and fuzzy' (p.139). However, within this 'premodern' concept of elastic territorial borders, there were some attempts to incorporate a 'modern' notion of geography-based, fixed borders (pp.138–149).

[7] There is no doubt that, from the British perspective at the time, Burma was seen as being of the utmost importance as a source of food (rice) for British India. The primary reason why Britain annexed lower Burma after the First Anglo-Burmese War was precisely to fulfil this goal. As a result, Burma lost its geographical access to the open sea.

[8] This was an attempt to limit the influence of regional feudal lords and regional governmental officials and to consolidate control over citizenry by the central government (Watanabe 2001: 135).

[9] The system for compensation of the royal family and of high officials was abolished and replaced with a salary system, and the judiciary system was revised to enable the central government to better enforce its will (ibid.: 135).

[10] This included the invitation of Western technicians to construct state-owned factories (for the manufacture of silk textiles, cotton textiles, weapons and ammunition, as well as dyeing and sugar refining), the modernisation of army by employing military advisors from France and Italy and the sending off of students to study in France, Italy and Great Britain (ibid.: 135–136).

In addition, under the commercial treaty of 1867, the right of state monopoly—an important source of revenue for the royal family—was restricted to oil, lumber and precious stones and under British pressure was subsequently (in 1882) completely stripped.

In order to stand up to the British, the Burmese dynastic government attempted (unsuccessfully) to establish closer ties with France. In 1885, arbitrations regarding the financial penalty imposed by the Burmese authority on the Bombay Burmah Trading Corporation for the under-reporting of teak production broke down. The Corporation had previously (since 1862) enjoyed an exclusive right to the timber harvest in the kingdom. The failure of the arbitration was taken by the Viceroy of India as an opportunity to send an ultimatum to the Burmese dynastic government. The refusal of the latter to submit to the former's rule led to the outbreak of the Third Anglo-Burmese War (November 13), which resulted in the surrender of the capital Mandalay, with no exchange of fire, on the 28th day of the same month, and the arrest and imprisonment of King Thibaw in Bombay (ibid.: 137).

3 Burma Under Colonial Rule

In January of 1886, Britain decided to annex Upper Burma, which it had occupied for some time.[11] Although resistance movements erupted throughout the country, each of these had been suppressed by force by 1895, with reinforcements coming from India or the police. Royalty was abolished, and thereafter, an entirely new bureaucratic system—one that did not utilise any dynastic governmental structures—was put in into place (ibid.: 138). The British, having encountered so much trouble in getting Burma to surrender, had come to the conclusion that it would be disadvantageous for them to rely on the institutions and practices that had been permeated with the vestiges of the dynastic rule. Specifically, *myo*[12]—the regional administrative units developed during the Konbaung Dynasty—were dismantled and individual villages reorganised into terminal administrative units, which were then directly connected to the central colonial government. The traditional ruling class, who had held together the indigenous society by acting as representatives for regional interests in the dynastic ruling, was replaced by the cold bureaucracy of

[11] There was some discussion among the British government, Indian office and the branch office in Lower Burma, of making Burma a protected territory rather than annexing it. However, given the bitter history of British-Burmese relations, it was decided that it would be difficult to gain control of an Upper Burma under dynastic control (ibid.: 137–138).

[12] *Myo* were defined not by their territorial relationship but by interpersonal connectivity (ethnic/military). Comprising several villages (*ywa*), the concept of *myo* did not include criteria such as land area or production output. The village chief (*myo daji*) collected taxes from villagers, which he donated to the king after having withheld a certain portion thereof as a handling fee. During times of war, he was obliged to mobilise troops as well as to help fund the war effort (Saito 1991: 120, 123–125, 133). The law dismantling of *myo* was officially enacted in 1897 in Upper Burma and later codified in the Burma Towns Act of 1907 (Watanabe 2001: 149).

colonial government clerks. These clerks had won their positions by passing tests in English proficiency and knowledge of administrative procedures and whose purpose was to transmit and carry out the will of the colonial authorities.

The Indian Civil Service (ICS) was charged with the mission of governing colonial Burma. While it was not surprising that a large number of British civil servants were sent to administer the ICS, the actual management and day-to-day governance were largely performed by Indian government officials under the direction of the ICS. The ICS comprised diverse groups with differing values, including Indians and Karen Christians, who functioned as police. These changes in social environment shocked and evoked anxiety among the Burmese peasants, leading to the aforementioned resistance movements which served as the undercurrent for subsequent grass-root resistance movements (ibid.: 149).

The new British (or Indian)-style bureaucratic system, which was overly reliant on rules (legal rationality), differed in essence from the hereditary style of Burmese governance, which was based on respect for personal networks. The former seemed 'heartless' to the native Burmese who came under its rule. National holidays that were associated with the dynastic regime were eliminated or barely allowed to continue after having been stripped of their meaning (e.g. through the changing of dates upon which the holidays were held). On the other hand, British holidays were celebrated only by the British and were not assimilated into Burmese culture.

Numerous British, Indians and Chinese came to live and work in Burma under colonial rule, so that Burma was, in a way, transformed into a pluralistic society. However, each of these groups formed its own intra-group communities with little intergroup interaction. In this sense, Burmese society could be characterised as a 'multitiered' society.[13]

Burmese society was comprised of a number of ethnic minorities in addition to the majority Burmese. The British strategy was to respect the autonomy of these ethnic groups and to manipulate their reciprocal interests in order to conciliate their resistance towards the colonial authority.[14] It can be said that 'national unity was prevented by segmenting ethnic groups' (Nu 1952: 9). As a result, conflicts and rivalries were fomented and even intensified among ethnic minorities, as well as between ethnic minorities and the majority Burmese. These conflicts easily disrupted cooperative relationships between ethnic groups.[15] Previous conflicts

[13]The expression used by Furnivall is 'two-tier society' (explained below). This is related to the argument by Boeke (explained later) that Indonesia was a 'two-tier society' (explained later) . Furnivall used 'two-tier society' to describe the separation *and* coexistence of Burmese and non-Burmese. There was a clear discrepancy between the two groups of residents in Burma in terms of income and participation in society. In other words, Burmese and non-Burmese were differentiated within the society. As a result, there existed a division in the labour markets for Burmese and non-Burmese that could not be crossed, and there was a clear difference in the economic remuneration between groups even for workers doing the same job.

[14]This was also the reason why ethnic Karens, many of whom were Christians, were appointed to important posts within the colonial government.

[15]According to Robert Taylor, the reasons why national unification was difficult for Burma following independence in 1948 included the fact that (a) Burma's regional boundaries were established

between ethnic groups, which had been quelled by the beginning of the nineteenth century, were thus reignited under the British rule. Finally, the majority of the colonial army consisted of Indian soldiers, while the members of Burmese and Shan ethnic groups, having been designated as 'dangerous people' by the colonial government, were excluded from the army (Hagen 1956: 27).

According to U Nu (1952: 4), the guiding principle of the British rule was to make profit. To achieve this goal, Britain monopolised profitable economic activities, accumulated raw materials and sent them home and forced its colonies to import finished products manufactured in Britain at as high a price as possible.

At the time of British colonial rule, four major profit-making activities were under British control: (1) milling and selling of rice, (2) the extraction of oil and of mining resources, (3) timber and (4) domestic marine transport. While (1) was profitable for Burma, it was under the control of British merchants,[16] and (2) was difficult for locals, as it was a capital-intensive activity that required specialised management skills and information about the international market. Moreover, even if the Burmese had wanted to nationalise (2), (3) and (4), it would have required permission from the colonial governor (ibid.: 6–8).[17] Finally, while the operation of domestic marine transport was simple and the Burmese would have liked to have operated it, this would also have required permission from the governor (ibid.: 8).

By the start of the Second World War, Rangoon (now called Yangon) had been transformed into one of the world's most advanced harbour cities through the development of natural resources, the creation of a railway system and a network of roads and the construction of a harbour under British rule. Although rice plantations were not established, the local farmers had to hand over their rice harvest, which was intended for export, to foreign rice millers and exporters. From 1886, the teak harvest was managed by the Ministry of Forests. Burma's natural resource exports also included oil and minerals. These, however, amounted to only 2–3 % of the world's production and paled in comparison to its export of rice (Hagen 1956: 16–17).

At the beginning of colonial rule, agricultural income started to increase. Yet it is doubtful that this trend continued after 1880. The oil and mineral industries employed Indian and Chinese workers, and the profits ended up in the hands of the British rather than in the coffers of the Burmese government. Burma did however profit indirectly from increased employment and spending. The development of means of transportation and a reduction in transportation costs led naturally to urbanisation, and thanks to the increase in foreign trade, the number of employed

---

under British rule; (b) India was engaged in indirect governance; (c) Britain had utilised conflicts among ethnic groups as part of its strategy to consolidate power with the consequence that the ethnic minorities developed a sense of being protected groups; and (d) the influence of the royal family and Buddhism had been eliminated (adapted from Ganesan and Hlaing 2007: 5–6).

[16] '…the rice trade was not subject to any severe international competition. … If exploitation of the rice by a handful of British capitalists had been prevented, the crores of rupees in profit from this undertaking would have remained in Burma to benefit the masses….' (U Nu 1952: 6).

[17] 'Like rice, too, the timber market was not very competitive and the buyers vied with each other to buy our teak' (ibid.: 7). This indicates that Burma held a strong position in the timber market.

urban dwellers increased. In spite of this, the incomes of urban workers failed to increase much beyond three times that of the rural workers (ibid.: 17).

Being based on the political principles of the rights and freedom of individuals, British rule (1) reaffirmed Burma's traditional individualism, (2) introduced the concept of contracts, (3) transformed the foundation of regional government from that of tribal (ethnic) rules to one based on geography and (4) introduced the concept of a nation state by way of a parliamentary system. This, however, was accompanied by a number of problems such as the following:

(a) As little effort was made to increase productivity in agricultural as it was in indigenous industries.[18]
(b) A small number of manufacturing activities, all conducted by foreigners out of the reach of the Burmese,[19] employed Indian workers at low wages. The Burmese worked under these Indian workers and therefore suffered from a double layer of managerial control.
(c) Primary education which had previously flourished when provided by Buddhist temples regressed under British rule. While numerous schools were established through funding from the colonial government, they were not great enough in number to make up for the loss of the temple schools. Neither did they provide any vocational training.[20]
(d) Western business practices were not readily accepted by Burmese society as they were seen as contradictory to traditional Burmese customs and ethics.
(e) The traditional system of land tenure was abolished and the rights of tenant farmers eliminated, forcing them to leave their lands.[21]
(f) As the system of chiefs was abolished and replaced with the rule of foreigners, local self-governance was obliterated.
(g) The Buddhist class system and the administration of temple justice were ignored.
(h) The abolition of traditional social order led to social decay and an increase in crime (ibid.: 19, 21–25).

[18] However, improved rice seed was introduced and agricultural research initiated (Hagen 1956: 21).

[19] Little heed was taken of King Mindon's earlier efforts to create small enterprises. Foreign companies had no interest in small-scale industries (ibid.: 21).

[20] Rangoon University was established in 1920. However, as late as 1937, the vast majority of the 2,500 students enrolled (2,061 students) were first- or second-year students. This was due to a high drop-out rate. Moreover, most of the enrolled students were Indians, while Burmese made up only a small minority of the student population. Only a few students were sent abroad to study (approximately ten students during the 1930s) (ibid.: 22–23).

[21] In the early days of the colonial government, there was a mounting need to officially register land ownership as quickly as possible. For this reason, those who happened to be in the midst of cultivation were identified as land owners. Lands that were not being cultivated at the time and shared commons were assigned to the persons whose signatures appeared on documentation. Moreover, land, whose ownership was indeterminate, was handed over to money lenders. As a result, the rights of tenant farmers were forfeited (ibid.: 24).

4 Origins of the Nationalist Movement

The development of anti-British movements in the 1910s, under the leadership of Buddhist monks (*pongyi*), marked the beginning of Burma's nationalist movement. The 1920s saw the emergence of a large number of monk politicians and the establishment of the General Council of Sangha Association (GCSA),[22] which contributed to the publication of a newspaper, exerted its influence on the appointment of government officials and assisted with fundraising efforts for the nationalist movement (Ikuno 1973: 94).

With the onset of the Great Depression in 1929, Burma's young intellectuals 'decided on the achievement of complete autonomy for Burma as their singular goal' (ibid.: 97). In 1932 the 'Thakin party' (Thakin meaning 'master') was formed, and workers and farmers were called to join their nationalist movement. The party tended towards Marxism and had nothing to do with religion.[23] Its leaders, which included Aung San, Takin Mya, U Kyaw Nyein, U Ba Swe and U Nu, were all Western educated.

Takin was a proponent of Sun Yat-sen's Three Principles of the People (nationalism, democracy and socialism) and a proponent of a school of social democracy known as Fabian socialism. 'It is said that the ideology of the *Thakin* party members tended to be an amalgam of revolutionary nationalism, British-style socialism, Marxism, and Buddhist thoughts' (ibid.: 103; Yano 1968: 327). U Nu joined the party in 1937, after which he served, along with Aung San, as advanced guards for the nationalist movement. U Nu was fascinated with the communist theory advanced by Lenin and others and translated a variety of Marxist documents including *Das Kapital* (Ikuno 1973: 103).

In response to Japan's invasion of Burma in 1944, Aung San, U Nu and others established *hpa hsa pa la*, otherwise known as the Anti-Fascist People's Freedom League (AFPFL). The AFPFL brought together the Burmese Revolutionary Party (later called the Socialist Party), the Burmese Communist Party and other political parties, as well as individuals and groups of students, workers, farmers and military personnel, to form a united front against the Japanese (ibid.: 98).

Hpa hsa pa la primarily advocated secularism and had little interest in the religious nationalist movement. However, after gaining independence in 1948, some of its members recognised that it would be politically unwise to ignore religion. Prior to independence, the participants of the nationalist movement were united in the goal of Burmese autonomy, with a shared motivation to evict a foreign power. After independence, however, they realised that 'a new positive agenda was needed to

[22] Among the monk politicians was high Buddhist priest Ottama, who had observed Japan's feverish efforts to modernise after the Meiji Restoration. Ottama was '… impressed by the possibility of a nationalist movement based on non-violence as demonstrated by Gandhi' and himself advocated for a non-violent revolution in a variety of locations (Ikuno 1973: 94–95).

[23] This may have also been motivated by a desire to distinguish their movement from that of the Buddhist politicians or may have been a reaction to the adoption of policies that emphasised Buddhism by pro-British-Burmese politicians (Yano 1968: 328–329).

unite the Burmese people in the creation of a new Burma' (ibid.: 99). The person who most ardently argued this viewpoint was U Nu.

5 Trends in Modern Burma as Seen by Furnivall

Despite being a member of the ICS and on the side of ruling government, John Sydenham Furnivall was a keen observer of Burmese economy and society. He was an Englishman who continued to speak from a viewpoint critical of British rule in Burma. After graduating from Cambridge University, he was sent to Burma as a British official. There his potential was recognised and he was promoted relatively quickly, overtaking his former superiors and eventually being appointed Assistant Commissioner and Settlement Officer. Unlike other ICS officers, he proactively pursued social interaction with the local Burmese, organising, for instance, a sports club for local residents. During one such social exchange, he met a Burmese woman, Margaret Ma Nyun, whom he married in 1906 and with whom he had two daughters. In addition, Furnivall established the Burma Research Society (BRS) in 1910. The journal published by the society—*Journal of Burma Research Society* (JBRS)—is an example of the cultural mark he left.

Furnivall's passion for studying Burma came from his desire to understand the 'truth' about Burma and the Burmese people by 'becoming an insider of Burma'. The BRS was an extension of that desire, and while being a platform for the neutral, scholarly investigation of Burma, it was rife with latent political implications and stimulated a variety of reactions from its readers. Naturally Furnivall was seen by his fellow bureaucrats as being ultra-pro-Burma. Nonetheless, there were a few ICS bureaucrats who shared Furnivall's views and took turns in succeeding him as chairman of the society (Pham 2004: 248–249).

The scholarly passion that could be seen among the members of the society reflected both the Imperial Idea and a romanticism held by a relatively large number of ICS bureaucrats—a type of paternalism or a nostalgic feeling on the part of the imperialists to protect Burmese culture.[24] This romanticism was perhaps a projection of the desire of the ICS bureaucrats to recover the 'lost past' of their own country. In that sense it was, to borrow Furnivall's expression, 'ghost hunting'.[25] Be that

[24] The colonial government recognised the rising tide of Burmese nationalism amidst the social anxiety following the conclusion of the First World War. Realising the importance of this trend, the colonial government established 'A Special Committee on the Imperial Idea'. The Committee argued that the members of the Empire (the Commonwealth) should, based on the principles of 'freedom, justice and human rights', cooperate together and that their obligations as members of the Empire and the development of their own countries were compatible. The Committee, taking in the opinions of the ICS members such as Furnivall, argued that nationalism was an essential element of the Empire and not vice versa. However, the view failed to include the possibility of an independent Burma (Pham 2004: 249–250).

[25] What was lost was the 'good old days', i.e. 'pre-industrial, pastoral society and village community' (ibid.: 249).

as it may, the JBRS and the *Burma Gazetteers* (a settlement report by ICS) served to bind the Western-educated Burmese (who were relatively conservative) and those Britons who were interested in learning about Burma (those who held a favourable view towards Burma) (op. cit).

Among Furnivall's most famous books is *Leviathan*, which criticises the colonial rule of Burma (Furnivall 1939). He was critical of the British system, which forcibly applied the same rules wherever they reigned without much concern for the local region and its residents. He likened it to the Leviathan in the Old Testament (Isaiah, Chapter 27, verse 1). According to Furnivall, once the Leviathan (i.e. colonial governance) had assumed power, the most effective agent to remove its power, and to recover freedom for the Burmese, was the Leviathan itself. This was Furnivall's own paradox, namely, his rationale for supporting the imperial governance while opposing rule by the ICS.

Furnivall's life and thinking provide an insight into some aspects of social economic thought and development in twentieth century Burma. After retiring from the ICS in 1923, he endeavoured to contribute to the cultivation of Burmese nationalism by working with the Burmese youth and starting a book club. All the while, he immersed himself in the study of Burmese society, serving as chairman of the BRS and editor of the society's journal, the JBRS, as well as working to nurture his successors.

It has been said that Furnivall's lifestyle and ideal for the unification and self-reliance of Burmese society were reminiscent of those of Christian missionaries (Pham 2004: 250–253). After arriving in Burma, he became a Buddhist for a short period of time, but later (ostensibly after considerable deliberation) converted to Christianity. He went so far as to state that the work of Christian missionaries would provide a model for the effort of rebuilding Burma (op. cit.).

Furnivall returned to England in 1931 and moved to the Netherlands a few years later (1933). Here he studied Indonesian society at Leiden University under Julius Herman Boeke, an expert on Indonesian society and the proponent of the two-tier society theory.[26] Furnivall then moved on to Indonesia (Java) to directly observe Dutch colonial rule, the results of which were contained in his book published in 1939. According to Furnivall, Java, like Burma, was a 'plural society'. However, Dutch colonial rule differed from that of the British. The Dutch placed importance on contact with, and the social development of, the local population, and adopting a more generous view on colonial rule than the British did not strictly enforce the rules. The local population could freely criticise the colonial bureaucracy and its rules. In contrast, Furnivall likened the British bureaucratic system to a 'machine', as it stubbornly adhered to the principle of rule by law which was mechanically imposed from above. According to Furnivall, the difference between the two systems lay in the difference between continental and British laws. While the former, based on the Roman legal tradition, encouraged improvements in the social welfare of colonies under its rule, the legal principles of the latter prevented its colonial

[26] In contrast to Boeke's 'two-tier society', Furnivall argued that Indonesia was a 'pluralistic society'. It is said that the two men never came to agree on this point.

officials from taking an active part in the social activities of the regions where they reigned, as this was outside of its jurisdiction. For this reason, unnecessary misunderstanding and friction existed between the colonial government and the local Burmese population (ibid.: 257–258).

Having completed his research in Indonesia, Furnivall returned to England and, dispatched by ICS, taught Burmese language, Burmese history and Burmese law at his alma mater, Cambridge University, between 1935 and 1942.

In terms of economic thought, Furnivall was greatly influenced by Fabian socialism.[27] According to Pham (2005), it is not possible to sufficiently understand Furnivall without taking this fact into consideration. Furnivall was a proponent of moderate socialism and was a supporter of the Fabian Society's criticism of *laissez-faire* economics.[28] According to the Fabian Society's thinking, for a society to function sufficiently as an organic organisation, there must also exist a 'community'. That is because its members believed that democracy functioned only when there was a community forged by a common bond. Furnivall's description of Burma as a 'pluralistic society' was an extension of this argument closely connected to his criticism of British rule in Burma. His criticism of British colonialism was that it lacked the understanding of local communities and dismissed the local population as if they were an inorganic assembly of people sharing only ethnicity.[29] According to his judgement, because of this the British colonial government created animosity among the local population, and the locals were justified in feeling the way they did.

These ideas notwithstanding, Furnivall believed that if Burma was to stand on its own as an independent modern nation, it would require Britain's assistance (op. cit.). As is laid out in his Leviathan argument, this was a reason why he valued the institution of the British Commonwealth.[30]

---

[27] From shortly before his appointment to Burma until his death, Furnivall was a regular member of the Fabian Society.

[28] According to Furnivall, land was a free good provided by nature, and people should not arbitrarily claim or transfer ownership of it (Furnivall 1909).

[29] On this point, he believed that the British could learn something from the Dutch rule of Indonesia. British-style colonial rule, when compared with its Dutch counterpart, was quite *laissez faire*. That is, after gaining control of its fundamental interests, the British colonial authority delegated local rule to trusted representatives who could act as they pleased. That did not mean, however, that the profits from colonial rule materialised in windfall fashion. In contrast, the system ensured that returns on investment of the Empire as a whole would flow into British coffers.

British-style colonialism clearly contrasted with Japanese colonialism where colonies were subject to assimilation into Japan. In the case of the latter, serious effort was made to transform its colonies into an essential part of the suzerain. For this reason, wherever nationalist sentiments were strong, resistance to the new style of colonialism was also strong and the Japanese were despised. The antipathy of the Japanese, who were met with such resistance, resulted in a synergistically increasing mutual distrust.

[30] As a result of the Statute of Westminster by the British Parliament on 11 December 1931, the principle of British colonialism changed from vertical, top-down rule, to the horizontally structured Commonwealth of equal partners. That is, British colonies transformed themselves into sovereign territories and became equal members of a collective body connected to the British homeland through their pledge of loyalty to the British monarchy.

In 1943, Furnivall, through a fortuitous turn of events, came to write a plan for Burmese reconstruction after the Second World War ('reconstruction for Burma').[31] At the time, he was of the opinion that, for the sake of improving its economic welfare, Burma should remain within the British Commonwealth after achieving independence and, with Britain's help, endeavour to increase the productivity of its domestic industries (Pham 2004: 262).[32] His argument was that Burma could benefit from the accumulated technology and human resources offered by Britain, as well as from its know-how regarding the management of government bureaucracy and its advice on foreign relations. Furnivall was a realist and his assessment of Britain's ability to govern and its experience was very positive.

It seems that Furnivall's views represented a possible and realistic choice. However, in Burma, which at the time was occupied by Japanese forces, the proponents of independence (including Aung San and U Nu) were not about to accept Furnivall's proposal.

In 1948, 17 years after leaving Burma, Furnivall had the opportunity to return to Burma as a planning advisor and developed, among other things, an economic vitalisation programme in close association with Hla Myint as his right-hand man. Furnivall worked in this capacity for approximately 10 years but lost his position when U Nu stepped aside and was succeeded by Ne Win.[33] Even then, Furnivall continued writing a report titled the 'Social and Economic Development of Modern Burma', entrusted to him by U Nu, which was to remain unfinished as the Ne Win administration ordered Furnivall's expulsion in 1960. He left Burma in April of the same year for a brief residence in England, with an intention to return to Burma to take up a new post as a visiting professor of economics at Rangoon University. However, he passed away 3 months later in Cambridge. He was 82 years of age (Pham 2004: 262–266).

6 Progress Under the U Nu Administration

The Japanese occupation (beginning in April 1942) marked a turning point in the political history of the Burmese nationalists' movement. The Burmese elite represented by the General Council of Burmese Associations (GCBA), which had held influence since the turn of the century, were replaced by a new group of Burmese

[31] 'Secret report on reconstruction for the fortnight ending Tuesday the 4th May 1943', Arnold Papers, MSS Eur. F145/7, item 1, OIOC.

[32] From the sole standpoint that political stability is a necessary condition for economic development, Furnivall's thinking was not incorrect (at least as one alternative). It is clear from Pham's description (2004: 263) of the conditions after Burma's abrupt independence and formation of the Republic that the departure of a large number of British bureaucrats and technicians had a significant negative impact on Burma's economic development. Added to this was the distrust towards the colonial government by the Burmese people, who had long been under colonial rule without any political representation.

[33] First Ne Win administration, 1958.

elite, the *Thakin* party ('Our Burma Association'). These elites began to pursue the 'ideal of an independent Burma (i.e. a nation in which the economic power is held and led by Burmese)'. One camp within this group, the *hpa hsa pa la*, began organising anti-Japanese uprisings in August of 1944, gaining momentum under the leadership of General Aung San. These uprisings were limited in scope but were politically effective; thus they benefited the *Thakin* party and ultimately bolstered Aung San's reputation.

After Japan accepted the terms of the Potsdam Declaration and the civil government was restored in Burma under the British Governor-General (October 1945), the British government invited General Aung San to Britain to solicit his opinion on the debate in England over whether Burma should be kept within the Commonwealth for a short period of time or immediately granted independence as a sovereign nation. Having taken off his military uniform and assumed chairmanship of the *hpa hsa pa la*, Aung San subsequently signed the Aung San-Attlee Agreement in London (January 1947). Under the agreement Britain agreed to allow Burma to decide whether it would become a self-governing dominion within the British Commonwealth or a completely independent republic unassociated with the British Commonwealth (Nemoto 2002: 189). Among Burmese intellectuals (particularly the leaders of the *hpa hsa pa la* movement), the call for immediate independence was overwhelming.

Upon returning home from London, Aung San met with representatives of Burma's remote regions and:

> ...arrived at the agreement (*Panglong* Agreement) that Burma would become an independent federation comprising both regions under the jurisdiction of the Burmese government and frontier areas. In April of the same year, elections were held to choose members of parliament to write a new constitution, which *hpahsa pa la* won readily, ...[and] work was begun on establishment of a new constitution that presumed a federal republic (ibid.: 190).

In this process, power was handed over by the older GCBA elite to the (relatively younger) *Thakin* elite.

However, in July 1947 seven leaders of the *Thakin* party, including Aung San, were assassinated by former Prime Minister U Saw, who had opposed Aung San.[34] The new Burma, which had attained independence in January 1948, now had to move forward without Aung San.

U Nu, acting chairman of the administrative council and deputy chairman of *hpa hsa pa la*, neither possessed the same managerial ability nor enjoyed the same high level of popular support and trust from the people of the frontier areas as Aung San had before him (ibid.: 191).

Aung San had a vision of a socialist Burma, arguing that '...Burma should make clear its anti-imperial/anti-capitalist stance and an independent Burma should strive to progressively nationalise all land and important industries, including agriculture,

[34] Aung San was an exceptional leader whose sincere character was admired even by colonial officials. If he had survived and coordinated the political milieu in the post-independence period, Burma may have experienced a markedly different path of economic development in the 1950s and 1960s.

and thereby realise 'highest well-being for the greatest number of people' and 'a direct democracy" (ibid.: 195). According to him, Burma had not yet reached the capitalist stage and capitalism could be tolerated for the time being. However, he argued that the constitution needed to include provisions to prevent capitalists from exploiting the workers.

U Nu inherited Aung San's vision, but neither U Nu nor his supporters in the *Thakin* party could create a concrete plan for the establishment of a socialist regime.[35] According to Nemoto (2002: 197), the policy ideals announced by the *Thakin* party evoked considerable anxiety among the business community and were therefore primary factors inhibiting Burma's economic development.

U Nu's administration (1948–1962) faced numerous problems, including an unsuccessful coalition with the Communist Party. These problems in turn lead to the Party provoking violent internal confrontations throughout the country over demands for self-governance by highland ethnic groups, in particular the Karen National Union (KNU) and its military wing, the Karen National Defence Organization (KNDO). In the first half of 1949, internal battles were fought on the outskirts of Rangoon. However, the U Nu administration, using a combination of military and political tactics, 'endeavoured to unify the nation under the flag of political principles based on tradition' (Ikuno 1973: 101) and narrowly managed to regain control over the country in the middle of the 1950s.

After assuming premiership, U Nu remained leader of *hpa hsa pa la*; although by this time, it had lost any form of coherence. Worse still, a factional dispute arose between the 'Clean' faction, represented by U Nu, and the 'Stable' faction, led by U Kyaw Nyein and U Ba Swe. The former faction prioritised agriculture, while the latter placed equal emphasis on agriculture and manufacturing industry (or placed greater emphasis on manufacturing). This dispute eventually led to a split in the *hpa hsa pa la* in June 1958. In addition, U Nu's emphasis on the role of Buddhism as a foundation for a welfare state and the rejection of Marxism as the guiding principle for *hpa hsa pa la* became the main cause of his rift with U Kyaw Nyein and U Ba Swe. As a result, the parliament fell into a state of chaos. Unable to gain control of the situation, U Nu entrusted the interim cabinet for administering the election to General Ne Win in October 1958.

A main point of dispute between the rival *hpa hsa pa la* factions during the 1960 general election was U Nu's proposal to establish Buddhism as the state religion. The Federation Party, led by U Nu, won a majority of parliamentary seats and

[35]According to Nemoto's interpretation (2002: 174, 193–194), the Constitution of 1947 does not explicitly indicate the intent to form a socialist state. Nemoto states that 'because Burmese legal experts and the Burmese high civil officials who participated in crafting the text of the Constitution had studied in Britain' (ibid.: 195), the document contained the language of liberalism and the principles of equality reminiscent of those of the British Labour Party and did not explicitly include elements of socialism. U Nu emphasised socialist principles in his speeches of 1952, precisely because these ideas were not necessarily strongly represented in the Constitution (ibid.: 196). According to this interpretation, the reason why Burma tended towards socialism after independence was not due to the Constitution, but to the political leanings of U Nu and his supporters in the *Thakin* party.

formed the third U Nu administration (1960–1962). The 'Law Designating Buddhism as the State Religion' (17 August 1961) was subsequently enacted (ibid.: 104).[36] Soon thereafter the 'Law to Promote the State Religion' was drafted/introduced/enacted and concrete plans for instating Buddhist socialism were announced.

However, the authority of the U Nu administration faltered in the face of demands for autonomy by Shan and other frontier states, internal disputes within the Federalist Party and calls for radical state religionism by Buddhist monks. Military leaders, fearing a collapse in governance, staged a *coup d'etat*. As its justification for this move, they cited the non-functioning parliament and the possibility of the collapse of the state federation (2 March 1962).[37] As chairman of the 'Revolutionary Council', Ne Win became head of the state. He criticised the religious policies undertaken by U Nu and abolished those provisions in the Constitution relating to religion that had been approved by the parliament under the U Nu administration (Nemoto 2002: 198–199; Ikuno 1973: 125).

7 Burma's Economic Development After Independence

At the time of gaining independence (May 1948), Burma was not in a position to immediately initiate steps towards economic development. As discussed previously, individuals associated with the Communist Party revolted against the independent government, but the government army was too weak to gain control over the uprisings. Externally, tense relations with China were a source of consternation. This was due to the fact that, in 1950 when the Chinese Communist Party gained full control over the mainland, one to two thousand *Kuomintang* (KMT or Chinese Nationalist Party) soldiers, aided by the US Central Intelligence Agency (CIA), had fled from Yunnan province along the Chinese border and mounted a large-scale attack on Northeast Burma (Nemoto 2002:197–198).[38] While they were not very strong as a military force, they were in possession of US dollars; therefore, their political implication could not be ignored. As apparent in these examples, Burma's society and external relations following independence were unstable,[39] and it faced numerous physical threats arising from this state of social chaos. As a result, by 1950 self-governing, self-defence forces had been established by young Burmese, and efforts had begun to restore order and safety. In 1954, an attempt was made to give political autonomy to local regions (Hagen 1956: 27–33).

[36] Yes's 324; No's 28; Abstentions 19 (ibid.: 104).

[37] 'Throughout the 1950s, by virtue of their deployment to and occupation of various regions around the country, the national army were instrumental in creating a national network centred in Rangoon and, thus, already possessed the ability to manage the federation' (Nemoto 2002: 198).

[38] Burma presented its case before the United Nations in 1953. While the majority of the soldiers had left Burma by the end of 1954, some stayed behind.

[39] (As discussed previously) the system of land ownership and village self-government had already been dismantled during colonial rule (Hagen 1956: 32).

Even after the end of the Second World War, the Burmese concept of capitalism was underpinned by that of colonialism. It seems that some were of the mistaken understanding that, owing to the large investment required, if large industry was deemed necessary, it would have to be state-run. Prime Minister U Nu, himself an advocate of Fabianism, was opposed to an economy based on capitalistic principles. He declared that all agricultural land and all businesses associated with major industrial activities should be nationalised.[40] Given these circumstances, the government advocated socialism, although its ideological character was fairly moderate. In June 1955, a policy directive was publically announced welcoming capital formation based on foreign investment in all the areas except for munitions and the mining of natural resources. Nonetheless, the government viewed the activities of the domestic Communist Party with disapprobation (ibid.: 40–42).

Economic development following independence progressed at a slow pace. Moreover, the government lacked understanding that agriculture required special attention and care (Myat Thein 2004: 28). In 1955, per capita gross income was roughly $65/year (conversion at market exchange rates).[41] The adverse impacts of the civil wars, which had continued for a total of 9 years after the end of the Pacific War, were most evident in the period from 1945 to 1950. Even as late as 1950, the economy had not recovered to its pre-war levels. While advances were made in capital formation, these gains were mostly the result of depleting foreign currency reserves, and the money was largely expended on building social infrastructure, such as construction of transportation networks and airport runways. The memory of pre-war economic management which, by relying exclusively on rice exportation, failed to stimulate economic development, led to an emphasis on import substitution (ibid.: 29). In addition to state-run cotton spinning, pulp and steel factories, government services made up 10 % of GDP. Half of this was spent on military expenditures, while the other half was spent on public services such as education and medical care. Private investment was mostly limited to small projects in rural regions (ibid.: 47–52).

In September of 1950, the United States signed an agreement to provide technical support to Burma. Around this time the scope of the US assistance was on an upward trend. However, due to the need to suppress domestic communist forces associated with the KMT (discussed above) in 1953, US assistance was eventually terminated at the request of the Burmese government. Meanwhile, war reparations paid by the Japanese had a significant economic impact after 1954.[42] In 1956, Burma signed an agreement with several countries, including the former Soviet Union, for trade assistance. Additionally, in the same year, the Soviet Union agreed to provide

---

[40] U Nu's thinking regarding the economy is evident in one of his long speeches cited here, which also reflected his gentle personality (U Nu 1952: particularly, pp. 16–22).

[41] A comparable figure for the United States in the same year was $2,350.

[42] Reparations of $20 million were paid annually over 10 years and $5 million in loans were paid annually for technical assistance. The first project paid for by the reparation funds was the Baluchaung hydroelectric plant (costing a total of 19 billion yen)—the research, design and construction supervision of which was undertaken by Nippon Koei Co. Ltd. (Sawai 2012: 15).

material and technical support to Burma in exchange for the latter's rice exportation to the former (ibid.: 77–80).

Burma's first 5-year economic plan was introduced in 1956–1957 and the second plan implemented between 1960 and 1964 (Suehiro 1998: 22).[43]

8 U Nu, the Man and His Beliefs

U Nu was a devout, practical Buddhist. He believed that Buddhism '…would endow Burma's unique political system with authenticity as well as authority' (Ikuno 1973: 101). His devotion to Buddhism was not superficial, but had come from strict adherence to the five precepts of Buddhism. He wrapped himself in the traditional *longyi*, covered his hair with a *gaung baung* (a kerchief unique to Burma), wore sandals and walked among and interacted directly with the common people (ibid.: 106). He was a mild and amiable person. Jawaharlal Nehru described him as possessing a 'radiant personality—it wins him friends wherever he goes' (Butwell 1963: 63).

U Nu was capable of attracting the attention of the masses. Ikuno (1973) believes that his personal appeal originated in the ideology of Setkya-Min. Setkya-Min was said to be the mythified form of Ashoka the Great, who unified India and declared that he would 'conquer the earth and rule by law, not by punishment or with weapons' (Ikuno 1973: 110). According to a Buddhist legend passed down through ages, King Ashoka, a devout and sincere Buddhist, ruled his earthly kingdom based on the principle of reincarnation (the endless cycle of death and rebirth) and brought peace and material happiness to the world through the practice of Buddhist compassion.[44]

Some aspects of this philosophy align well with the ideals of Fabian socialism. It is not mere coincidence that Buddhist socialism was advocated by the U Nu administration. 'It seems that, in the modern age, 'Setkya-Min' and the ideal of the country live on in the public's understanding of politics and political stance of populist politicians, and can serve as a model for what is expected of leaders and nation' (ibid.: 110).[45] The high political support for Prime Minister U Nu may be ascribed

---

[43] Prior to this, in 1948, Furnivall and Hla Myint developed a 2-year economic plan, and in 1952, technicians and economists from the American Knappen Tippetts Abbett Engineering Company drafted an 8-year economic plan. The former plan was not implemented due to political instability in Burma, and the latter was suspended for similar reasons, as well as for the shortage of personnel capable of executing it (Myat Thein 2004: 16–20).

[44] It is said that under the reign of King Ashoka: (1) material goods were plentiful, and the people led extremely easy and comfortable lives; (2) the people maintained, and aspired to, the high moral character taught by Buddhism and adhered to the law; (3) geographical movements were easy and villages drew close to each other as the world was not divided by mountains or rivers; (4) the spirits of the people were joined together and different languages assimilated; and (5) no one paid particular attention to precious stones since they were so abundant.

[45] The ideal quality of Burmese kings is said to have been embodied in King Mindon (Mindon Min, 1858–1878). He 'arrived on the throne to protect the teachings of the victor by the benevolent

to a combination of his personality and his actions, overlapped with the reincarnation ideology discussed above, which must have appealed to the masses. Perhaps this is why U Nu was able to maintain his administration over a relatively long period of time.[46]

9 'Inward-Directed' Economic Policy

Ne Win was concerned with removing the religious tone from U Nu's political ideology. However, Burma's socialist ideology had inherited a Buddhist-like tenor. According to a declaration by the Revolutionary Council in April 1962 entitled the 'Burmese Way to Socialism', in order to improve people's material well-being, it was not only possible but highly essential to adopt a rational/scientific view of the world as the fundamental national goal, without relying on supernatural powers.[47]

However, shortly after the declaration, the Revolutionary Council formed the Burma Socialist Programme Party (BSPP, 1964–1988) (a single-party system). According to the outline of its platform:

> All material things and souls exist fleetingly and experience changes based on the 'principles of reincarnation, as the inevitable consequence of the unending and invariable cycle of deaths and rebirths.' A human society, too, is subject to perpetual changes; …neither are the 'eternal' social system nor the 'just' economic system (be they slavery, feudalism, or capitalism) exempt from this absolute law of changes. For this reason, those who endeavour to advance the interest of the masses, must not be dependent on social political systems or the classes that support such systems. It is necessary instead to stand by, and think first and foremost for, the farmers and the industrial workers who labour for the interest of the society. (cited in Ikuno 1973: 127)

According to this passage, it may be said that Burma's socialism was not simple materialism but intended to achieve a morally sound nation and spiritual well-being of its people. It was 'deeply rooted in the tradition of syncretising Buddhism and

---

authority that had been accumulated by a long series of previous generations, and was revered as he was capable of enlightening people on the causes and effects of one's desires and pains' (Ikuno 1973: 112).

[46] In order to unify the Burmese nation, it may well have been a reasonably viable choice to merge the Buddhist philosophy of reincarnation with political ideology.

In the Middle East (e.g. Egypt, etc.) after the Second World War, the political leadership erected as a result of the secular nationalist independence movement, gradually acquired dictatorial power. This coupled with their corruption, caused the leadership to lose the trust of the people and it eventually ended in failure. At this time, Islam surfaced as a rallying point for national unity, and was to a certain degree successful in attaining its purpose (Katô 2010: 34–35). U Nu's efforts to establish Buddhism as the state religion may have been motivated by a desire to trod a similar path.

U Nu's life up to 1962 is documented by Butwell (1963). U Nu died in 1995, at the age of 87.

[47] At the same time, the declaration revealed the Council's intention to avoid close interaction with foreign countries.

Marxism...' (op. cit.).[48] In this sense, there was no absolute rift between the thinking of Ne Win and that of U Nu.

'Burmese Socialism' continued up to 1988, with the nationalisation of all industries except agriculture, the exclusion of all foreign investment and the expulsion of all foreign industrialists. According to Nemoto (2002: 199), when, after a period of political chaos, the military seized power and established Burmese-style socialism, it

> turned off not only the indigenous capital accumulation, but also the path to prosperity and political representation of the middle-class elite that had supported the nationalist movement since 1920, installing in its place a system of political rule by a new class of people made up of the Burmese military and those associated with it.[49]

The trend towards complete isolation from the international community began under the Ne Win Administration.[50] Economic development remained sluggish. Instead of utilising civil officials with experience in economic development, military staff with little exposure to economic management were put in charge of formulating economic policy. Moreover, in order to ensure loyalty to the military elite, military staff were from time to time replaced with equally inexperienced staff (Myat Thein 2004: 63). Under these circumstances, the potential for cultivating devoted civil officials and bureaucrats passionate about improving the nation's material welfare was severely limited.

The two utmost reasons for the stagnation of Burma's economy were the slow pace of development in agriculture and the inefficiency of state-owned enterprises. The government intervened excessively in agriculture in order for rice to be provided to the government at low prices. This allowed the government to continue its supply of rice to public employees as a form of payment in kind. Moreover, it seems that the government lacked the sufficient understanding of the importance of the financial sector. The People's Bank of Burma, serving as Burma's central bank, was a carbon copy of the Soviet National Bank (*Gosudarstvenny* Bank USSR) which had little to do with the nation's monetary policy (ibid.: 67). One may conjecture that Burma's neglect of financial policy inherited some aspects of the Soviet economic ideology on economic planning. In any case, the financial sector was underdeveloped, and there was great difficulty in accumulating the funds necessary for capital investment. The state-owned banks could do nothing to improve these circumstances.

While the investment rate in neighbouring countries was on the rise, Burma experienced an opposite trend (ibid.: 70). With the exception of a rise between 1973

---

[48] The quoted text was excerpted from Heinz Bechert, *Buddhismus, Staat und Gesellschaft II*, 1967, S. 154. 'Syncretism' refers to an attempt to reconcile contradictory theories and/or ideologies.

[49] The U Nu administration recognised the low efficiency of the state-run enterprises and came to the conclusion that if the country continued on this 'socialist' path, the result would be pitiful; however, this recognition was not passed on to the military leadership (Ne Win administration) (Myat Thein 2004: 43).

[50] It is said that the impetus for isolationism came from the invasion, in 1950, of Shan State by a part of the *Kuomintang*, aided by the United States (Ganesan and Hlaing 2007: 1).

and 1983, the ratio of exports and imports to GDP between 1961 and 1988 was in constant decline. Despite the severity of the economic situation, the government was not about to solicit either foreign investment or official development assistance (ODA) (ibid.: 76–77).[51]

Nonetheless, Burma's economic performance during the 1970s was considered relatively commendable (Hill and Jayasuriya 1986: 1–65). However, its growth was in large part achieved by improving the economy's substandard operating rates and, according to Hill and Jayasuriya, would have been impossible to maintain after the 1980s unless new production methods and/or new factors (such as structural reforms) were introduced. It was inconceivable, for instance, that exports from Burma would increase dramatically in the 1980s. While domestic demand for rice—Burma's principal export prior to independence—was on the rise due to the increasing population, the international rice price fell rapidly. Moreover, Thailand and the United States came to be increasingly competitive players in the rice market. Meanwhile, the primary rice-importing countries in the Middle and Near East, and in Africa, were experiencing shortages in foreign reserves (op. cit.).

Given the high interest rates and the lack of economic know-how, even if Burma had tried to introduce foreign investment as a way of strengthening its economy (e.g. by restructuring), things would not have turned out as planned. Had Burma ventured into new businesses, such as labour-intensive manufacturing, its connection with international markets would have been too fragile for it to succeed. Furthermore, it would have faced fierce competition from other Asian economies such as India, Indonesia and China. In the agriculture, forestry and fishery industries, Burma's greatest potential for exports lay in teak. However, teak production had already reached its upper limit and a further increase was not expected.

For these reasons, Hill and Jayasuriya (ibid.: 66–88) foresaw that after the 1980s, Burma's economic policy would again turn inward. Their predictions were, unfortunately, quite correct. During the period of the early to mid-1980s, while the country was politically stable, the 'inconsistencies' of Burma's economic structure became strikingly obvious. The agricultural sector stagnated. The nonagricultural sectors saw the emergence of a two-tiered system that comprised a public sector with state-owned enterprises as its core and a black-market economy. At the same time, the exercise of isolationist policies resulted in the stagnation of exports. Whereas 'the flourishing of the underground economy was a direct indication of the failure of Burma's socialism' (Nishizawa 2000: 54), the government 'twice implemented demonetization policies, once in 1985 and again in 1987, in order to deal a blow to the 'evil businessmen' who ran the underground markets' (op. cit.).[52] It was

[51] Burma's contribution to the total exports of the ASEAN region continued to fall from 12 % in 1937 (the greatest contribution that year coming from Malaya at 34 %), 6 % in 1955, 5 % in 1965, 0.7 % in 1980 and 0.5 % in 1995 (Booth 2003: 146). There must have been an ideological backdrop to this situation.

[52] Demonetisation had been tried in 1964 (Myat Thein 2004: 66, 70). Among all the policies adopted since independence, this represented the most serious blunder in the running of the economy. Many years were necessary to regain the public and international trust lost through its implementation.

assumed that the black markets were operated by Chinese and Indian immigrants, and it appears that non-Burmese businesses were a prime target for punishment. In any case, the demonetarisation dealt a severe blow to the general public and clearly led to the plummeting of the public's trust in government economic policies.

Capital investment in the manufacturing industry made little headway. The promotion of textile exports also failed to progress as hoped.[53] One reason for the stagnation of the manufacturing industry was that the provision of investment funds did not proceed smoothly. Another reason was the continual hesitation of businesses to commit to capital investments, given the considerable uncertainty regarding the future of the economy. The financial market was state-run-oriented, overly bureaucratic and too rule based and was averse to quick action. It was not therefore in a position to ameliorate the hardships of the private sector. The state-run enterprises, despite being short of good managerial oversight, showed some improvement in their performance following the reforms of the late 1970s, but their operating ratios began to fall again after 1982 (Nishizawa 2000: 51). Furthermore, the government printed money in order to remedy budget deficits, which accelerated the pace of inflation. The economic growth rate in real terms became negative in the latter half of the 1980s.

In March 1988, near the end of the Ne Win administration, democratic movements erupted in the form of student demonstrations. This brought about a rising tension within the society. In this tense atmosphere, Ne Win resigned, making way for the establishment of a new administration led by Sein Lwin (July 1988), who abruptly stepped down after only 16 days. Lwin was succeeded by the administration of Maung Maung.

Having experienced the enforcement and the repeal of martial law, the democratic movement led by the National League for Democracy (NLD) with Daw Aung San Suu Kyi as its leader gained momentum. However, in the midst of this, the military, fearing the loss of political order, staged a *coup d'etat* (September1988) and established the State Law and Order Restoration Council (SLORC). While the democratic movement was allowed to continue, Aung San Suu Kyi was put under house arrest. Nevertheless, in the general elections—held as planned on 27 May 1990—the NLD won by a landslide victory (Ino 1996: 9–40).

However, SLORC refused to relinquish its power and sought to re-establish political, social and economic stability. The conditional lift of the ban on foreign investment in November 1988 marked a turning point in the basic stance of the government economic policy. It was publicly announced that the long-advocated principles of a socialist economy would be abandoned and replaced by

[53] In addition, it is reported that in1982–1983, the informal imports and exports amounted to as high as 75 % of the formal imports and exports (Myat Than 1992: 58). Smuggling must have been quite common. It seems desirable, however, to carefully analyse the method of estimation employed by Takamura and Mori (title unknown, 1984: 134), on which the above-cited figures are based.

market-economy principles. The 1965 Law of Establishment of the Socialist Economic System was repealed in March 1989.[54]

The effect of the transformation from socialist to market economies was striking. At the beginning of the 1990s, the real GDP growth rate increased from 6 to 10 % per annum. Additionally, the contribution of the private sector to GDP rose from 69 % in the period 1986–1987 to 76 % in the period 1998–1999. However, major industries remained under state control and the macroeconomy continued to suffer from budget deficits, current-account deficits, inflation and low saving rates (which meant low investment rates) (Thein 2004: 123–29).

10 Search for a New Development

With the general elections held in 1990, the world's attention turned to Myanmar's future. The rise of Aung San Suu Kyi as leader of the NLD, which happened to coincide with the collapse of the Soviet Union, bolstered expectations of a change both within and outside Myanmar. In the West, which at the time was in the midst of celebrating the victory of free democracy, Aung San Suu Kyi was widely acknowledged as a courageous leader of the democratic movement.[55] However, the change that had been hoped for was not realised. Internal political battles erupted, during which many members of the democratic movement were arrested. Aung San Suu Kyi was again placed under house arrest. Myanmar faced severe criticism from the international community, particularly from the United States and the European Community.

Since 1988 internal warfare was gradually resolved under the military leadership. This was particularly so in the 1990s. Nonetheless, Myanmar's economic development was inhibited by difficulties in attracting foreign investment as a result of the continuing civil war, isolation from the international community and the imposition of international economic sanctions following the arrest of Aung San Suu Kyi in June 2003. Although in 1997 ASEAN expressed its willingness to accept Myanmar as a member, this did not immediately lead to political reforms within Myanmar.[56]

[54] The following slogan appeared on the bottom of a poster hung around the University of Yangon campus on the occasion of the above mentioned anti-government student demonstrations: 'We will fight for a meaningful and prosperous new socialist society' (Ino 1996: 11). It may be that the young intellectual class at the time did not necessarily believe that socialist ideology should be rejected.

[55] Daw Aung San Suu Kyi had resided in England for a long time and married an Englishman. The starting point of her involvement in Myanmar politics was her return to Myanmar in 1988 to care for her ailing mother. She was placed under house arrest in July 1989 while still the leader of the NLD and was not permitted to run for public office despite having Myanmar citizenship.

[56] Among ASEAN members, there was some concern that Myanmar's obstinate attitude would lower the confidence in, and international reputation of, ASEAN as a whole (Ganesan and Hlaing 2007: 3).

It would be useful at this juncture, to compare Burma's record of economic development since independence with that of other Southeast Asian countries. If one takes the view articulated by Suehiro (2002: 1–2) as a reference, the course of economic development in the region in the twentieth century consisted of four mutually overlapping stages, namely:

1. *From the beginning of the twentieth century up to the 1950s*: the rise of nationalism, the realisation of political independence, the establishment of nation states and liberalisation from colonial domination
2. *From the end of the 1950s to the 1980s*: departure from parliamentary democracy and the increasing dominance of authoritarian political regime, which came to characterise the period
3. *From the latter half of the 1970s to the end of 1980s*: remarkable economic growth of a new breed of industrial countries (Hong Kong, Singapore, Taiwan, Korea etc.) with export growth as the driving force, following economic restructuring after the two oil shocks
4. *The period beginning in the latter half of the 1980s*: the collapse of the Cold War regime, a rising trend in economic liberalisation, the economic transformation of planned economies, the inevitable re-evaluation of state-led industrial development and the termination of the age of 'developmentalism'

With respect to stage (1), repulsion of colonial rule nurtured nationalism. Evolving political movements sought political independence and the establishment of nation states. In stage (2), criticism of parliamentary democracy became overwhelming and authoritarian regimes became dominant.[57] Developmental dictatorship emerged, under which the introduction of foreign investment was expanded.[58] Out of these dictatorships, the keywords 'the Cold War regime', 'economic development' and 'nationalism' emerged as characteristic of Southeast Asia in the 1960s. The political system that embodied these three characteristics was called 'developmentalism'.[59] In stage (3), faults of the import substitution model of

[57] For example, Thai-style democracy, Burmese-style socialism, Indonesian-style new order and Filipino-style revolution from within

[58] The reason countries moved towards developmental dictatorships was (according to Suehiro) due to the widely held perception that, in order to oppose internal and external political threats, it was necessary to increase the country's power (through economic development) under a system of crisis management. That is, in stage (2), there was the external 'threat' of the communist influence and the internal threat of anti-government movements. The ruling regime decided that in order to achieve a developmental dictatorship, it would be necessary to concentrate authority in the central government.

[59] The systematic presentation of the concept of developmentalism is derived from Murakami (1996). The developmental regime was implemented and bore fruits under the direction of capable technocrats. It was executed by assimilating social movements such as the top-down movements in the Philippines (as in the case of the *Kilusang Bagong Lipunan* ('New Society Movement'), the *Yushin* (revitalisation-reform) system in Korea, the Politics of Survival in Singapore etc.). The developmental regime put in place in Indonesia after it had established a developmental dictatorship—'the restructuring of state socialism' through economic growth—is said to have been the model for Myanmar (Iwasaki 1998: 134).

development were recognised and the countries that succeeded were those capable of enacting export-driven policies, tailor made to their resource endowments. Finally, with regard to stage (4), as the economies under the planned economic regions were liberalised and transformed to market economies, state-planned industrial development faced inevitable overhauling. This marked the end of the age of developmentalism.[60] The three central concepts characterising the 'post-developmentalism era' were globalisation, economic liberalisation and democratisation (op. cit.).

With the adoption of policies emphasising agriculture since the end of the 1980s, it has been demonstrated that Burmese farmers respond swiftly when provided with the proper incentives. The new emphasis on the importance of taking such things as minority groups and environmental protection into consideration brought about a refreshing change (Myat Thein 2004: 178–182). In the early 1990s, both imports and exports increased dramatically and with the establishment of the Privatization Commissio n in January of 1995, efforts aimed at privatisation were stepped up (although it cannot be said that the desired progress was easily achieved) (ibid.: 151, 156–157).[61] The end of the same decade saw a growth in the export of textile goods.

Meanwhile, after the SLORC changed its name to the State Peace and Development Council (SPDC) in November of 1997, government intervention into the market increased (ibid.: 6, 175). As for industrial policy, while touting the industrialisation of agriculture and respect for small businesses, the government maintained its import substitution policies (Chit So 1999: 139). In light of the increase in the contribution of Burma's primary industries (agriculture and forestry) to the GDP from 47 % in 1980 to 60 % in 2000 (in current-year prices),[62] one could hardly say that Myanmar experienced remarkable industrialisation in the last decades of the twentieth century.

Although Suehiro's stages (1) and (2) apply loosely to Myanmar, the country's political path during the respective periods differed in some important aspects from those of other East and Southeast Asian countries (e.g. Thailand, Singapore, the Philippines and Korea). For example, Myanmar never explicitly declared development as its guiding principles and never showed explicit interest in developing and managing such groups of professional bureaucrats and technocrats as represented by NEDA (the National Economic Development Authority) in the Philippines. Additionally, it did not proactively pursue private investment or foreign direct

[60] Based on the experience in Asia, it can be said that once developmentalism succeeded, its political usefulness declined. Developmental dictatorships supported by developmentalism tended to fall apart once the underlying system of single-party rule collapsed. Business groups nurtured under developmental dictatorships became disobedient and people started to criticise the government. Pressure to democratise came from both within and outside of the country. Although their specific circumstances differed, Singapore, Indonesia, Malaysia, Thailand, the Philippines and South Korea all experienced similar transformation processes (Iwasaki 1998: 134–41).

[61] Between 1990 and 1999, the ratio of exports and imports to GDP fell continuously (according to reports from the IMF and UNCTAD, as quoted by Myat Thein (2004: 156–57).

[62] According to the *Key Indicators of Developing Asian and Pacific Countries*, published by the Asian Development Bank

investment (FDI) and never officially announced an anti-communist stance, instead advocating a socialist path. It appears that neither a growth-oriented value system nor the Islamic concept of 'sharing' has ever taken root in the country as a common bond for national unity. Perhaps Myanmar stood as a rare case in which the militarily leadership could push forward national unification based on a principle of socialism.

After the 1990s, Myanmar remained at stage (2) for a long time. It then jumped to stage (4), under the impacts of the rapidly changing international environment and without having experienced the socioeconomic structural transformations that were characteristic of other East and Southeast Asian nations in stage (3). This, however, did not mean that Myanmar has arrived at stage (4). The clear difference between Myanmar and other East and Southeast Asian states was that the former's 'developmentalism', if anything, was not sufficiently successful to register improvements in the low level of personal consumption (both relatively and absolutely).[63] Myanmar's urban middle class most likely remained politically immature, and in that sense, the foundation for establishing parliamentary democracy has remained incomplete.

Two factors contributed to the emergence of developmentalism in Asia after the end of the Second World War. Firstly, few of the Asian countries that had been under colonial rule until the end of the War were able to easily achieve economic growth during the period from the late 1950s to the early 1960s. According to Suehiro (1998: 28), 'developmentalism, which had come to be seen as an inescapable requirement for nation building', won the support of the people, in spite of developmental dictatorship. This was not necessarily because of fear of the tyranny exercised by developmental dictatorship. In the newly independent Asian countries, parliamentary democracy was introduced at a stage when preconditions for a self-reliant economy had not yet been met. Their attempts to manage the economy with liberalist, market-oriented principles resulted in all manner of confusion in the economy, including hyperinflation, high unemployment, corruption, macro-mismanagement and illegitimate elections throughout the region. For this reason, people grew disillusioned with party politics. It is important to keep in mind that these circumstances have made the conservative politicians, as well as the military leaders, keenly aware of the need for an ideology for regulated economy (Suehiro 2002: 12–13).

A second major factor contributing to the flourishing of developmentalism was the commencement of a peace offensive by the Soviet Union against the United States in the latter half of the 1950s. For example, Soviet assistance to developing countries increased approximately 100-fold between 1954 and 1956. This led to a

[63] Even if, hypothctically, the economy had successfully been grown, a significant amount of time would have been required for such success to be reflected in the consumption levels of the public. For example, in reference to Thailand, Suehiro states: 'to be exact, the consumption patterns and lifestyle of the people (and, similarly, per capita GDP) significantly changed in the 1990s (similarly per capita GDP); indeed 30 years after the *Sarit* administration had executed its plan for 'National Development" (Suehiro 2002: 19).

change in the ideology held by the United States. Specifically, justification was made for state-planned developmentalism (even under developmental dictatorship), exemplified by the stance adopted by the US Kennedy administration (Suehiro 1998: 25–27).

11 Concluding Remarks

In view of the insights gained from the historical records and ideological developments, it seems a meaningful exercise to return to the point of independence and to re-examine the conditions at the time. Consideration can then be given to what Myanmar's ideal economic policy would be in the twenty-first century. As Aung San appropriately pointed out in 1947, it would have been impossible to successfully implement a socialist economy in Burma around the time of independence, when Burma's capitalism, if existent at all, was still immature. By now it has been conclusively demonstrated that, compared to market economies, planned economies are less efficient, are more wasteful and grow at a slower pace. As discussed at the beginning of the present essay, in light of the past experiences and the theoretical understanding of socioeconomic development processes, there seems to be no choice for an economy to grow but to take a path of market development.

However, this by no means implies the adoption of a *laissez-faire* system in which all economic activities are entrusted to the market. Historically markets were formed as a result of the intricate interplay between institutional and cultural factors in the context of social development. In the early stages of economic development, for instance, governmental economic policy plays an important role in nurturing market systems. In mature market economies, there is also an important role for public policy: to support, watch and direct market performance in order to make sure that the market functions appropriately in light of the society's development goals. Needless to say, the nature and the extent of such governmental actions vary depending on time and circumstances. Still fresh are the memories of the financial crisis (the so-called subprime loan crisis) brought on by the overheating of market transactions due to excessive liberalisation of Western financial markets from the end of the twentieth to the beginning of the twenty-first century. The second decade of the twenty-first century in fact marked the beginning of a reassessment of the Reagan/Thatcherism that held the market economy as omnipotent.

It would be appropriate to re-evaluate the economic thoughts of Furnivall and Hla Myint, who had developed a plan of moderation under the U Nu administration. At the same time, it would be important to maintain a clear and objective view of the political and economic aspects of the country's economic development. Looking back on the modern economic history of Japan and that of other Asian countries after the Second World War, one is reminded that it was the initiation of economic development (Rostow's 'takeoff') and its material fruits that provided a condition for generating the political process of democratisation. It is often said that the presence and the growing maturity of a robust middle class is a necessary condition for democracy to blossom. However, democracy does not constitute an initial condition for economic development. The economic sanctions by Western countries and Japan against the government of Myanmar from the last part of the twentieth century, however justifiable they may have been, functioned as a major factor constraining the country's economic progress. As a result, this undoubtedly contributed to the prolonging of the oligarchy.[64] On the other hand, it was the general public who suffered the most from the sanctions.

References[65]

Booth, A. (2003). The Burma development disaster in comparative historical perspective. *South East Asia Research*, 11 (July), 141–171.

Butwell, R. (1963). *U Nu of Burma*. Stanford: Stanford University Press.

Chit So. (1999). Industrial development and reforms in Myanmar. In M. Kiryû (Ed.), *Industrial development and reforms in Myanmar: ASEAN and Japanese perspectives*. Bangkok: White Lotus Press (cited in Myat Thein 2004: 257).

Cœdès, G. (1962). *Les peuples de la Pénisule indochinoise, histoire-civilisations*. Paris: Dunod.

Furnivall, J. S. (1909). Land as a free gift of nature. *The Economic Journal, XIX*, 552–558.

Furnivall, J. S. (1939). *The fashioning of Leviathan: The beginnings of British rule in Burma*. Rangoon: The Burma Research Society.

Ganesan, N., & Kyaw Yin Hlaing. (2007). Introduction. In N. Ganesan & Kyaw Yin Hlaing (Eds.), *Myanmar, state, society and ethnicity*. Singapore/Hiroshima: Institute of Southeast Asian Studies/Hiroshima Peace Institute.

Hagen, E. E. (1956). *The economic development of Burma* (National Planning Association, Planning Pamphlet No. 96). Washington, DC: National Planning Association.

Hill, H., & Jayasuriya, S. (1986). *An inward-looking economy in transition: Economic development in Burma since the 1960s*. Singapore: Institute of Southeast Asian Studies.

Ikuno, Z. (1973). U Nu to bukkyô shakaishugi no seiritsu [U Nu and the establishment of Buddhist socialism]. In Y. Takahashi (Ed.), *Tounan Asia no nashonarizumu to shûkyô* [Southeast Asian nationalism and religion]. Mimeograph copy, Chapter 3.

Ino, K. (Ed./Trans.). (1996). *Aung San Suu Kyi enzetsushû* [The speeches of Aung San Suu Kyi]. Tokyo: Misuzu Shobô.

Ishikawa, S. (1990). *Kaihatsu keizaigaku no kihon mondai* [Fundamental problems in developmental economics]. Tokyo: Iwanami Shoten.

Iwasaki, I. (1998). Kaihatsu taisei no kigen/tenkai/henyô, Higashi/tonan Ajia wo chûshin ni [The origins, development, and evolution of the economic development structure in East and Southeast Asia]. In *Tokyo Daigaku Shakai Kagaku Kenkyûsho* [Tokyo University Institute for

[64] In David Steinberg's opinion, the popular evaluation in Myanmar of the political legitimacy of a given administration has differed subtly from that in the West, particularly since the BSPP administration. In addition to the number of votes garnered in an election, the evaluation depends on the exercise of personal influence and authority. It is in that sense similar to that of the traditional concept of legitimacy. Be that as it may be, Khin Zaw Win notes that after the general elections in 1990—in contrast to the international assessment—there were some signs of improvement in the domestic political environment (both observations are quoted from Ganesan and Hlaing (2007: 6, 9)).

[65] Followings were particularly influential in the writing of this essay: Ganesan and Kyaw Yin Hlaing (2007), Hagen (1956), Ikuno (1973), Myat Thei (2004), Nemoto (2002), Pham (2004), Suehiro (2002), Watanabe (2001).

Social Science]. Nijusseiki shisutemu 4: Kaihatsu shugi (Series on the Twentieth Century System No. 4: Developmentalism). Tokyo: University of Tokyo Press, Chapter 4.

Japanese Association for Canadian Studies. (Ed.). (2009). *Hajimete deau Canada* [The first steps in Canadian studies]. Tokyo: Yûhikaku.

Katô, Hiroaki. (2009). Canada no kokuseki gainen to senkyoken – Eikoku shinmin kara Canada jin e [The Canadian concept of citizenship and voting right – From a British subject to a Canadian]. *Daitou Hougaku* (Journal of Law and Politics), *19-1* (October Issue), 1–33.

Katô, Hiroshi. (2010). *Isuramu keizai ron, Isuramu no keizai rinri* [Islamic economic theory and Islamic economic ethics]. Tokyo: Shoseki Kôbô Hayama.

Murakami, Y. (1996). *An anticlassical political-economic analysis: A vision for the next century*. Translated with an introduction by Kozo Yamamura. Stanford: Stanford University Press.

Mya Than. (1992). *Myanmar's external trade, an overview in the Southeast Asian context*. Singapore: Institute of Southeast Asian Studies.

Myat Thein. (2004). *Economic development of Myanmar*. Singapore: Institute of Southeast Asian Studies.

Nemoto, T. (2002). Biruma no dokuritsu – Nihon senryôki kara U Nu jidai made [Burma's independence – From Japanese occupation to the time of U Nu]. In S. Ikehata et al. (Eds.), *Iwanami kouza Tôunan Ajia shi dai 8 kan, kokumin kokka keisei no jidai* [Iwanami lecture series on the history of Southeast Asia No. 8: The age of nation states]. Tokyo: Iwanami Shoten.

Nishizawa, N. (2000). Biruma-shiki shakaishugi no hôkai [The collapse of Burmese socialism]. In N. Nishizawa (Ed.), *Miyanmâ no keizai kaikaku to kaihou seisaku – Gunsei 10 nen no sôkatu* [Myanmar's economic reforms and its open policy – An overview of the decade of the military regime]. Tokyo: Keisô Shobô, Chapter 3.

Pham, J. (2004). Ghost hunting in colonial Burma, nostalgia, paternalism and the thoughts of J.S. Furnivall. *South East Asia Research, 12*(2), 237–268.

Pham, J. (2005). J.S, Furnivall and Fabianism: Reinterpreting the 'plural society' in Burma. *Modern Asian Studies, 39*(2), 321–348.

Saitô, T. (1991). Konbaung-chô Biruma no tochi hoyû seido to shakai kousei – Zaigen chôsho no bunseki wo chûshin ni [The system of land ownership and social organization under the Konbaung dynasty – An analysis of financial records]. In H. Umehara (Ed.), *Tônan Ajia no tochi seido to nôgyou henka* [Land policy and agricultural transformation in Southeast Asia] (Institute of Developing Economies Series No. 406), Tokyo: Institute of Developing Economies, Chapter 4.

Sawai, M. (2012). Sengo Nihon ni okeru gijutsushi no tanjô (The advent of consulting engineers in postwar Japan). *Osaka Daigaku Keizaigaku* (Osaka Economic Papers), *61*(4), 1–24.

Suehiro, A. (1998). Hatten tojoukoku no kaihatsu shugi [The developmentalism in developing countries]. In *Tokyo Daigaku Shakai Kagaku Kenkyusho* [Tokyo University Institute for Social Science]. Nijusseiki shisutemu 4: Kaihatsu shugi (Series on the Twentieth Century System No. 4: Developmentalism). Tokyo: University of Tokyo Press, Chapter 1.

Suehiro, A. (2002). Sôsetsu [An overview]. In S. Ikehata et al. (Eds.), *Iwanami kouza Tounan Ajia shi dai 9 kan: 'kaihatsu' no jidai to' mosaku' no jidai* [Iwanami lecture series on the history of Southeast Asia No. 9: The age of development and the age of exploration]. Tokyo: Iwanami Shoten.

U Nu. (1952). *Towards a welfare state*. The speech of Prime Minister U Nu delivered on the opening day of the Union Welfare State Conference on August 4, 1952, Ministry of Information, Government of the Union of Burma.

Watanabe, Y. (2001). Konbaun-chô Biruma to 'kindai' sekai [The 'modern' world and Burma under the Konbaung dynasty]. In S. Ikehata et al. (Eds.), *Iwanami kouza Tounan Ajia shi dai 5 kan: 'kaihatsu' no jidai to' mosaku' no jidai* [Iwanami lecture series on the history of Southeast Asia no. 5: The reorganization of Southeast Asia]. Tokyo: Iwanami Shoten, Chapter 5.

Yano, T. (1968). *Tai/Biruma gendai seiji-shi kenkyû* [An investigation of modern political history in Thailand and Burma]. Kyoto: Kyoto University Center for Southeast Asian Studies.

Chapter 2
Remnants of the Colonial Period and Economic Policies of Post-Independence: Through the Study of Hla Myint

Asuka Mizuno

1 Introduction

In 2008, 20 years after the Socialist Constitution of Myanmar had been suspended, a new constitution was enacted; in November 2010 a general election was held, and in March 2011 the reformist candidate Thein Sein became president. Myanmar was finally on its way to becoming a democratic nation with a market economy. The year 2012 may well have been the second point of national foundation. With the land law reform and the transition to a managed floating currency exchange system, the legal system that had been maintained for nearly 60 years was experiencing reform. In fact, the slogan for 2013 was 'Let's build the country with the power of the people'. Against this backdrop, this chapter will review the first point of national foundation, when the country gained its independence from British rule and began its ascent as a modern nation. This chapter will also review the essence of economic policies through and immediately following the socialist era, with a focus on academic contributions by Professor Hla Myint.

The purpose of this chapter is to examine why the Burmese government failed to achieve economic development and to identify those tasks that remain unaccomplished. At the same time, this chapter will outline the characteristics of Myanmar's development process. Hla Myint has spent his career heeding the Burmese situation; as a result, he has conceived of a unique economic developmental theory—namely, the necessity of improving the economy's organizational framework in order to improve its efficiency.[1] Since many excellent empirical studies have been

[1] In the outstanding textbook, *Pioneers in Development*, Hla Myint has been noted as one of the pioneers in development economics and credited with the explanation of economic growth through export orientation, with an emphasis on the importance of an institutional framework for the smooth functioning of market mechanism (Meir 1987). His model of economic development by

A. Mizuno (✉)
Faculty of Economics, Asia University, Tokyo, Japan
e-mail: amizuno@asia-u.ac.jp

K. Odaka (ed.), *The Myanmar Economy*, DOI 10.1007/978-4-431-55735-7_2

made of Myanmar's economic policies and political economics after independence, this chapter will focus on Hla Myint's theoretical studies.[2]

Hla Myint was born in the Lower Burma delta, in 1920. He attended the University of Rangoon in the mid-1930s. Having graduated from the University, he was sent in 1940 as a state scholar to study for a doctorate at the London School of Economics (Brown 2013: 125–126), where he studied under Friedrich August von Hayek. In 1943 he earned his doctorate with a thesis on the history of economic doctrines, from the classical economics of Adam Smith, David Ricardo et al. to the neoclassical economics of Arthur C. Pigou, with an emphasis on welfare theories for economic policies. After earning his doctorate degree, Hla Myint became a research fellow at the University of Manchester, where he received scholarly guidance from John Richard Hicks (Hla Myint 1948: v).

In the debate over the implementation of a socialist economy, von Hayek claims that it is impossible for a government to collect all the information it needs for its economic planning and that socialism will either deteriorate into totalitarianism or a rampantly corrupt bureaucracy. It should be noted that Hayek's concept of the role of government was to support the market by maintaining the rule of the law (Hayek 1948). Hicks, on the other hand, is well-known for *The Theory of Economic History*, which illuminates the development process of market economy (Hicks 1969). From these intellectual intercourses, it would be easy to infer how Hla Myint's theoretical and practical interest was nurtured with regard to the mechanism of the market economy and its development.[3]

After obtaining his degree in the United Kingdom, Hla Myint returned to Burma in 1947 to support the independent government, but went back to the United Kingdom in 1949 to teach at Oxford University (Walinsky 1962: 166, footnote 2). Under the auspices of the United Nations, he served as an economic advisor to Burma for the year 1954–1955, and in 1958, Ne Win 'personally wired' Hla Myint in Oxford, persuading him to become rector of Rangoon University and serve as economic advisor to the government. But Hla Myint left Myanmar in 1960, deeply frustrated and disappointed, and wouldn't go home for long time (Brown 2013: 127). His outstanding work, *Economic Theory and the Underdevelopment Countries*, is a compilation of the articles he published during the years spanning 1954–1970.

The section to follow will examine Burma's first economic plan that Hla Myint was involved in, namely, the 'Two-Year Plan of Economic Development'. The Plan was laid by the 1947 Constitution and formed the basis for Burmese economic policies of the 1950s and many subsequent projects (Walinsky 1962: 64). In light of the analytical papers that Hla Myint published in the 1950s, Sect. 3 will examine the economic changes that occurred during the Colonial Period, which formed the initial stumbling block for following economic policies; this study will be supplemented by Sect. 4 and the empirical research conducted on village documents during the

way of 'vent for surplus', as discussed in Sect. 3, continues to be referenced in modern textbooks of development economics (e.g. Todaro and Smith 2011).

[2] Recent examples are Myat Thein (2004), Tin Maung Maung Than (2007) and Khin Maung Kyi et al. (2000), Brown (2013).

[3] For Hla Myint's own summary of his own research transitions, see Hla Myint (1987).

Colonial Period. Finally, Sect. 5 will make use of Hla Myint's papers from the late 1960s to provide an understanding of why and how the Burmese socialist economic policies, based on experiences from the Colonial Period and the 1950s, evolved in the proscribed manner.

2 The Principle of Economic Policy at the Beginning of Independence: Democracy and the Establishment of a Welfare State

On May 23, 1947, the eve of independence, the Anti-Fascist People's Freedom League (AFPFL or *hpa has pa la* by its Burmese acronym), the group of key players for political independence, held a convention at the Jubilee Hall in Rangoon. During the gathering, in conjunction with the constitution, a post-independence economy was conceived. In a speech, General Aung San expressed his earnest desire for democratic nation building, for which the establishment of an economic basis would be essential. General Aung San's speech began with an explanation of the meaning of 'state', the relationship between the state and its people and his definition of what a true democracy represented:

> True democracy alone must be our basis if we want to draw up our constitution with the people as the real sovereign and the people's interest as the primary consideration. Democracy alone is the basis upon which the real progress of a nation can be built. (AFPFL Convention Brochure (date unknown): 4)

What is illustrated here is the idea that true democracy represents the interests of the people. Behind this was the fact that while Burmese independence had been declared in 1943, it was with the backing of Japan. In view of the situation, AFPFL used the term 'democracy' as a form of resistance against the Japanese.

> Following his talk on 'true democracy', General Aung San continued on the subject of economic management as 'the basis of Burmese democracy'.
>
> How shall we lay the foundations of such a democracy? (1) Ways must be found that will lead to the nationalisation of important industries and means of production. (2) Workers must have definite rights regarding their working and living conditions, health, social insurance, etc. (3) Land must be in the hands of those who work on it and there must be no large land-holdings whatsoever. (4) Various national minorities must be able to enjoy proper rights due to them....
>
> Now you will want to ask, 'isn't it socialism that you are propounding?' Not quite. In fact, however anxious we may be to set up socialism in our country, the country's present economic position is such that socialisation at the present stage is by no means possible. (AFPFL Convention Brochure (date unknown): 5–6)

General Aung San's speech propounds that need for the nationalisation of important industries, primarily because those were British firms. In addition, he had a vision for a mixed economy, which was a general policy trend in Southeast Asia at the time.[4] For General Aung San, the objective was to achieve genuine economic

[4] Khin Maung Kyi, et al. (2000) state that the Burmese economy in the 1950s was a typical example of mixed economy, which was popular in Southeast Asia at the time.

independence to establish democracy. He was realistic enough to allow capitalistic corporations to stay on. One should take note, however, that he defended the rights of cultivators and workers.

Hla Myint also gave a lecture on the first day of the constitutional convention (UHRC 1999: 59). Details of the lecture are lacking, but from the contents of his later papers, we can infer that Hla Myint spoke of the 'disequalizing factors' that resulted from Burma's open-door process to an isolated economy under the reign of Burmese kings, but that he would not deny the role of foreign capital or foreign trade.[5] In a 1945 interview with the *Far Eastern Survey*, Hla Myint commented that he could no longer envision the domination by foreign capital, but that future Burma would definitely require foreign trade, foreign capital and foreign technology, so that its government could ensure the nation's economic welfare (*Far Eastern Survey* [May 23, 1945], p. 128). At the time, socialism was clearly identified as the Burmese nationalist ideologies; nevertheless, political leaders had the wherewithal to invite Hla Myint to give a lecture at the convention (Taylor 1987: 244).

The 1947 Constitution was enacted on the basis of socio-democratic principles aiming to build a welfare state. Section 30 (1) and (2) stipulate that the state is the ultimate owner of all lands and that the state has the right to regulate, alter or abolish land tenure and to distribute the same to collective (or cooperative) farming or to agricultural tenants. Meanwhile, Section 23 (1) establishes the right of private property and of private initiatives in economic spheres, and Sections 13–19 stipulate the rights of citizens for equality and liberty, as well as the need for the protection of farmers and workers. In order to ensure these objectives, Section 41 announces that economic planning will be introduced with the aim of increasing the public wealth of the Union, improving and raising the material conditions and cultural level of the nation and consolidating the independence and strengthening the defensive capacity of the Union (Walinsky 1962: 61; Maung Maung 1961: 259–262).[6]

In addition, General Aung San called for a conference on economic reconstruction, to be held at Sorrento Villa in Rangoon on June 6, 1947, a month after the convention.[7] With his assassination, the conference was prematurely concluded, but not before the Economic Planning Board had been established,[8] to which John

[5] See next section.

[6] The 1947 Constitution was abolished in 1962 after Ne Win's *coup*. In 1973, a Socialist Constitution was passed by a referendum, with which Ne Win's government held elections the following year, making a transition to civilian rule. The Socialist Constitution was terminated in 1988 by the army that suppressed the national democracy movement of 1988. In 2008, Myanmar passed its third Constitution since independence was declared.

[7] The economic reconstruction conference was divided into five sections: (1) statistics, (2) planning, (3) finance, (4) ways and means and (5) coordination. Statesmen, government officials and experts in various fields were invited to contribute to the reconstruction plan (Burma, Economic Planning Board (1948) foreword).

[8] In 1946, before independence, the National Planning Department was established to oversee the reconstruction of the cities from war damages. It was, in 1947, reorganised into the National Planning Board, which was further reorganised as the Economic Planning Board in order to draw up the national development plan (Tet Tun 1957: 1–2).

Sydenham Furnivall and Hla Myint were invited as planning and economic advisors, respectively. Soon after independence, in April 1948, the Board announced the 'Two-Year Plan of Economic Development'.

The introductory chapter of the 'Two-Year Plan' quoted Section 41 of the Constitution, explaining the Plan's economic vision on the basis of its interpretation of the Burmese economy during the Colonial Period. During the Colonial Period, according to the Plan, products such as rice, oil, lead, silver and wood were developed and exported, but under the then-dominant *laissez-faire* doctrine, economic transactions were almost exclusively dominated by the interests of foreign capitalists. While the wealth of the nation undoubtedly increased, the lives of most villagers remained poor.

However, the Plan declared, the nation's destiny was once again in the hands of its people, who had gained an opportunity to develop the economy in order to suit their needs. The Plan had been drafted with the intent of increasing the national wealth in a manner that would improve the people's standard of living, while laying the foundation for a balanced economy (Burma, Economic Planning Board 1948: 1–2). This plan, to which Furnivall and Hla Myint had contributed, presented a long-term vision. It did not specify any numerical targets for economic growth or industrialisation, but repeatedly stressed the need for investigation and analysis prior to drawing up a practical plan for development. While recognising the role of the market, it emphasised the importance of improving the income and welfare of people in the rural areas of the nation.[9]

The Two-Year Plan was never put to practice, due to the deterioration of the political situation, but it formed a basis for the plans of the 1950s.[10] It also made a significant impact in the area of statistical compilation. As the Plan stressed the essential need for statistics and national income figures in order to perform economic planning, the Central Statistical and Economic Department was established under the Ministry of National Planning, where for the first time statistics were collected, and national income figures were calculated with the help of a United Nations technical cooperation programme (Burma, Economic Planning Board 1948: 30–35, 54–55). This effort culminated in 1951, with the publication of *The Economic*

[9]The Plan was composed of the following 12 chapters: (1) Introduction, (2) Agriculture, (3) Forests, (4) Industrial Development, (5) Fisheries, (6) Technical Education, (7) Electricity, (8) Labour, (9) Transport and Communications, (10) Finance, (11) Survey of Natural Resources and (12) Economic Research. As for its contents, the main topic was agriculture (Chap. 2), which consist of three pillars (i.e. land reform, the development of agriculture and the recovery of pre-war output level), accounted for a quarter of the total Plan. The establishment of rural industry was proposed as a source of subsidiary employment opportunities for villagers. As for manufacturing, the Plan suggested that research identify the industries that take best advantage of the country's rich natural resources. Regarding capital ownership, it took the stance that basic industries should be state owned and operated, but that, with respect to consumer industries, there should be room for profit motives and consumer preference for product choice. All in all, it was a proposal that was very much ahead of its time (Burma, Economic Planning Board 1948: 4–17, 21–22).

[10]Namely, a report in 1953 by KTAM (Knappen Tippetts Abbett McCarthy), a group of American engineers and consultants, and '*Pyidawtha Plan*' in 1952 (Walinsky 1962: 64–67).

Survey of Burma, a predecessor to the contemporary *Statistical Yearbook*. In addition, professors of Oxford, Cambridge and Manchester universities were invited to discuss the problems of Burma's economy, using these statistics (Economic Survey of Burma 1951 (1951), introduction).

At the same time, the Two-Year Plan contained ideas that would constitute a cornerstone of economic planning under the 'Burmese Way to Socialism'. It would also hint dissent within the Economic Planning Board, with regard to the extent to which market mechanism would be utilised.

Directly originated from the Plan was the institutional control of marketing and trading of agricultural products by the State Agricultural Marketing Board.[11] There was, however, a predecessor: the Agricultural Project Board, established in 1945, was intended to address the food shortage immediately after the Second World War. Having changed its name to the State Agricultural Marketing Board in 1946, it monopolised the collection and exporting of rice under the supervision of the International Emergency Food Council (Tinker 1959: 255–256).

In the opinion of the Two-Year Plan, paddy could be considered the country's currency, such that violent fluctuations of its price would result in national chaos. For this reason, control of the rice trade in both domestic and international spheres should be entrusted to the State Agricultural Marketing Board as a temporary means to stabilise rice prices and protect the livelihood of the citizens.[12]

The treatment of money and finance in the Chapter 10 of the Two-Year Plan, the prospective cornerstone for the economic recovery of the entire nation, is quite unlike the style of any other chapter. For one thing, it is only a page long and contains hardly any discussions on the monetary details; it simply declares that the government's financial policy should be brought in line with the general policy of state socialism, the only time the term 'socialism' is used in the entire Plan. When the chapter was written, there was no plan to modify the previous currency system; rather, the nation's leaders were willing to issue the currency as in the Colonial Period, through negotiations with India and the United Kingdom. Moreover, it was thought that the country could acquire substantial saving of monetary reserve in the course of its diplomatic negotiations (Burma, Economic Planning Board 1948: 46).

To sum up, the economic policy immediately following the nation's independence was to form a self-sustained economy, such that democracy and the interests of the villagers would be maintained. Economic planning, or the control of market transactions, was considered necessary in order to attain these objectives. Put another way, the laissez-faire attitude of the Colonial Period was criticised as having inhibited the realisation of these objectives. Hla Myint reports that the Burmese government had high expectations of its economic planning (Hla Myint 1971: 279).

[11] Cf. Burma, Economic Planning Board (1948: 14).

[12] However, the Plan suggested that alternative, longer-term methods be devised for stabilising prices (Burma, Economic Planning Board 1948: 13–14).

Both the 1947 Constitution and the Two-Year Plan shared the same idealistic philosophy, which was referred to as welfare statism (state-controlled national welfare plan) (Trager 1958: 4). Section 3 will review the economic changes in and burgeoning philosophy of the Colonial Period, which lead the Burmese economy to stumble in the 1950s, by utilising mainly three papers written by Hla Myint in the 1950s.

3 Economic Failures in the 1950s and Implications of the Theory of 'Vent for Surplus'

In the 1950s, Hla Myint wrote three papers on the export-led, open-door process of economic development; he did so bearing in mind the precedence of land clearing in the lower Burma delta, which was transformed during the Colonial Period from a semi-empty, sparsely populated area to a rice-exporting, flourishing region, by the initiation of foreign trade. Of these three papers, two that were published in 1954 pointed to the existence of 'dis-equalising' factors that hampered the participation of indigenous people in economic activities other than the production of agricultural products. These papers differed in tone from his later writing, but they led to his famous paper of 1958, 'The Classical Theory of International Trade', in which he presented the famous 'vent for surplus' theory. His intension for these papers was the belief that, as a new national government emerged, its leaders' ideas concerning the past would surely influence their international trade policies of the future. Throughout his work, there is a consistent desire to defend against extreme economic nationalism by debunking antiforeign-trade convictions, which had resulted from the colonial trade pattern of exporting primary products and importing manufactured goods (Hla Myint 1971: 91, 94, 145).

It is useful to take a look at Hla Myint's understanding of land clearing during the Colonial Period, by way of examining his 'vent for surplus' theory. 'Vent for surplus' is a notion that, due to foreign demand, 'semi-empty' areas with sparse populations can expand by exporting their products without technical innovation or large-scale investment.[13] This idea was inspired by a passage from Adam Smith, which consisted of two parts: (1) the 'vent for surplus' theory, which claims that international trade helps a country overcome the limited size of its domestic market by providing an outlet for surplus products, and (2) the 'productivity' theory, which argues that international trade will raise the level of domestic productivity by promoting the division of labour. Specifically, Hla Myint took note of the first part of the theory (Hla Myint 1971: 119–120).

---

[13] It so happened that Burmese trade had surplus from the start. This was the reason why Hla Myint thought Burma had not benefited from foreign investment. If, on the other hand, foreign investment flows in large quantity during the initial stage of development, the trade balance usually falls into deficit (Hla Myint 1971: 109).

The reason why the arable land in the delta rapidly expanded without any technical innovation or large-scale investment was that economic resources had been underutilised when demand for Burmese agricultural products increased, so that the growth process started from somewhere within the production possibility curve theoretically attainable. This was because the economy's organisational framework had not been developed to promote the proper allocation of its resources. The incomplete development of 'organizational framework' meant:

1. The rudimentary state of its domestic exchange economy, leading to the underdevelopment of internal trade and the underutilised production potential of the subsistence agriculture
2. Underdeveloped social infrastructure, leading to poor internal transport and communication
3. Underdeveloped administrative and fiscal systems, leading to inadequate public services, including the maintenance of law and order and the enforcement of contracts and property rights (Hla Myint 1987: 120)[14]

According to Hla Myint, the Colonial government did contribute to the improvement of the 'organisational framework'. Even at the height of the laissez-faire era during the latter half of the nineteenth century, he argued that the development of the British colonial hemisphere was never completely left in the hands of the private sector. There was always considerable encouragement of export production by the government, with the goal of increasing its revenue in order to finance the development of social overhead capital in the form of modern administration, transport, health and education services etc. (Hla Myint 1971: 93 n1, 144).

Once the development of organisational framework was underway, it was necessary for foreign trading companies to play a crucial role in creating trade channels between small farmers with the world market, in order to utilise underemployed resources. In fact, these foreign firms provided two functions. First, the foreign trading firms introduced new wants and a wider range of consumer goods to the farmers, and second, the desire for these imported consumer goods spurred the farmers to expand the production of the export crops (Hla Myint 1973: 31–32).

Because of these two factors, rice cultivation expanded rapidly in the hinterland of the delta with the spread of the monetised economy. Hla Myint divides this process into two phases. In the first phase, the farmers were engaged in export crop production as their subsidiary activity, while maintaining their subsistence farming. In this phase, money was merely a means of exchange between imported and exported goods (Hla Myint 1973: 35–36). The existence of surplus resources enabled the farmers to start monetised transactions; that is, the surplus resources made it possible for them to hedge against the risk of entering into trading activities, while safely securing their minimum subsistence (Hla Myint 1971: 134–135).

However, the situation changed significantly in the second phase. Some farmers began to specialise in producing export production. As a result, they had to buy

[14] The word 'economic organisation' is used in Hla Myint (1971: 127). More detailed explanations are available in his later papers.

foods from other farmers, who produced commercial crops for the domestic market, thus creating a demand for money with which to buy foods and other merchandise. In this manner, the money economy was extended from the foreign trade sector into the domestic sector – even to the transactions of labour services, because employment was necessary with the shortage of family labour, and to that of land property, because sales and rentals had been permitted (Hla Myint 1973: 35–36). In other words, the process of market development began with the opening of its door to foreign countries during the Colonial Period, resulting in the birth and expansion of monetary transactions and of the division of labour.

However, the local residents were placed at a serious disadvantage. Firstly, economy of underdeveloped country 'specialise' on crops which they have traditionally produced, and it left the local resident in unspecialized roles as producers using traditional methods of production. Secondly, for foreign enterprises, the process of opening up a new territory for trade was an extremely risky and costly business. Only fairly big firms with sufficiently large reserves could venture into the new territory. Therefore, only large European firms came to buy the native products, acting as a monopoly. Thirdly, numerous Asians served as intermediaries between the local residents and the large European firms, filling the gap between the highly specialised economy of the Western nations and the relatively primitive, unspecialised economy of the local farmers and providing an essential service for the rapid economic development of the area. Not only did these intermediaries play an important role in collecting the agricultural produce from, and selling the imported goods to, the farmers, they also acted as money lenders to local residents. In this manner, a pyramid-shaped social structure developed, with Europeans at the top, the intermediaries in the middle and the local residents at the bottom (Hla Myint 1971: 76–81).

The open-door features of the Burma delta created the 'dis-equalising' factors, as exemplified by the farmers' ignorance of market conditions that could be extremely unstable, their lack of economic power to stand up against the possible tyrannies of speculators and middlemen and their need to borrow money at high interest rates, all of which led to a decrease in the relative share of income attributable to the indigenous population. Hla Myint cited Furnivall's opinion that the free play of economic forces under the conditions of fluctuating export prices had resulted in rural indebtedness, land alienation and agrarian unrest (Hla Myint 1971: 83).

It is important to understand that Hla Myint's basic intention was to safeguard his readers against falling into undue, irrational economic nationalism (e.g. recklessly nationalising foreign companies) by demonstrating the causes of economic suffering of the indigenous people.

As a logical consequence of his understanding of the Burmese colonial economy, Hla Myint recommended that the State Agricultural Marketing Board keep control of the domestic marketing of, and foreign trading of, agricultural products, in order to stabilise agricultural product prices. Furthermore, he suggested that the Burmese government be entitled to retain the country's export surplus, which the foreign trading firms had previously remitted to their home countries.

However, in later years Hla Myint severely criticised the State Agricultural Marketing Board for treating agricultural cultivators as mere 'milk cows' for the sake of government investment in state enterprises. He also warned against the danger of excessive reliance on countervailing measures against foreign economic domination, as they could degenerate into excessive economic nationalism, and the danger of an unduly nationalistic policy (Hla Myint 1971: 34, 90).

If a country were prevented from stimulating contact with the outside world, heavy losses would be incurred in a wide sphere of economic activities, because the country would lose all the indirect gains from foreign trade – namely, the introduction of new technology and new methods of production, improvement in internal transport and communication systems, the extension of public services financed out of increasing government revenues from foreign trade and, last but not least, the growth of a market for merchandise and for the factors of production (Hla Myint 1987: 121). In other words, if the first part of the 'vent for surplus' (i.e. foreign trade) were lost, its second part (i.e. gains realised from the enhanced domestic division of labour) would also be lost.

The paper published in 1958, which advocated the 'vent for surplus' theory, strongly endorsed an export promotion policy. Hla Myint wrote this against the backdrop of a foreign exchange crisis. When import was liberalised in the early 1950s, after the implementation of the Import Control Act of 1947, foreign exchange reserves, accumulated during the Korean boom, were frittered away. By 1954, when the boom of Korean War had expired, the reserve had been reduced to half its original amount.[15] Subsequently, the government was forced to impose import restrictions and to change its development plans (Walinsky 1962: 172–173). By 1958, when Ne Win was placed in charge of a caretaker cabinet, a vicious cycle had already begun between the shortage of foreign exchange, import restrictions and inflation, a characteristic of the Ne Win economy in later decades.

First to have noted the foreign exchange crisis was Hla Myint, who had, after leaving Burma once, returned to Rangoon for the year 1954–1955 to serve as an economic advisor under the auspices of the United Nations. He advised the government to prevent its agency from having the right to receive foreign exchange allocations to finance the capital-intensive development programmes (Walinsky 1962: 166–167, 172–173). However, to his great disappointment and frustration, his advice was 'politically impossible' for the new independent government to accept, given the atmosphere of deeply rooted economic nationalism and anticolonialism at the time, the government had already committed itself to its development programmes (Hla Myint 1971: 146). Hla Myint defined the economic policies of Burma in the 1950s as 'inward-looking', ascribing this perspective to the political and psychological atmosphere that had been moulded by the country's experiences stretching far back into its colonial days. In particular, he suspected that the great depression of the 1930s had had a profound influence on forming the political leaders' future outlooks (Hla Myint 1971: 273).

[15] Hla Myint 1971: 277; Walinsky 1962: 163–166. For more detail on the Import Control Act of 1947, see Tinker 1959: 259.

4 Legacy of the Colonial Period as Viewed from the Study of Economic History

The process of economic development in the delta during the Colonial Period will be easier to understand when it is placed in historical context. This section will complement Hla Myint's analyses by briefly reviewing the early development of the Irrawaddy delta.

During the time of the *Kong Baung* dynasty, people were basically self-sufficient – although, as recent studies have shown, rice exportation had already begun and money was being widely circulated (Coclanis 1993; Toe Hla 1987). In that era, the delta was a sparsely populated, 'semi-empty' area, with an estimated population of about 700,000. In those early days, the expansion of land reclamation was a slow process, so that the colonial government, when it came in, promoted public investment to induce internal migration to the area. By 1873, the roadway of 500 km (800 miles) had been completed, and in 1877, Burma's first railroad was laid out. The water transportation system, which connected the inland districts, was constructed with a subsidy provided by the Irrawaddy Flotilla Company in 1868. Important canals were excavated in the delta, such as Twante, Pegu-Sittang and Pegu-Kyaikto, and annulus embankments for the Irrawaddy River were constructed. The improvement in transportation infrastructure brought immigrants, seasonal labourers, money lenders and merchants to the delta (Adas 1974: 34–35).

With the arrival of the British colonial government, a land tax system was established for the purpose of securing the government's revenue and encouraging the reclamation of the delta. By the 1870s, when land reclamation had started to rapidly expand, the Colonial Government had adapted 'the squatter system', which allowed people to settle freely on any vacant land without obtaining official permission, so long as the settlers kept paying the land tax on the occupied area. The government also used 'the lease system', by which the cultivators were offered lease tenure for a period of 5–10 years, during which time they might extend their cultivation without having to pay additional taxes.

After the 1870s, the land policy was modified: peasant proprietors were encouraged by 'the *patta* system', which granted a small area of land, usually 15–50 acres, to selected cultivators. The system was expected to effectively promote peasant proprietors, since applicants for *patta* licenses needed to show that they were 'genuine' cultivators – which is to say, equipped with the necessary resources for reclamation, such as seeds, tools, cattle and cash, without recourse to money lenders. Under any of these arrangements, and approved by the Land and Revenue Act of 1876, the occupants were given the landholder's right (which was assimilating to land property right), provided that they kept paying the land tax for 12 years.[16] From the

[16] Furnivall 1957: 50–54. The land acquisition system was composed of a total of five parts. In addition to the three parts mentioned in the text, it also included 'the grant system', which permitted capitalists to obtain large areas, and 'the colonisation system', which encouraged people moving into the new frontiers after the beginning of the twentieth century.

1870s to the 1880s, the land revenue settlement operation was conducted at a rapid speed, and detailed settlement maps were drawn for the flatlands plains called Burma Proper. However, the land was not legally registered, and the land revenue roll was used in place of land registry throughout the Colonial Period (Burma, Government Publication 1922: 44–45).

These policies helped boost the area of cultivated land, which doubled from 1.3 million acres in 1860 to 3 million acres in the span of only 20 years. By 1880, the upper delta and the area around Rangoon had been completely cleared, and the wave of reclamation moved into the south-western part of the delta (Cheng 1968: 241). This occurred far faster than the land clearing at Thailand's Chao Phraya, or at Indochina's Mekong Delta, both of which were conducted at around the same time (Johnston 1975: 414–421). Funding for reclamation was provided by the relatives or friends of migrants in Upper Burma until the 1880s.[17] The reclamation was a process of 'scramble for land', or 'struggle for survival', because people could sell as much paddy as they produced (Furnivall 1957: 42, 55). The paddy was carried to the large mills by the port and, until the first decade of the twentieth century, exported to Europe. Large rice mills were built with European capital; while there was only one large mill in 1861, that number increased by 1881 to 49, 41 of which were owned by Europeans.[18] Hla Myint's theoretical model of the land reclamation process matches well with the historical record.

However, there is some reservation about the 'indigenous farmers' specialisation in traditional agriculture', as will be made clear by examining the land revenue roll or the registers of holdings (Register IA, *U pain hmatpoun sayin*). Let us now focus on one particular village tract, namely, the Ngagyigayet in the Maubin District in the centre of the delta (hereinafter the G village). The register of holdings was a record that contained the land holder's name, occupation (agriculturist or non-agriculturist), the size of the cultivated area, amount of revenue, tenancy, mortgage, the sale of land etc., all of which were annually prepared and updated by the local staff of the Land Record Department of the British colonial government. Registers were solely written in the Myanmar language and maintained until the late 1920s (Mizuno 2011: 406).

Land clearing for the G village became possible after the Maubin embankment was established by the British colonial government in 1884 for the purpose of preventing floods during the rainy season. After the completion of the embankment,

[17] Adas 1974: 40, 59, 65. This means that there had been domestic capital formation in Burma under the dynasty.

[18] Cheng 1968: 81–83. It should be noted that the four large European-owned rice mills (Steel Brothers Inc., Bulloch Brothers Engineering, Inc., Ellerman's Arakan Rice and Trading Co. and Anglo-Burma Rice Co.) had formed an alliance called *Bullinger Pool*, the name of which came from the telegraph address of their companies in Rangoon. They milled roughly 30 % of the rice for export from Burma. They consigned paddy milling to other smaller mills, thus gaining a strong monopolistic power on the determination of paddy price (or so their critics argued). The Pool was severely criticised by Burmese nationalists when rice prices drastically fell during the great depression and disbanded (Cheng 1968: 67–68).

the area, which had been described by a colonial officer in 1879 as 'a swamp, producing nothing but myriads of mosquitoes and a few fish', attracted a multitude of immigrants from Upper Burma and was transformed to a relatively densely populated area around Rangoon, as its population rose from 139,498 in 1881 to 210,235 in 1890. The reclamation of the land transformed the Maubin district into 'a flat alluvial plain, devoid of any striking feature to relieve the monotony of its paddy fields beyond the occasional green patches of coconut, bamboo and mango gardens to mark the sites of village lands'. Paddy was cultivated in 85 % of the sown area in the district (Mizuno 2011: 415–416).

The oldest register of holdings of the G village tract that still remains today is for the years 1894–1895, only 10 years after the establishment of the Maubin embankment. Considering that it took 4–5 years after reclamation before the planting of paddy to become possible, the register represents a very early stage of the development of the village. A map, drawn at the same time as the tract, shows that the land holdings were divided into perfect rectangles, each with the area of 20 acres (8 ha). One may safely assume that this area was cultivated under the *patta* system, though no explicit evidence remains to date (Mizuno 2011: 417).

According to this register of holdings, 88 % of the total arable land of 1,687.88 acres (or 1,486.87 ha) was owned by those whose occupations were recorded as *le lout* or *le ya lout sa thu*. Literally translated, *le lout* means 'the one who does paddy fielding' and *le ya lout sa thu* 'a person whose livelihood depends on paddy fielding'. In the British colonial administrative documents, these words were both translated as 'agriculturalist'. However, the original words differed in nuance from the English term (agriculturist), which suggests a person who was engaged in agriculture in general or a peasant. In those days, immediately after the land clearing, some *le lout* were already renting out their lands, amounting to nearly half of the total area, while some other *le lout*s owned a hundred acres of arable land without renting it at all. One realises from these examples that *le lout*s who obtained the land in the 1890s included a wide range of farmers, from those who hired workers and 'do paddy fielding' on a large scale to those who 'do paddy fielding and eat with its earnings' (Mizuno 2011: 406–408, 417–420).

Land ownership in the G village went through a major change in years 1903–1904. The area of land owned by traders (called *koungthe*), who were classified in the colonial statistics as 'non-agriculturalists', reached 893.11 acres, more than half of the cultivated field in the village. Of the land that had come to be owned by *koungthe*, 382.60 acres were, as often suspected, the land whose ownership categories had been transferred from *le lout* to *koungthe*. This, however, was not the whole story. Noteworthy here is that the owners of the remaining 329.62 acres had shifted their occupational categories from *le lout* to *koungthe*.[19] The categories of *le lout*

[19] In 1894–1895, the area owned by *koungthe* was 201.01 acres. Adding to this the total of 712.22 acres (382.60 + 329.62) of land which came to be newly owned by *koungthe* by 1903–1904, as mentioned in the text, the gross total becomes 913.23 acres. As there was one holding that had been sold by a *koungthe* to a *le lout*, the total area of land owned by *koungthe* in 1903/1904 was 893.11 acres.

(agriculturalists) and *koungthe* (non-agriculturalists) were not clearly distinguishable, as they were mutually interchangeable.[20]

The occupational activities of *koungthe* were supposedly paddy brokerage. Until the beginning of the twentieth century, many cultivators, having harvesting the paddy, transported the products by wooden ships with low, flat floors (called *sampan*) or paddy gigs to nearby seaports, where the paddy was sold to mill brokers. Such a practice was no longer common in the twentieth century, when a multitude of merchant-cum-brokers came to act as intermediaries between the primary producers and the mill owners. Included among the intermediary agents were landlords (Cheng 1968: 50–54, 59). According to the colonial report, many of the farmers ('agriculturists') were engaged in speculative paddy trade in the early part of the twentieth century. Having borrowed money by mortgaging their land, they would erect warehouses and store not only their own paddy but also others', purchased from nearby villages at the lowest possible prices during the cropping season, with the goal of resale during the pre-harvesting season (Couper 1924: 8–9).[21] The fact that Burmese farmers participated in paddy trade was quite different from the Thai experience, where Chinese-Thai traders called compradors were hired by the European rice mills to control the entire market transaction of paddy. In addition, the Burmese farmers also participated in rice milling. Small mills owned by the Burmese grew from the beginning of the twentieth century, accounting for 60 % of the total number of rice mills in the 1920s (Cheng 1968: 82–85).[22] Contrary to the situation described by Hla Myint, the indigenous people's specialisation in agriculture had begun to change after the turn of the century.

This does not deny, of course, that 'disequalizing factors' were still at work: large mills, export traders, shippers, insurers etc. were all dominated by oligopolistic European corporations, while overseas financial funding, originating from foreign exchange banks, had deeply penetrated many agricultural villages by way of *chettyars* (Indian money lenders).

It was also true that the farmers were exposed to extremely unstable market conditions. In the G village, almost all of the cultivated land was mortgaged after the beginning of the twentieth century, and 5 % of them transacted annually. Not many landowners kept their land titles for longer than 10 years. By the same token, no tenants kept cultivating the same piece of land for more than a decade. The price of

---

[20] Mizuno 2011: 421. The determining factor in the original record of the category of landowners was, in the opinion of the writer, the place of their residences. For instance, a large landowner who resided in a neighbouring town was registered as a *koungthe*, whereas the same person was entered as a *le lout* when the residence moved to a village not very close to the G village.

[21] The speculative action often led to the loss of the land properties by the farmers.

[22] Note, however, that the Burmese-owned rice mills were small in size. Compared with European-owned rice mills, which employed 40 % of the total number of the workers in rice milling, accounted for only 6.4 % of the total number of milling establishments, whereas the employees working at Burmese-owned rice mills represented approximately 30 % of their total numbers. In terms of the quantity of the product, output per day at large European-owned mills was 100–250 tons, whereas small Burmese rice mills averaged 10–70 tons per day (Cheng 1968: 82–85).

land and the amount of money offered for mortgaged land were considerably high. Especially when grain prices globally increased in the 1920s, the frequency of land transactions went up, and the value of land mortgages soared to more than ten times the average farmer's annual monetary income, inclusive of the value of crops for home consumption. Furnivall reported that land was actively transacted not only to acquire its produce (paddy) but also to earn profit (capital gains) from the only source of investment (land asset) at the time. A cultivator with 5 acres of land, for instance, would borrow money in order to expand his land to 15 acres, then to 40 acres, or even to 400 acres (Furnivall 1957: 58–59, 107).

However, debts accumulated in this manner could not possibly be paid back when paddy price fell during the Great Depression, resulting in foreclosures by *chettyars*. The collapse of the paddy price was a major blow for the tenants who subsisted under the *sabape* loans, whereby they had borrowed cash which they planned to pay back in paddy; it also affected the agricultural labours, who were paid in paddy. During the 1930s, Burma was hit by the sequence of agrarian rebellions (Adas 1974: 185–190).

The stagnation of agriculture and the deterioration of social security in the rural areas were serious problems for the government to deal with. In 1937, the Land and Agriculture Committee was established, to adjudicate agriculture and rural-area issues. In the following year, the committee presented a four-volume report which recommended that the government should regulate tenancy rent, prohibit the transfer of farm lands to non-agriculturists and purchase the farm lands owned by absentee landlords and redistribute them to cultivators (Burma, Government Publication 1938). The proposals were enacted as the Tenancy Act, Land Alienation Act and the Land Purchase Act, respectively, and passed the Burmese Parliament before the Second World War. The Rice Control Board which was empowered to directly control rice exportation was also established (Cady 1958: 390–391; Levin 1960: 215–216). In other words, economic policy directions of the independent, post-Second-World-War government were already underway during the late Colonial Period.

5 Market Distortions during the Period of Burmese Way to Socialism

When the Ne Win regime came about as the result of the *coup d'etat* in March 1962, it advocated socialism, but it was more appropriately characterised by its xenophobia and controlled economy (Khin Maung Kyi et al. 2000: 10; Myat Thein 2004: 7). It has been said that Burmese socialism had its antecedents in the economic history of pre- and early post-Second-World-War years (Thet Tun 1990: 20). The 'inward-looking' economy became even more inwardly drawn during the 1960s. With the help of Hla Myint's papers, this section will look at how 'inward-looking' economic policies were tied to economic control and why Burmese socialism failed.

An overview of the economic characteristics of the decade spanning the 1960s to the 1970s is necessary. The economic policies of the Ne Win military government started with the nationalisation of foreign and domestic companies, which was considered essential for Burmese economy (Thet Tun 1990: 20). In 1963, Burma Oil Company was nationalised, along with joint venture companies, banks, trading companies and other companies that were owned by foreigners and still in business after the 1950s. Also included were some wholesale and retail companies owned by the Burmese. In the case of the manufacturing sector, a plan was announced to proceed with import-substituting industrialisation on a state-owned basis; it was also declared that while new factories would be constructed, there would be no room for expansion by the private sector. All the privately owned manufacturing enterprises of any significant size were nationalised, and the remaining un-nationalised smaller concerns came under administrative control (Myat Thein 2004: 52, 104). According to Hla Myint, the reliance on state-owned enterprising and administrative control was due to the ideological distrust of market mechanism (Hla Myint 1971: 307).

With regard to the agricultural sector, land reform based on the Land Nationalisation Act of 1953, which had been suspended since 1957, was abandoned, and an attempt was made to terminate the landlord system by designating tenants as 'state tenants' and ruling out land rent (Tenancy Act of 1965). The cultivators were now obliged to plant crops according to the directions of the government and to offer their produce to the Union of Burma Agricultural and Marketing Board (or UBAMB, previously entitled as SAMB, or State Agricultural Marketing Board, and renamed in 1963) at far below their market values, depriving the cultivators of their incentive to increase production. While the population was increasing, the growth in rice production was sluggish, and rice exportation had decreased (Mya Than and Nishizawa 1990: 90–97). This entailed the underutilisation of state-owned factories, since the shortage in foreign exchange availability had resulted in a decline of raw materials and spare parts being imported, upon which the factories heavily relied. By this time, the Burmese economy had been caught in a vicious cycle: stagnant exports led to difficulties making payments and worsened budgetary constraints, necessitating low rates of investment, slow industrialisation and low growth, which resulted in stagnant exports. The low rate of production at state-owned factories and the priority given to the importation of raw materials for these nationalised enterprises over the importation of merchandise for consumption led to the shortage of domestic consumer goods and encouraged black markets for contraband goods.[23]

Hla Myint captured these conditions in his paper, *Market Mechanism and Planning*, published in 1968, which explained the reason why an 'inward-looking' policy led to enlarged economic control. In this paper, he categorised economies into two types: 'outward-looking' and 'inward-looking'. The former was characterised by its openness, making use of indirect controls through market mechanism such as foreign

[23] Myat Thein 2004: 59, 81, 106–108. It is pointed out here that a shadow economy was a necessary component of the socialist economy and that the government had seemingly adopted a 'two-wheeled' policy of silent approval.

exchange rates, interest rates, tariffs, taxes and so on, whereas the latter, in contrast, is noted for its insulation, characterised by direct administrative controls such as quotas, licensing, rationing and so forth (Hla Myint 1971: 293–294).

According to Hla Myint, the inherent interdependence between the world and domestic economies established the broad pattern of relationship between direct and indirect controls with economic policy measures. Under the openness of an economy, there was limited opportunity to use arbitrary direct controls to affect it. He also called the readers' attention to the open economies of Asia, which had pursued fiscal and monetary policies that successfully controlled the rate of inflation and kept the external values of their currencies in line with their domestic prices and economic costs. By contrast, the rate of domestic inflation and the overvaluation of domestic currencies at the official exchange rate had been much greater in the insulated economies than in the open economies (Hla Myint 1971: 294–295).

Interestingly, Hla Myint noticed that, at a starting point of directly controlled, insulated economy, the quantitative controls of imports were imposed first in response to a short-run balance of payments crisis. In the 'openness' economy, import control would be used only as a short-run emergency measure, whereas in Burma quantitative controls on imports, once introduced, tended to perpetuate themselves as an integral part of its 'planning' and to spread to the rest of the economy. The tendency was aggravated by the 'inward-looking' policy of domestic industrialisation, due to a failure to clearly distinguish the type of import controls necessary to deal with the short-run balance of payments from the type which was necessary to promote long-run domestic industrial development (Hla Myint 1971: 295–296, 299).

According to Hla Myint, it is easy to understand why direct administrative controls tended to perpetuate and proliferate themselves in 'inward-looking' economies. For instance, the government would find it 'politically unacceptable' to raise the prices of imported goods as a result of quantitative import controls, either because a raise would increase the cost of living and invite demand for higher wages or because it would increase the cost of capital goods and of raw materials for industrialisation programmes. Consequently, the government would control both the quantities and prices of imports, while suppressing the disequilibria that arose from excess demand, using administrative means such as licensing and rationing. Without making drastic changes to improve the international balance of payments, continued control would be inevitable. As the effects of the disequilibria spread to the other parts of the economy, Hla Myint predicted that there would be further need to impose more extensive and comprehensive controls over the rest of the economy (Hla Myint 1971: 296).

Hla Myint also spoke of a well-known defect of the direct control system; that is, it required elaborate bureaucracy in order to operate. Inefficiency and delays due to red tape, such as we see even in developed nations, would be notorious in developing countries. As a result, corruption became prevalent. In addition, when the extensive system of direct control is employed, it becomes necessary to coordinate various controlling measures in order to avoid serious contradictions and to eliminate loopholes that will lead to the growth of black markets (Hla Myint 1971: 299–300).

By pointing out these problems, Hla Myint acknowledged the role of government, which is to encourage the growth of the market economy and to use it as a means to make economic policy. Only through the growth of a well-articulated market economy with a wide taxation base can a government expect to exercise effective controls over the economy and promote economic development. If anything, the government's reliance on market mechanism, which is not equivalent to adopting a *laissez-faire* policy, would improve the organisational framework of underdeveloped countries (Hla Myint 1971: 301).

In the 'inward-looking' economy of Burma, market development was retarded because of the inappropriate policies of maintaining the overvalued domestic currency, setting artificially low rates of interest in the state-enterprises sector and maintaining an unfavourable agricultural price policy for the development of the farming sector.

The retardation of market development was particularly pronounced in the capital markets. Because of complicated government controls, the informal credit market, which actually was a genuine, free credit market, was downgraded to the status of a black market. To begin with, there was a chronic tendency for capital to escape abroad, since the overvalued exchange rate of the domestic currency (kyat) led to domestic inflation. If the government succeeded in blocking the leakage of capital outflows, domestic currency would not come into the formal credit market, but rather be diverted to the purchase of gold, jewellery, real estate and speculative activities. That is to say, domestic funds would not be utilised for economic development (Hla Myint 1971: 304, 327).

In the end, the government could no longer control its economy and reached the verge of a collapse. As for the internal economy, the underground (black) economy grew to a scale as large as the gross domestic value added (in nominal terms). By the middle of the 1980s, the proportion of foreign trade dealings that existed outside official control had expanded to anywhere between 50 % and 85 % of the total trade values (Myat Thein 2004: 80), and rice price in the free market had risen to five times higher than the official procurement price (Tin Soe and Fisher 1990: 128).

Throughout this period, the Burmese government did not succeed in resolving its international balance-of-payment problems by itself. Due to the deterioration of economic conditions, it was left with no choice after the mid-1970s but to change its inward-looking, self-reliant policy of isolation. The first thing the government did was to look for international loans including ODA (official development assistance); however, foreign assistance did not lead to a fundamental solution of the problems, while it did assuage some of Burma's strains. In as much as the country's international debt had reached enormous proportions, the government applied to the United Nations for the status of a 'least less developed country (LLDC)' in order to receive debt relief. The status was duly granted in December 1987.

As the economic growth stagnated again in mid-1980s, the government began its attempt at an economic reform. In August 1987, Ne Win called for a joint meeting of the Central Committee of Burma Socialist Programme Party and various People's Councils and, acknowledging Burma's economic failure, instructed them to devise a plan of economic and political reforms within a year. A month later, on

September 1, 1987, the government announced the removal of controls on domestic trading of nine major agricultural products, such as paddy, maize, *mappe* etc. Moreover, on September 5, 1987, the government launched a demonetisation policy, which became one of the factors that led to the political upheaval of 1988 (Brown 2013: 156–157, 160; Myat Thein 2004: 122–123). All in all, these unfavourable economic circumstances lay behind the uprising of a pro-democracy movement, which eventually inspired the collapse of the socialist regime (Myat Thein 2004: 4–6, 122–123; Brown 2013: 160).

6 Concluding Remarks

After toppling the pro-democracy movement in September 1988 by *coup d'etat*, the State Law and Order Restoration Council (SLORC) turned to the open-door policy. In November 1988, the Foreign Investment Law was introduced, to coincide with the removal of restrictions on private sector participation in domestic and foreign trade. During the 1990s, the government accepted foreign investments in natural resources, which it had hitherto stubbornly refused – a major breakthrough, for the first time since the nation's independence (Myat Thein 2004: 123, 162–163). As a result, Myanmar was freed from a shortage of foreign exchange for the first time since mid-1950s, and its balance of trade at last turned to surplus in 2000.

However, even after the year 2000 with its current trade turning to surplus, it was not easy for the nation to remove all the economic controls, despite the publicly declared, market-oriented policy orientation. As Hla Myint remarked a long time ago, market economy would not grow automatically, irrespective of whatever actions were taken by the government (Hla Myint 1971: 301).

Even in the early years of the twenty-first century, the market mechanism of Myanmar was still developing; it was not difficult to find distortions of resource allocations, artificially created by various forms of past controls. Nevertheless, the adoption and execution of properly designed, new open-door policy will surely shine a bright light on the political economy of Myanmar. Even eliminating the ill-directed legacies of the past that have hindered market development may serve as a kickoff point for fresh, new development (Hla Myint 1971: 304).

References

Adas, M. (1974). *The Burma Delta: Economic development and social change on an Asian rice frontier, 1852–1941*. Madison: University of Wisconsin Press.

AFPFL Convention Broche. (year unknown). *Pamana pyinsin hmu nilakhan hmat than*, Rangoon.

Brown, I. (2013). *Burma's economy in the twentieth century*. Cambridge: Cambridge University Press.

Burma, Government Publication. (1922). *Report of the committee appointed to examine the land revenue system of Burma* (vol I). Rangoon: Government Printing and Stationery.

Burma, Government Publication. (1938). *Report of the land and agriculture committee, part I, II, III* (Reprint, 1949). Rangoon: Government Printing and Stationery.
Burma, Economic Planning Board. (1948). *Two-year plan of economic development for Burma*. Rangoon: Government Printing and Stationery.
Cady, J. F. (1958). *A history of modern Burma*. Ithaca: Cornell University Press.
Cheng Siok-Hwa, C. S. (1968). *The rice industry of Burma: 1852–1940*. Kuala Lumpur: University of Malaya Press.
Coclanis, P. A. (1993). Southeast Asia's incorporation into the world rice market: A revisionist view. *Journal of Southeast Asian Studies, 24*, 2.
Couper, T. (1924). *Report of inquiry into the condition of agricultural tenants and labourers*. Rangoon: Government Printing and Stationery (reprint (1966): Rangoon: Central Press).
Furnivall, J. S. (1957). *An introduction to the political economy of Burma* (3rd ed.). Rangoon: Peoples' Literature Committee & House.
Government of the Union of Burma. (1951). *Economic survey of Burma 1951*. Rangoon: Superintendent of Government Printing.
Hayek, F. A. (1948). *Individualism and economic order*. London: Routledge and Kegan Paul.
Hicks, J. R. (1969). *A theory of economic history*. London; New York: Oxford University Press.
Hla T. (1987). *Money-lending and contractual Thet-Kayits: A socio-economic pattern of the later Kon Baung period, 1819–1885*. Ph.D. dissertation to Northern Illinois University, University Microfilm Series.
Hla Myint. (1948). *Theories of welfare economics*. New York: Augustus M. Kelley. (Reprints of Economic Classics, 1965)
Hla Myint. (1971). *Economic theory and the underdeveloped countries*. New York: Oxford University Press.
Hla Myint. (1973). *The economics of the developing countries* (4th Rev. ed.). London: Huchinson University Press.
Hla Myint. (1987). The neoclassical resurgence of development economics: Its strength and limitations. In G. M. Meier (Ed.), *Pioneers in development, Second Series*. New York: Oxford University Press for the World Bank.
Johnston, D. (1975). *Rural society and the rice economy in Thailand, 1880–1930*. Ph.D. dissertation, Yale University.
Khin Maung Kyi, et al. (2000). *Economic development of Burma, a vision and strategy*. Singapore: The Olof Palem International Centre.
Levin, J. V. (1960). *The export economies, their pattern of development in historical perspective*. Cambridge Massachusetts: Harvard University Press.
Maung Maung. (1961). *Burma's constitution*. The Hague: Martinus Nijhoff.
Meier, G. M. (Ed.). (1987). *Pioneers in development: Second series*. New York: Oxford University Press for the World Bank.
Mizuno, A. (2011). Identifying the 'agriculturists' in the Burma Delta in the colonial period: A new perspective on agriculturists based on a village tract's registers of holdings from the 1890s to the 1920s. *Journal of Southeast Asian Studies, 42*(3), 405–434.
Mya Than, & Nishizawa, N. (1990). Agricultural policy reforms and agricultural development in Myanmar. In M. Than & J. Tan (Eds.), *Myanmar dilemmas and options*. Singapore: ISEAS.
Myat Thein. (2004). *Economic development of Myanmar*. Singapore: ISEAS.
Tin Soe, & Fisher, B. (1990). An economic analysis of Burmese rice-price policies. In M. Than & J. Tan (Eds.), *Myanmar dilemmas and options*. Singapore: ISEAS.
Taylor, R. H. (1987). *The state in Burma*. London: Hurst.
Tin Maung Maung Than. (2007). *State dominant in Myanmar, the political economy of industrialization*. Singapore: ISEAS.
Tinker, H. (1959). *The Union of Burma, a study of the first years of independence* (2nd ed.). London: Oxford University Press.
Todaro, M., & Smith, S. (2011). *Economic development* (11th ed.). Harlow; Tokyo: Addison-Wesley, Pearson.

Trager, F. (1958). *Building a welfare state in Burma, 1948–56*. New York: Institute of Pacific Relations.

Tet Tun. (1957). *A review of economic planning in Burma*. Rangoon: typescript.

Universities Historical Research Centre (UHRC). (1999). *The 1947 constitution and the nationalities* (Vol. 2). Yangon: Innwa Publishing House.

Thet Tun. (1990). The Myanmar economy at the cross road: Options and constraints. In Mya Than & Joseph Tan (Eds.), *Myanmar dilemmas and options*. Singapore: ISEAS.

Walinsky, L. (1962). *Economic development in Burma 1951–1960*. New York: The Twentieth Century Fund.

Chapter 3
Growth Structure and Macroeconomy Under Twenty Years of Junta Regime in Myanmar

Fumiharu Mieno and Koji Kubo

1 Introduction

The economy of Myanmar in the first part of the twenty-first century has been typified by drastic reforms. Since the middle of 2011, Thein Sein's new government moved forward to engage in economic reforms under the newly established parliamentary system. Observing this new trend, the international community started to cooperate with the reforms, and various economic cooperation projects and development research projects were initiated.

However, the structure of the economy of this country has remained largely unexamined at the time of writing. Since the early 2000s, only a few articles and books on Myanmar's economy have been published. For example, Mya Than (2004) and Taylor (2008) have presented relatively comprehensive analyses. They pointed to various points of distortion in the economy without describing the nexus of the distortions that lead to inefficiencies in the economy as whole. After the reforms of 2011 started, some efforts to grasp a more holistic picture of the economy have been made in research such as that by Turnell (2011), ADB (2012), and Mieno (2013).

F. Mieno (✉)
Division of Economic and Political Dynamics, Center for Southeast Asian Studies,
Kyoto University, Kyoto, Japan
e-mail: fmieno@cseas.kyoto-u.ac.jp

K. Kubo
Bangkok Research Center, Institute of Developing Economies-Japan External Trade
Organization (IDE-JETRO), Bangkok, Thailand
e-mail: koji_kubo@jetro.go.jp

K. Odaka (ed.), *The Myanmar Economy*, DOI 10.1007/978-4-431-55735-7_3

Yet, the main purpose of these efforts continues to be updating the details of the past and providing newly unveiled information on the current situation.[1] Since previous studies on the Myanmar economy suffered from a paucity of information, even in terms of the official statistics, these recent efforts have certainly improved our knowledge of Myanmar's economic situation. However, another type of difficulty seems to lie in the fact that there are few comparable examples of countries like Myanmar that have experienced such a variety of extreme swings in the economy and economic policy. For instance, the extremely closed economy before the 1980s was almost unique in the world. Furthermore, the persistence of an unrealistic foreign exchange system over 30 years may be considered a very rare policy, too. More recently, it is not easy to find reference examples in Southeast Asian countries for Myanmar's sudden and quick transformation into the resource-exporting economy it became in the 2000s.

In the search for general characteristics of Myanmar's economy, this chapter focuses on three key economic aspects. First, Myanmar's economy during the 20 years of the junta period had been in the nature of a market transition economy comparable to such economies in Asia and Eastern Europe. Therefore, the military government in the early 1990s faced the challenge of breaking away from the former socialist regime, implementing policies for separating the fiscal and financial sectors, privatizing state-owned enterprises (SOEs), and encouraging private economic activities.

Despite the initial intentions of the military junta, the reforms in the government sector mostly failed or at least remained incomplete. Meanwhile, the private sector had grown primarily through commodity exports and the domestic service sectors. As a result, a gap that emerged between the growing private sector and the government sector became a fundamental cause for macroeconomic instability. The growing private sector became an important element of the financial system in establishing banking businesses, contributing to the privatization of the financial sector, although the fragility of the infant banks subsequently became another cause for the macroeconomic instability.

Second, despite the moderate economic growth after the junta's reforms in the 1990s, signs of industrialization had been rather limited up until the late 2000s. Known as an "open door policy," the junta government took on a policy stance of waiving its traditional isolation from the international economy, "authorizing" foreign trade, and encouraging foreign direct investment (FDI). Economic growth in this early stage was through the export of natural endowments, including timber, precious gems, noble metals, and marine products. Although FDI expanded in the 1990s, this was mostly toward the service sectors, such as energy, construction, and real estate, whereas the share of the manufacturing sector in economic activity

[1] For the studies on specific sectors in the junta period, please refer to Turnell (2009) for the financial sector, Kudo and Mieno (2009) for trade and FDI, and Kubo (2007) for price and currency. As a work for understanding the whole picture of Myanmar economy, Fujita et al. (2009) and author's papers published in the book provide the bases of this chapter.

barely increased, remaining at less than 10 % until the 2010s. The slow growth of industrialization arose, at least partly, through distortions stemming from an incomplete reform process in the government sector, including an unfavorable exchange rate and heavy taxation on exports.

Finally, particularly after the mid 2000s, the Myanmar economy began to more clearly take on the features of a resource-exporting economy, in all likelihood most comparable to some African countries.[2] From the export of precious gems and noble metals in the early stages of economic development, the export of natural gas has rapidly expanded in the 2000s, contributing to improve the condition of the government sector and therefore helping to regain macroeconomic stability.

The present chapter aims to grasp the structure of the Myanmar economy as a whole by retrospectively examining the process of its formation during the 20 years of junta period. In doing so, the chapter tries to derive implications for the ongoing reforms. The organization of the chapter is as follows: Sect. 2 (following) examines the reforms that have occurred since 2011. Section 3 provides an overview of the changes in the economic structure of Myanmar over the two previous decades, i.e., 1990–2010. The first subsection explains the "reform" by the junta government in the early 1990s, and the second and the third subsections show the growth performance and sectoral development at the time. Section 4 discusses macroeconomic conditions and examines the basic reasons for economic instability while touching upon on the issue of the formation of financial sectors at the time. Section 5 discusses the ways of understanding Myanmar's economy and confronting existing policy challenges. Section 6 offers some conclusions to the chapter, stating the agendas and suggesting a sequence for economic reform in Myanmar.

2 Economic Reforms Since 2011

Political and economic reforms in Myanmar accelerated in the 2010s. A general election based on the new Constitution was held in November 2010. Even though the Constitution contains various rules favorable to the military government, the election was successfully conducted and new representatives were elected. In March 2011, the General Assembly was convened, electing Thein Sein as "President," a post created by the new Constitution. General Than Shwe, who had long chaired the State Peace and Development Council and was Head of State, retired, passing on the position to the new President.

Since the first Assembly, reforms in both the political process and economic policy have accelerated. Thein Sein, in his first presidential address to the Parliament in March 2011, emphasized democratization and economic reform. In May, the first comprehensive amnesty that included an amnesty for political offenses was imple-

[2] For the arguments related to resource-exporting economy such as resource curse or Dutch diseases, refer to Corden (1984), Davis (1995), or Katz et al. (2004), for example.

mented, and in August a direct dialogue between the President and Daw Aung San Suu Kyi took place. The political party registration law was amended to make it easier to form a political party. Under this improved political climate, the National League for Democracy (NLD), the largest opposition party, decided to join the political process under the new Constitution in October 2011. In November 2011, Myanmar was selected as the chair country for the ASEAN general meeting to be held in 2014, as a symbol of Myanmar's return to the international society. At a by-election in April 2012, Daw Aung San Suu Kyi was elected as a congress member, and emerged as an "authorized" opposition leader in parliament.

Along with the improvements in the political process, senior officials and advisers enthusiastically advocated the need for drastic economic reform and succeeded in the gradual lifting of unreasonable economic regulations that had constrained Myanmar's economy over a long period. In April 2013, the exchange rate system was significantly changed, unifying the multiple rate system into a near-market rate, thereby virtually realizing a managed float system. The new central bank law to establish its independence from the budgetary department was enacted in August 2013. Accompanying the exchange system reform, the need for drastic SOE reforms had become inevitable and was duly put on the agenda. A survey on the development of port infrastructure at three sites, Dawei, Thilawa, and Kyaukpyu, and surrounding industrial estates is being conducted. New investment laws in preparation for an expected increase in FDI were enacted in April 2013. Further proposals for the restructuring and enhancement of infrastructure of the financial system are being examined at the time of this writing (January 2015) with the cooperation of the World Bank, Asian Development Bank, and the government of Japan.

Despite the process of democratization and economic reform since March 2011, conflicts in areas where there are significant racial minority have occasionally broken out (such as Rakhine and Kachin States—both in June 2012), and groups opposing reform remained in both the government party and the army. However, President Thein Sein gradually strengthened his political position, which was partly due to obtaining the cooperation of the opposition parties, including NLD.[3]

On the other hand, the early twenty-first century the macroeconomy showed some signs of weaknesses. It was forecast that in the near future, the deregulation of imports would bring the trade balance into negativity after 2012, even though exports would continue to grow. The market exchange rate for local currency, which had been appreciating since 2006, turned into devaluation in early 2013. The first steps of the reform were successfully undertaken, but the environment of the reform was in fact, still fluid.

[3]In June 2012, he reshuffled the cabinet to promote major pro-reform members to higher positions.

3 Economy in the Junta Regime

3.1 Reform in the Early 1990s and Trends in the Economy

Reform in the early 2010s aimed at eradicating various economic distortions. To trace the distortions to their origins, this section reviews the profile of the Myanmar economy in the 20 years of the junta rule.

The starting points for any examination can be found in the "reforms" by the junta government in the early 1990s. Having captured the power in September 1988, the junta government declared its intention to abolish "the Burmese way of socialism" and undertake various reforms. In short, a series of reform policies were oriented to market transition economy reform.

The fiscal and financial sectors were separated. For the financial sector, the mono-bank of the socialist economy was divided into the central bank and other specific state-owned banks that provided services such as foreign exchange and agricultural development. The commercial banking sector was opened up for private capital entry under license, and private commercial banks were established by the mid 1990s. While the financial sector's reform went smoothly, by comparison, reform in the fiscal sector stalled. Reform of the SOEs remained incomplete, with only small factories and retail shops being privatized, but for the most part, the sector remained unchanged. Nonetheless, the autonomy of the SOEs was weakened under the integrated account system introduced in 1990.

The external economic relationship was largely liberalized. Trade, which had been strictly limited under "the Burmese way of socialist regime", was totally liberalized under the import licensing system, including trade in border areas. The authorization of trade had a fundamental impact on the economy in terms of Myanmar's historical context. Also, the institutions for accepting foreign direct investment (FDI) were gradually built: New laws—Foreign Investment Law (1988), Myanmar Citizen Investment Law (1994)—were enacted, and the Myanmar Industry Development Council was established in 1995.

Meanwhile, the junta government's attitude toward reforms for macroeconomic stabilization was very passive. In general, formation of the financial sector and the deregulation of trade and capital flow inevitably complicate the demand and supply of the money and foreign exchange. In Myanmar, however, in spite of the change of real and financial sectors, the system for control of money and foreign exchange remained unchanged. The exchange rate had been virtually fixed to 5–6 % against the US dollar, and directly holding foreign currency was prohibited in the private sectors: All exporters were obligated to deposit foreign currency at either the Myanmar Investment and Commercial Bank (MICB) or Myanmar Foreign Trade Bank (MFTB).

In many ways, these reforms brought about a degree of dynamism to growth in the 1990s. The "start" of trade realized a vast *surplus of trade*, particularly in exports from the primary sector such as agricultural and marine products and precious metals, which accelerated capital accumulation in the private sector. The expanding exports triggered greater diversification of crops in the agricultural sector (Fujita and Okamoto 2009). FDI also grew—mainly in the construction, tourism, and mining sectors. Under such stimulation of economic and financial reform, private banks were established one after another by the growing private business capital in mid 1990s, forming a domestic financial system.

Meanwhile, the halfway reforms brought confusion to the economy. While the reforms achieved market-based economy to a degree in trade, finance, and investment, strong state control over policies in the fiscal sector including SOEs, the monetary sector, and the foreign exchange system remained little changed. In particular, the stiff foreign exchange system continued to keep in place an unrealistic official exchange rate, thereby fostering a large-scale black currency market. Attempts by the government to unify the multiple rate system into a managed float system at a level near the market rate in 1997–2001 by manipulating foreign exchange certificates (FEC, introduced in 1993) further worsened confusion in the macroeconomy. The two separated markets, one for the private (black) market and the other for public sector, continued to coexist throughout the junta period. The official and market exchange rates diverged increasingly due to the large depreciation of the domestic currency caused by accelerating inflation.

While the economic structure persisted on this basis until 2011, it was sometimes challenged by external changes. The Asian financial crisis (AFC) in 1997–1998 suddenly caused exports and FDI inflow to stop, worsening the inconsistency of state policies. The government, facing a serious shortage of foreign reserves, resorted to direct import restrictions and strict controls on foreign currencies gained through the private sector. By doing so, the government adhered to the existing system and was able to avoid any drastic reforms. In 2003, Myanmar's economy experienced a serious recession triggered by bank runs. The situation was converted again in around 2004, as natural gas production, which had been developed since the early 1990s, came online. Gas exports enabled the government to accrue large foreign reserves and increase its fiscal revenues. This rescued the economy from the crisis and brought about some stability.

3.2 Growth Performance

It is noteworthy that although economic performance over the 20 years of the junta's reign may not be interpreted as highly successful, the economy was not always in a state of misery—and sometimes even went well. Table 3.1 shows the real economic growth rate in Myanmar. As the official estimates of GDP are generally considered to be less reliable after 1999, we included in the table alternative estimations by the International Monetary Fund (IMF), the Economist Intelligence Unit (EIU), and Regional Outlook (RO). While there is substantial variation between the alternative estimates, we can readily observe a few common trends and note that the process of economic change in Myanmar over the two decades may be divided into three distinct periods, i.e., (i) 1988–1996, (ii) 1997–2003, and (iii) 2004 and after.

Table 3.1 GDP growth rate (real, annual, percentage)

	Official	EIU	IMF estimate	Regional outlook
1989	3.7			
1990	2.8			
1991	−0.7			
1992	9.7			
1993	6.0			
1994	7.5			
1995	6.9			
1996	6.4			
1997	5.7			
1998	5.8			
1999	10.9	10.9[a]		
2000	13.7	13.6[a]		5.5
2001	10.5	5.3		5.0
2002	12.0	5.3	5.5	4.5
2003	13.8	−1.0	0.0	3.2
2004	13.6	−1.1	5.0	3.0
2005	13.6	1.1	4.5	3.7
2006	12.7	3.4	7.0	
2007	12.0	0.9	5.5	
2008	10.3	1.1	3.6	
2009	10.6	1.8	5.1	
2010	10.1	3.3	5.3	
2011	12.0	3.2	5.5	
2012			6.3	

Source
Official: 1993–1994: Key Indicators 2003, Asian Development Bank, 1995–2008: Statistical Yearbook 2008, Central Statistical Organization, 2008–2011: Regional Outlook, ISEAS, 2012–2013, p. 171
EIU: Economic Intelligence Unit, 1999–2001: ver. Nov. 2002–2005, ver. Sep. 2005, 2006–2007: ver. April 2009, 2008–2011: Regional Outlook, ISEAS, 2012–2013, p. 171
IMF estimate: IMF Country Report and others
[a]EIU estimate followed the official statistics until 2000

Here, together with the growth rate, we briefly touch upon the key developments of the economy in each of these three periods. Firstly, during (i), the period from 1988 to 1996, the government implemented reforms to transform the Myanmar economy from a socialist regime to a market-based regime, as described above. As a result of these reforms, after 1992, the Myanmar economy attained a reasonable level of economic growth of about 6–8 % annually, driven mainly by commodity exports and FDI.

Secondly, during (ii), the period from 1997 to 2003, the economy experienced a significant external shock in the form of the Asian financial crisis (AFC). Consequently, after 1998, export growth slowed and FDI declined sharply.

The expanding current account deficit and the disappearance of foreign capital inflows brought about a serious shortage of foreign reserves in Myanmar, and this worsened the level of macroeconomic instability. Despite this, the economy continued to grow at least for a short time, mainly through the strong performance of the domestic service sector (i.e., the real estate and construction boom) and the emergence of a vibrant export garment industry. The booming domestic economy, however, resulted in a bank run in 2003 in the still infant private banking sector, leading to overall economic depression.

The official statistics reported a slight decline in the growth rate between 1997 and 1998. Then after 1999, the official statistics showed a very high growth rate that was inconsistent and inexplicable based on the circumstances at the time. EIU and IMF started to adopt their own alternative estimates after 2001 or 2002. Still, up until 2003, even these alternative GDP estimates showed moderate growth (around 5 %). The economy was presumed to have continued moderate growth until the end of 2002, probably led by the service sector and then frozen by the bank run in late 2002. As indicated by some of the alternative GDP estimates (EIU and IMF), the economic growth rate in 2003 may have even been negative.

However, during (iii), the period after 2004, the economy recovered in an unexpected way. The natural gas industry, having developed through the assistance of FDI in period (i), commenced stable production in 2003–2004 and became a large source of export revenues. Owing to natural gas exports, the current account turned to surplus after 2002, and the problem of foreign reserve shortages disappeared. As a result, the economy recovered to attain a growth rate of 2–6 % (though the rates varied across the range of estimates), and the macroeconomy returned to a position of stability. The newly elected Thein Sein Government was able to kick off its reforms in 2011 in significantly more favorable economic and fiscal conditions.

3.3 Sectoral Structure

As explained above, any macroeconomic growth which had been realized was based on sectoral development. Needless to say, this is closely related to changes in external economic relationships: trade and FDI. Table 3.2 and Fig. 3.1 show the composition of GDP and FDI inflow by sector from the 1990s through to the 2000s. Figure 3.2 details the trends in trade classified by export products and trade balance (in Myanmar kyat). These three figures indicate the characteristics of the sectoral development in Myanmar's economy during the 1990s.

During the early 1990s, period (i), when Myanmar's economy grew rapidly, the largest industry in terms of value added was agriculture (representing about 50–60 % of total GDP), followed by the gradually growing value added of trade (some 20 % of total GDP). In contrast, the share of the manufacturing sector in overall economic activity was only 6.8 % in 1993, and it increased only slightly during the 1990s.

Figure 3.1 indicates that, in spite of the accelerating FDI inflow following the relevant legal institutional arrangements, the inflow was mostly toward the service sector, such as hotels, real estate, and mining, including gas and oil, and very little

Table 3.2 Sectoral composition of GDP (percentage)

	Agriculture	Mining	Electricity, gas, and water	Manufacturing	Construction	Trade	Others
1988	57.4	0.7	0.4	7.5	1.1	20.8	12.2
1992	60.5	0.5	0.2	6.9	1.8	22.6	7.4
1996	60.1	0.6	0.3	7.1	2.4	22.6	6.8
2000	57.2	0.6	0.1	7.2	1.8	24.0	9.0
2004	48.2	0.6	0.2	11.6	3.9	22.3	13.2
2008	40.3	0.9	0.7	16.8	4.2	21.1	15.9
2009	38.1	1.0	1.0	18.1	4.5	20.3	17.0
2010	36.4	0.9	1.0	19.5	4.5	19.8	17.8

Source: Statistical Database System, Asian Development Bank, in December 2012

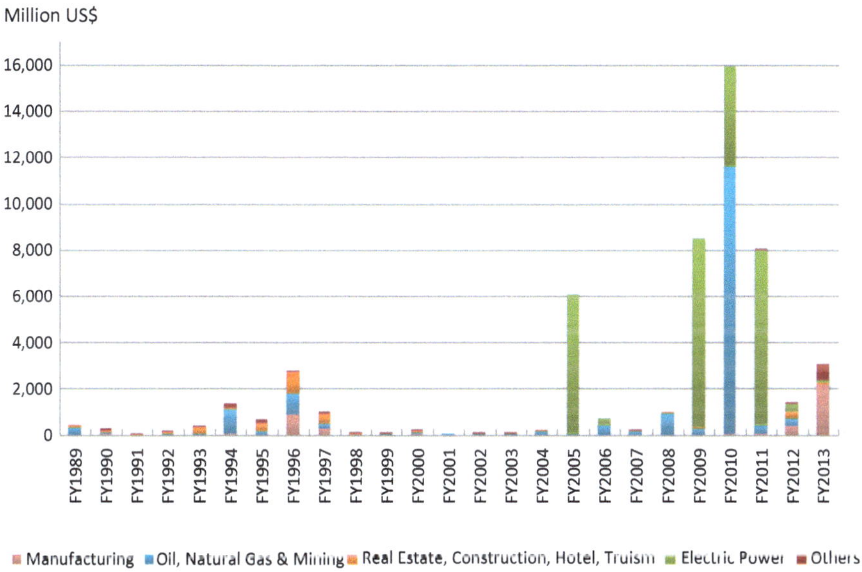

Fig. 3.1 FDI inflow (approval base) (*Source*: Selected Monthly Economic Indicators, CSO, various years). Note: the figure of 2013 is the forecasted value based on the performance in April–October

was toward the manufacturing sector. Economic growth in Myanmar in period (i) was instead mostly through the trade and domestic service sectors.[4]

The prevailing trade structure confirms this feature. As shown in Fig. 3.2, the major component of exports was agricultural and marine products and "others," which presumably included precious gems and noble metals. This indicates that the

[4] Note that there was a serious gap between the amount of approved investments and the aggregated amount of FDI in the balance of payment, as pointed out by Mieno (2009) and Kudo and Mieno (2009).

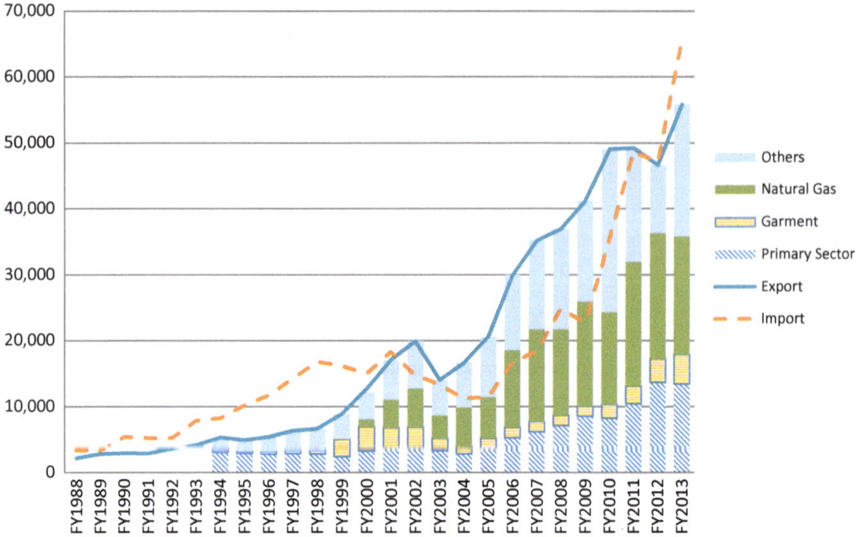

Fig. 3.2 The trend of export commodities and trade account (*Source*: Statistical Yearbook, CSO). Note: Million kyat. For the volumes of each commodity in 2011–2013 are estimated from the information in US dollar. The volumes of 2013 are forecasted based on the performance in April–October

growth process during the first period was mainly led by the expanding commodity trade under the condition that trade was openly "authorized" and the investment of foreign capital in the service sector was encouraged. Meanwhile, the state of industrialization at this time remains unclear.

In general, a growth structure deeply dependent on commodity exports and foreign investment in the absence of industrialization may lead to severe macroeconomic vulnerability. In the case of Myanmar, this was amplified by the external shock of the AFC during the second period. Since the early days of reform, the trade balance had worsened, and the trade deficit expanded. Under such conditions, the AFC suddenly stopped FDI inflow in 1998, which led to a shortage of foreign reserves for the Myanmar Government. The market exchange rate further declined as a result, so that the government strengthened foreign currency controls to enable transfer from the private sector to the government sector at a much appreciated value. To cope with the decrease in foreign reserves, the government in Myanmar moved to directly restrict imports after 1999. As shown in Fig. 3.2, any increases in imports were restricted from 1999 to 2005.

It is noteworthy that even in such an environment, the export sector showed a remarkable evolution; the garment sector emerged as a large exporter, leading to an increase in exports up until about 2002. As shown in Table 3.2, the share of manufacturing as a proportion of GDP slightly increased in the period of 2000–2002 from about 6 % to 7–9 %. During this period, there was a slight trend in that the Myanmar economy began the shift to a labor-intensive form of industrialization. As a result of the restriction of imports and such increase in exports, the trade account deficit shrank after 1999, finally achieving a surplus in 2001.

Oddly in a sense, although FDI inflow drastically slowed during this period, the domestic service sector appeared to remain active throughout and after the AFC. For example, real estate development continued to flourish in the Yangon area. Most of the private banks that arose in the 1990s formed through the affiliation of business groups in these service sectors and so were highly dependent on real estate and developer business. Such businesses were certainly booming until 2002. It was the bank run in late 2002 triggered by bankruptcies of informal financial institutions that moved the domestic service sector into recession leading to an overall slowdown in economic growth in 2003–2004.

Then, in period (iii) (2004 onwards), the economy exhibited yet another swing in activity, with the gas fields in Myanmar coming on line. Beginning in 2004, natural gas exports from Myanmar exhibited a stable and increasing trend, resulting in a dramatic surge in total exports. In fact, according to Fig. 3.2, the total value of exports tripled from 2004 to 2010, with natural gas exports accounting for between 30 % and 39 % of the total. This was, in fact, a late-coming fruit of the intensive foreign investment in the natural gas sector during period (i), the early 1990s. As shown in Fig. 3.2, the share of "other services" as a portion of total GDP also increased after 2004. Responding to the recovery of the economy, FDI inflow to Myanmar increased after 2005, mainly to the electric power and natural gas sectors, further accelerating the development of these sectors. Up to the end of the 2000s, the Myanmar economy reverted to its historical feature as a commodity-exporting economy.

In sum, since the junta reforms in the early 1990s, the growth of the Myanmar economy had been realized by expanding exports of primary products and by the investment in the nonmanufacturing sector. The AFC brought about a trade deficit and shortage of foreign reserves, but changes to the export sector kept the crisis to a minimum as a result. The changes in the export sector at that time were twofold: one was the emergence of the garment sector and another was the fruit of natural resource development. In the recovery process after 2004, the latter factor became overwhelmingly significant.

4 Financial and Monetary Systems Under the Junta Regime

4.1 Fiscal Deficit and Inflation

It is typically observed in market transition economies that the reform of the government sector remains insufficient, in contrast to the moderate development in private business. This causes vulnerabilities in the macroeconomy. In the case of Myanmar, the major problems were insufficient SOE reform, and adherence to an extremely inflexible foreign exchange system in circumstances where foreign currency transactions expanded explosively as trade and FDI were activated.

Incomplete reform by the junta gave impetus to informal economic activities in the private sector including the informal foreign exchange market. The pervasive informal economic activities were also associated with low tax revenue of the government, which eventually led to monetization of fiscal deficits and high inflation.

The mechanism of inflation incurred by the monetization of fiscal deficit is well-known. Although it seems apparent that this mechanism was the basis of Myanmar's macroeconomic instability during the junta period, the lack of consistent statistics have made the verification impossible. However, to provide some evidence of the situation at the time, Table 3.3 details the budgetary condition, the money supply, and the inflation rate during the period. The SOE account is available in official statistics only for the period of 1994–1999, since the government stopped disclosing the information after 2000. However, the deficit of SOE accounts shows a comparable level to the deficit of the central government deficit in the 1990s, and it relatively worsened in the late 1990s. It strongly suggests that the prevailing fiscal deficit remained at a substantial level, at least during the 1990s, in part caused by deficits in the SOEs. Since the SOE reforms stalled, apart from the privatization of small establishments in the early 1990s, as previously pointed out, the gradual increase of the SOE deficit after 1997 may imply that SOEs having lost competitiveness against private business and had thereby become a large factor in the fiscal deficits.

However, the size of the fiscal deficit may not solely have been caused by the problems related to SOEs. Above all, the size of total revenue in Myanmar continued to be very small, even compared with market transition economies in similar situations. Figure 3.3 shows a comparison of the size of general government including SOEs for Cambodia and Laos, both countries that had a similar level of per capita GDP. The expenditure of Myanmar was relatively small, implying that the problem lay with the revenue side. Tax revenues accounted for only 4 % of GDP, about a half of the level in Laos. Unlike Cambodia and Laos, the availability of official development aid and general external borrowing was limited for Myanmar due to the accumulated arrears. Such a condition was one of the basic causes of dependence on the monetization of fiscal deficit.[5] Meanwhile, the deficit of the central government remained almost constant through 1999, the latest year relevant statistics were available. In addition to the SOE problem, lack of the general tax reform to enhance the tax revenue may have been another cause of the serious deficit and hence of inflation.

The growth rate of both the money supply and inflation (CPI) lay in a range of 20–30 % and were apparently synchronized, suggesting that changes in the price of

[5] The ratio of tax revenue to GDP was apparently low by international comparison. According to Tanzi and Zee (2000), the rate in 1995–1997 was 37.9 % in OECD member countries and 18.2 % in developing countries on average.

Table 3.3 Fiscal condition, money supply, inflation

Fiscal balance to GDP (percentage)						Money supply (annual growth rate)		Inflation rate (CPI, % change)
	ADB	IMF	Government official statistics			ADB		ADB
Source	General government	General government	General government	Central government	SOEs	M1	M2	
1980			−5.3	1.8	−7.1			
1985			−4.5	−2.8	−7.4			
1990	−2.8		−6.4	−4.2	−2.3			
1991	−3.7					35.3	31.1	32.3
1992	−2.1					37.6	35.6	21.9
1993	−1.4					24.6	26.8	31.8
1994	−2.5		−6.5	−3.4	−3.1	31.1	33.9	24.1
1995	−3.3		−6.6	−4.2	−2.4	34.0	40.5	25.2
1996	−2.2		−6.6	−3.2	−3.4	32.8	38.9	16.3
1997	−0.1		−5.1	−0.9	−4.2	32.1	28.9	29.7
1998	0.8		−5.7	−0.4	−5.3	30.7	36.5	51.5
1999	−0.3		−5.0	−1.7	−3.3	22.6	29.6	18.4
2000	0.7					34.9	42.2	−0.1
2001						52.1	44.8	21.1
2002		−3.6				42.9	34.2	57.1
2003		−5.4				14.9	0.2	36.6
2004		−4.7				27.9	34.5	4.5
2005		−3.3				26.5	24.1	9.4
2006	−4.3	−4.2				26.5	27.2	20.0
2007	−3.8	−3.8				30.2	30.0	35.0
2008	−2.3	−2.4				11.5	14.0	26.8
2009	−4.6	−4.8				5.2	8.0	1.5
2010	−4.5	−6				32.1	42.5	7.7
2011		−5.5				20.5	30.5	5.0

Source: ABD: Statistical Database System, IMF: IMF Country Report, International Financial Statistics 2012, Official: Statistical Yearbook, 2002, 2007
Note: The year represents fiscal year (April to March)

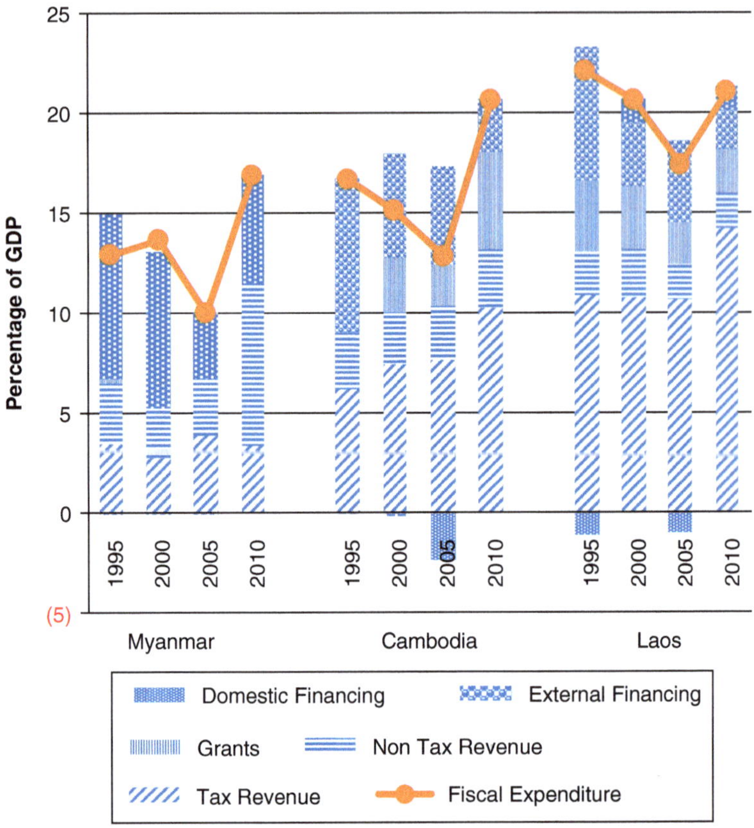

Fig. 3.3 Fiscal revenue, expenditure, and financing of deficit in Myanmar, Cambodia, and Laos (*Source*: IMF Country Report)

goods during this period clearly corresponded to changes in the money supply. Inflation surged further in the early 2000s, with the annual growth rate reaching 40 %. There was apparently a *quantity-theory-of-money*-type relationship between money supply and inflation.[6] On the other hand, the relationship between the fiscal deficit and money supply was less clear from the available information. Due to the lack of reliable statistics, we can only infer that although the deficit may be a fundamental factor in inflation, the causes of its fluctuation remain unclear.

[6] Ito and Kumamoto (2004) identified a clear co-integrative relationship between the money supply and inflation using data from 1997 to 2002. Kubo (2007) also confirms the same relationship using data from 1996 to 2006.

4.2 *Foreign Exchange System, Exchange Rate, and Rent Mechanisms*

The complicated foreign exchange system that operated in Myanmar during the period of the military junta is a clear indicator of the halfway progress of transitional reforms during this time. They effectively functioned as a serious impediment to the development of a healthy private sector.

Figure 3.4 plots the nominal exchange rate of the Myanmar kyat against the US dollar and other currencies. Since 1977, the official exchange rate was pegged to the IMF's Special Drawing Rate (SDR) at 8.50847 kyat and therefore in the range of about 5–6 kyat to the US dollar. Under this arrangement, the thick black market was formed. Kiryu and Nishizawa (1996) noted that the kyat market rate in the early 1990s went up to as high as 20 times the official rate, with the overvalued official rate mainly applied to SOEs in import substitution sectors.[7]

In February 1993, the Myanmar Government introduced foreign exchange certificates (FEC) and fixed it to an alternative official rate, sometimes called the exchange centre rate (ECR), which was close to the market rate at that time; ECR was applied to export transaction in private sector and the calculation for export tax.

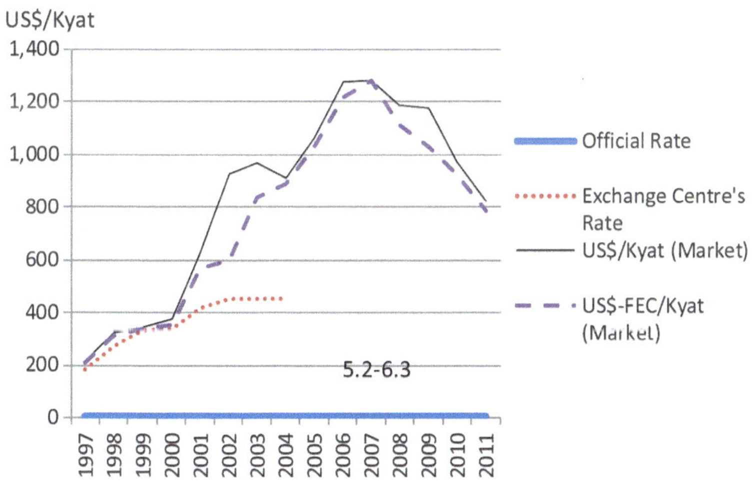

Fig. 3.4 Trend of nominal exchange rate (*Source*: Collected from various sources (including among information venders))

[7] Kiryu and Nishizawa (1996) report that the market rate in 1994 was 100–120 kyat against the US dollar and interpret the system as a part of the scheme for protecting SOEs. Until the mid 1990s, the level of the divergence between the official and market rate was moderate. During that period, the system may have functioned better to protect SOEs compared to that in 2000s when the level diverged unrealistically.

On the surface, the private sector's foreign currency holdings remained strictly controlled by the government, with exporters being obliged to deposit their gains in foreign currency into either of two foreign exchange banks: the Myanmar Investment and Commercial Bank (MICB) or the Myanmar Foreign Trade Bank (MFTB). Through these state banks, exporters were charged an export tax of 8–10 % and were obliged to exchange foreign currency into kyat at the ECR. Moreover, at that time, approval for importation was given in principle only when payment in foreign currency was made to the foreign exchange banks, i.e., the foreign currency (normally US dollars) which had been originally acquired through exportation. In response to the regulation, however, the prevailing practice in the private sector was done in an informal way that an exporter would provide their foreign currency earned from exports for an importer's payment under the exporter's name. Such an informal transaction or a black market for "export-earning foreign currency deposit" was formed and expanded.[8]

During the early stages of economic development in Myanmar, this system functioned as the mechanism for transferring foreign exchange from the private sector to the government (the SOEs) with moderate exploitation from private sector. It enabled the high official rate and the allocation of foreign exchange to the government sector to persist. For a few years after the AFC (during period (ii)), facing the critical decrease of foreign reserves, the government temporarily strengthened the control of foreign exchange in the way that the import was strictly controlled generally, being allowed only for the export firms.

The situation changed again when natural gas exports loosened the foreign exchange constraint of the government sector. After the mid 2000s, with the government creating its own foreign currency income source by exporting natural gas, the necessity for the government to exploit the private sector in terms of obtaining foreign exchange disappeared rapidly. The government largely loosened the controls on foreign exchange in the private sector and virtually abandoned intervention in market transactions. As a result, the foreign exchange market separated into (1) a "de facto pure float market" form of currency circulation for the private sector and (2) government sector circulation, where the a certain kind of official rate probably applied. These characteristics persisted in the foreign exchange markets until the time when the Thein Sein Government authorized the market rate in April 2012, to which the official rate quickly adjusted itself.

[8] Such a transaction custom persisted until the foreign exchange reform in 2012 and is regarded as one of major causes for high transaction costs in the foreign exchange market. But the real picture has been barely revealed due to lack of systematic research. The Box section of this chapter reports a snapshot of such transactions based on a survey conducted in 2009.

4.3 Emergence and Turmoil of the Private Banking Sector

Generally, in market transition economies, the management of the financial sector separated from the fiscal sector becomes a major issue and sometimes instigates an unstable macroeconomy. In particular, as is frequently the case, a newly privatized banking sector absorbs private deposits in a short time and expands very rapidly in terms of asset size, while the capacity of loan supply can hardly catch up with the speed of such expansion. As a result, the banking sector tends to direct its abundant assets to closely related sectors, typically the real estate and construction sectors. Such sectors are usually mother bodies of private banks, forming business groups together. Therefore, the loans to such sectors can be made without a skillful evaluation process or adequate information processing. In the early stages of market transition economies, this frequently brings about a surge in asset prices, with a resulting burst in prices.[9]

The case of Myanmar in the 1990s was also characterized by the malfunction of state banks born from the socialist mono-bank and by the rapid formation of private banks. In the latter process, 20 new private banks were established between 1992 and 1997, and they explosively increased their assets by absorbing deposits. Private banks played a central role in the temporary asset price surge in urban areas in the early 2000s, where active business transactions took place in the real estate and construction sectors, but then triggered a bank run in 2003 leading to a serious recession in the real estate sector.

Table 3.4 lists the private banks for which information was available in the early 2000s, along with more recent indicators in Table 3.5. The private banking sector in fact experienced both strong expansion and contraction activities in the first decade of the twenty-first century. The Myanmar Government enacted the Financial Institution Law in 1990 and granted licenses to 20 banks in 1992–1997. Large business groups operating in the nonmanufacturing sector sometimes established banks.

Examples of banks founded at the time include Yoma Bank, which was established in 1993 as a subsidiary of First Myanmar Investment (FMI) group, which had grown through investments in hotels, real estate, and import businesses. Asia Wealth Bank was established in 1994 under the initiative of the Olympic Group, one of Myanmar's largest construction conglomerates (Mieno 2009). It was Myanmar's largest bank in 1999 but was extensively damaged by a bank run in 2003. A more recent arrival, Kanbawza Bank was established by a ruby trader in Shan state in 1994. Known for its conservative management, it had few assets before the bank run in 2003 and grew rapidly after the run by absorbing the outflow of deposits from the damaged, frail banks, ultimately becoming Myanmar's largest private bank. In addition, there was also the so-called semigovernment banks such as Myawaddy Bank, which were funded and owned by holding companies associated with the army.

[9] Such a process occurred in Thailand in the 1950s, Russia in the 1990s, and Cambodia in the 2000s, for example.

Table 3.4 Private banks in Myanmar in the early 2000s

		Total assets	Deposits	Share of deposits	Established year	No. of branches
1.	Asia Wealth Bank Ltd.	52,051	12,698	27.32 %	1995	39
2.	Myanmar May Flower Bank Ltd.	14,937	8,261	17.78 %	1994	24
3.	Myanmar Oriental Bank Ltd.	11,180	3,559	7.66 %	1993	14
4.	Myawaddy Bank Ltd.	14,671	3,257	7.01 %	1993	6
5.	First Private Bank Ltd.	6,112	1,750	3.77 %	1992	15
6.	Myanmar Citizens Bank Ltd.	2,899	1,509	3.25 %	1992	1
7.	Myanmar Industrial Development Bank Ltd.	3,545	990	2.13 %	1996	2
8.	Co-operative Bank Ltd.	1,543	656	1.41 %	1992	8
9.	Yangon City Bank Ltd.	n.a.	4,302	9.26 %	1993	1
10.	Yoma Bank Ltd.	n.a.	4,551	9.79 %	1993	42
11.	Myanmar Livestock and Fisheries Bank Ltd.	n.a.	1,793	3.86 %	1996	7
12.	Innwa Bank Ltd.	n.a.	817	1.76 %	1997	8
13.	The Myanmar Universal Bank Ltd.	n.a.	815	1.75 %	1995	25
14.	Tun Foundation Bank Ltd.	n.a.	813	1.75 %	1994	5
15.	Sibin Tharyar Yay Bank Ltd.	n.a.	244	0.52 %	1996	1
16.	Asian Yangon International Bank Ltd.	n.a.	144	0.31 %	1994	n.a.
17.	Kanbawza Bank Ltd.	n.a.	136	0.29 %	1994	22
18.	Co-operative Promoters Bank Ltd.	n.a.	122	0.26 %	1996	n.a.
19.	Yadanabon Bank Ltd. (Mandalay)	n.a.	33	0.07 %	1992	n.a.
20.	Co-operative Farmers Bank Ltd.	n.a.	20	0.04 %	1996	2
Total		n.a.	46,471			
Base period		March, 1999	March, 1998			March, 2000

Source: Reprinted from Mieno (2009), Original Source, Total Assets: Balance Sheet of each Bank, Deposit: Mya Than and Myat Thein (2000: 89), Table A4.1, A4.2. Established Year: Wang (2004), No. of Branches: Wang (2004). The number is up to March in 1998 for Bank 8

Note:The total assets of 5 up to the end of 2000. Banks 8, 18, and 20 were merged into Co-operative Bank Ltd. in 2004

Million kyat for Total Asset and Deposit

Table 3.6 illustrates the trend in financial assets and operations of private banks in Myanmar up to 2008. As shown in the table, the assets of private banks and the amount of deposits rapidly expanded with the establishment of banks after 1992, as shown by the cash holdings to deposits in the M2 component. However, the ratio of M2 to GDP (Marshall's k) remained very low at around 30 %. Table 3.6 also shows

Table 3.5 Private banks in Myanmar in 2012 (March 2012)

		Total assets	Deposits	Share of deposits (%)	Year established
1.	Kanbawza Bank	1,774,444.86	1,580,206.11	37.0	1994
2.	Myawaddy Bank	732,786.29	610,981.83	14.3	1993
3.	Co-operative Bank	563,134.99	480,615.68	11.2	1992
4.	Myanmar Livestock and Fisheries Development Bank	397,370.22	296,455.00	6.9	1996
5.	Myanmar Apex Bank	275,867.19	214,257.07	5.0	2010
6.	Innwa Bank	245,094.28	215,229.33	5.0	1997
7.	Asia Green Development Bank	209,720.27	177,139.84	4.1	2010
8.	Ayeyarwady Bank	197,655.56	165,651.34	3.9	2010
9.	Sibin Tharyar Yay Bank	119,322.76	110,209.28	2.6	1996
10.	Small & Medium Industrial Development Bank	118,341.40	82,605.17	1.9	1996
11.	Myanmar Citizens Bank				1992
12.	First Private Bank				1992
13.	Yadanabon Bank				1992
14.	Yangon City Bank				1993
15.	Yoma Bank				1993
16.	Myanmar Oriental Bank				1993
17.	Asia Yangon Bank				1994
18.	Tun Foundation Bank				1994
19.	United Amara Bank				2010
Private bank total		5,126,387.51	4,273,480.81		

Source: Table 3.3 in CBM Annual Report (2011–2012: 26)
Note: Million kyat, Bank 4 was renamed to "Global Treasure Bank" in 2013, Bank 10 was renamed from "Myanmar Industrial Development Bank" in 2012

that the bank run in 2003 apparently hit bank operations on the deposit side, causing a substantial decline in the deposit rate. The figure also shows that lending operations did not catch up to the expanding level of deposits. Along with the increase in deposits, the loan-to-deposit ratio continually declined during the period of 1992–2000. Since the mandated allocation of treasury bonds to banks began in 1999, 20–30 % of deposits were transferred into treasury bond holdings. This effectively meant excess deposit in banks financed the fiscal deficit.

As previously noted, the explosive growth of the banking sector in Myanmar in those years occurred largely through the absorption of public deposits in the 1990s (in period (i)). In this sense, the formation process of private banks was consistent with the public demand for financial services. However, due to the high inflation rate and interest rate ceiling, the real interest rate was continually negative, making deposits at banks not necessarily an attractive method of asset holding. Table 3.6 shows how loans did not expand as speedily as deposits. The loan–deposit rate

Table 3.6 Financial position of private banks

	(1)	(2)	(3)	(4)	(5)	(6)	(7)	(8)
	Total asset	Deposit	Total asset/GDP	Deposit/GDP	M2/GDP	Loan/deposit	TB[a]/deposit	(6) + (7)
1992	522	230	0.2	0.1	31.2	78.1	0.0	78.1
1993	2,400	1,578	0.7	0.4	27.4	82.0	2.5	84.5
1994	6,676	4,840	1.4	1.0	27.9	72.6	0.8	73.5
1995	20,231	15,705	3.3	2.6	30.7	61.9	3.2	65.0
1996	48,966	37,014	6.2	4.7	32.5	70.8	3.1	73.9
1997	85,062	58,156	7.6	5.2	29.7	86.8	7.7	94.5
1998	139,849	110,784	8.7	6.9	28.2	54.9	8.3	63.3
1999	230,588	186,169	10.5	8.5	26.8	52.1	31.8	83.9
2000	384,101	324,580	15.0	12.7	32.7	49.2	31.1	80.4
2001	597,174	487,101	16.9	13.8	34.3	63.6	22.0	85.5
2002	846,215	644,692	15.0	11.5	28.9	72.3	15.8	88.1
2003	439,204	215,579	5.7	2.8	21.1	85.9	37.0	122.9
2004	531,387	346,245	5.9	3.8	24.1	60.2	31.0	91.2
2005	514,981	364,559	4.2	3.0	22.1	68.5	19.5	88.0
2006	711,435	519,366	4.3	3.1	20.2	62.6	20.7	83.3
2007	948,189	689,449	4.1	3.0	18.8	68.6	23.7	92.3
2008	1,331,262	928,091	4.6	3.2	17.2	63.2	28.8	91.9

Source: Statistical Yearbook 2002, 2007, ADB Key Indicators
Million of kyat for (1) and (2), percentage for (3)–(8)
[a]Treasury Bond

declined to 70 % level in 1993–1995, then further fell to 50 % after 1998.[10] As discussed before, nonmanufacturing business groups engaging in the real estate or construction sectors were mother bodies of private banks. The declining loan–deposit rate implied that their demand for funds from the private sectors was not expanding as speedily as deposit expansion. This gap was probably an indirect cause of the asset price surge in the 2000s.

These banks continued to expand even after the AFC in period (ii) along with the flourishing of the real estate sector.[11] In this financial bubble situation, informal financial firms known as "General Financial Companies," a type of informal financial institution, began issuing deposit-like certificates, which flourished around the period of 2000–2002, and the contagion of their bankruptcy triggered a bank run in the private bank sector. This bank run seriously affected three particular banks—the Asia Wealth Bank, the May Flower Bank, and Yoma Bank. The largest two of these, the Asia Wealth Bank and the May Flower Bank, were rumored at that time to have been involved in the drug business and money laundering and subsequently faced serious deposit outflows. The government froze the operation of these two banks under the Control of Money Laundering Law and eventually dissolved the banks entirely.[12]

Following the bank run in 2003, other banks with healthier finances or management reputations, such as Kanbawza Bank and Myawaddy Bank, replaced the position of the other major private banks. Following the bank run, the government tightened banking regulations to restrict bank deposits to ten times their equity value, which became a major impediment to the collection of deposits by Myanmar banks.

In sum, the emergence of the private banking sector, realized by the junta reform in the early 1990s, partially enhanced financial functions in the economy, as it provided a deposit service to the public and delivered a financial channel for treasury bonds. However, it brought with it an asset price surge particularly in the real estate market, which led to the financial turmoil in the early 2000s. The private banking sector recovered from its distressed condition fairly quickly, at least on the deposit collection side. However, through the 2000s, its overall development remained immature, as shown in the low loan–deposit rate after 2004 (Table 3.6). Capacities associated with financial intermediation such as information processing and monitoring were also not sufficiently developed in the period.

[10] According to an interview by one of the authors to a representative bank in 2004 and 2009, the major income source of the banking business at those times was mostly from the fees of domestic remittances.

[11] Wang (2004), for further details.

[12] For details, see Kubo et al. (2009).

5 Interpreting the Economic Structure Under the Junta Regime

The pathway of the Myanmar economy during the two decades of the junta was strongly distorted and somewhat chaotic, but it was also dynamic. In numerous ways, the economic situation was complex. In summarizing the policy challenges, however, we may generalize the overall characteristics into the following three points.

Firstly, Myanmar takes on the strong feature of a market transition economy shifting from its previous socialist regime. In fact, its performance from the early 1990s to the early 2000s was more or less similar to other transition economies. In the case of Myanmar, the framework building for the separation of fiscal and financial sectors was successfully carried out, and deregulation for FDI acceptance was conducted smoothly. FDI inflow was moderately activated, and the private financial sector was created, leading to substantial economic growth.

On the other hand, the reform was stalled in some sectors. In terms of SOE reform, as a part of fiscal reform, privatization was limited, and the autonomy of each SOE was rather weakened, becoming one of the major causes of the worsening fiscal deficit and therefore of inflation. The reform of the foreign exchange system and foreign currency control also ran into a stone wall, resulting in the conditions favorable for import substitution and unfavorable for export-led growth in real sectors. Excessively strict currency controls resulted in the emergence of the thick black market, leading to the loss of control and further confusion in foreign exchange transactions: a vicious cycle incurred by halfway interventions.

Secondly, throughout Myanmar's economic growth during the two decades showed very weak signs of industrialization. The growth was led by export of primary products in the early 1990s after the sudden lifting of the prolonged prohibition of private trade, in other words, by a suddenly realized potential "surplus of trade." Then, since the mid 1990s, the economy was characterized by the growth led by the nonmanufacturing sector such as construction, real estate, or hotels. In fact, FDI flew into such sectors, plus mining sectors, while the growth of the manufacturing sector was hardly observed except for the garment sector in the late 1990s.

It is natural to see that sectoral bias was, to a large extent, an effect of the distorted foreign exchange system. As discussed in Sect. 4, the highly controlled and extremely inflexible foreign exchange system and the export tax were designed to allocate cheap foreign exchange to the SOEs, which mainly shouldered the burden of the import substitution sector in the economy. Consequently, the export sector was forced to persist in unfavorable conditions. This seriously discouraged export manufacturing and resulted in a growth path biased toward nonmanufacturing or domestic sectors.[13]

[13] Furthermore, it is possible to see that growth biased toward the nonmanufacturing sector may have worked as a distant factor in the asset bubble and resulting bank run in the early 2000s.

Lastly, since the mid 2000s, the Myanmar economy has become increasingly dependent on natural gas exports, forming the characteristics of natural resource export economy, instead of shifting into export manufacturing. Since natural gas exports enable the government to gain foreign currency directly (through the SOE, Myanmar Oil and Gas Enterprise), it is presumed that they contribute to accommodating fiscal deficit and easing foreign reserve shortages. As shown in Table 3.3, the inflation rate has settled down and the market exchange rate stopped falling in around 2007.

The change of fiscal and foreign reserve conditions through natural gas export provided favorable conditions for economic reforms being undertaken by the current Thein Sein Government. Seemingly, it weakened the necessity for the government to exploit surplus in forms of foreign currency from the private sector. As noted, in parallel with the increase in natural gas exports, the control of foreign exchange by MICB and MFTB has largely loosened. The development of a market for foreign currency with a de facto free-floating market since the mid 2000s is indicative of the greater separation between the government sector and the private sector. It is possible to see that, thanks to abundant export income from natural gas in the government sector, the tension between supply and demand of foreign currency for SOEs had been relatively loosened. Such a situation might bring about preconditions that the government could go forward to foreign exchange system reform.

With the gas field operations showing a trend toward expansion, Myanmar's economy would further shift toward developing the features of a natural resource export economy in the near future. Although natural gas exports have played a role in rescuing the fiscal and foreign reserve tensions since the mid 2000s, the new features of the economy necessitate new policy considerations in terms of economic management: corruption associated with the distribution of the export surplus by government, vulnerability of the macroeconomy to fluctuations in commodity prices, and prevention of Dutch disease, which could become a major impediment to export-oriented industrialization.

6 Concluding Remarks: Implications for Current Reforms

Looking back at economic changes in Myanmar during the period of 1990–2010, it is possible to comprehend two fundamental problems that the Thein Sein reforms faced as initial conditions when they commenced in March 2011. First, macroeconomic instability in the 1990s and the early 2000s stemmed from insufficient reform of the government sector, particularly SOEs. The monetization of fiscal deficit was no doubt the main cause of economic instability. Although this was subdued temporarily after 2004 by a trade surplus from export of natural gas, this structure remained largely unchanged and was therefore a major priority on the reform agenda.

Second, the lack of appropriate foreign exchange management systems made the policy choice of an export-oriented industrialization strategy unfeasible. The complicated, irrational, and ineffective foreign exchange system bequeathed a trade structure that retained the features of import substitution, thereby delaying industrialization as a basic economic factor. This needed to be overhauled at the first step of the reform.

The current reform agenda appeared to have been widely shared during the process of implementation. As a first step of overall economic reform, the government implemented significant changes to the foreign exchange regime in April 2012 by accepting the market rate and introducing a managed float system. The government showed a strong will to radically reform the SOEs and the fiscal sector.

Given that such first priority issues had been already recognized and put in the process of reform, there remained various midterm policy challenges. Considering that much of the economy was formed in the junta period, the following challenges were important. The first is the necessity of policies to stabilize the macroeconomy and to construct a solid financial system, which was impeded for a long time by the monetization of fiscal deficit and malfunctions in the foreign exchange system.

As a prerequisite for reform, the independence of the central bank is crucial. In this regard, the new central bank law to separate the central bank from the Ministry of Finance and Revenue, passed in August 2013, was quite a significant first step. Under a prospective new regime of monetary and exchange policy, and of the supervision on financial sector, the healthy development of the private banking sector should be constructed with a positive real interest rate, proper prudential regulation, and competition control.

Another agenda associated with the financial system is to redesign the roles of the private and the public sectors or to redefine the role of policy-based banks. Although the financial sector should be led by the private sector, the supply of financial services should be complemented by the public sector, particularly in the early stages of economic development. The role of policy-based finance may be found in so-called financial inclusion needs such as small and medium enterprises and agricultural finance. Furthermore, the role of government may be crucial in constructing systems to supply the long-term capital necessary for industrialization. The experience of East Asian neighbors including Japan might provide useful insight in this area.

In addition to the issues on macroeconomic stability and finance, the balance between natural resource exports and industrialization is another central challenge for reform. It is probable that natural gas exports will continue to expand and play a significant role for growth in the midterm. Meanwhile, in general, there are various controversies for a resource export-dependent economy. Firstly, the macroeconomy can easily be affected by international commodity prices. Resource-based exports should be substituted by industrialization in the long run. Even in the short run, efforts to diversify exporting commodities from natural gas to other mining and agricultural products should be considered desirable. This should, in fact, be feasible for a country blessed by such abundant natural resources. Secondly, in what has become known as Dutch disease, a resource-based export economy always carries the risk that currency appreciation will weaken the competitiveness of export goods, thereby delaying industrialization. New policies should consider this trade-off in planning growth strategies. Desirably, the trade policy formation should be decentralized to guarantee the participation of a wide range of stakeholders, including the export-manufacturing sector. Lastly, a resource-based export economy can easily fall into corruption in the process of surplus allocation, since export income is usually concentrated in a particular sector. While guaranteeing transparency, an allocation channel should be preserved in a way that the export surplus is well directed into the reinvestment for sustainable growth.

Lastly, institutional development to overcome shortcomings in sectoral development and the financial system experienced in the junta period is also an important challenge. The emergence and growth of private capital in the period were dynamic, but at the same time, were confusing and chaotic in terms of the corporate system. The Myanmar Government would need to formulate a future prospective on the better corporate governance of ballooning private capital. Large business groups contributed to growth to a degree, even though it was biased toward the nonmanufacturing sector and the exports of primary commodities. We can well understand this as the early process of capital accumulation. By the early twenty-first century, corporate sectors such as banking and other modern service sectors grew to provide essential infrastructure for the economy. In the next stage of development, they would need to transform themselves to be more transparent, socially responsible entities. Carefully designed legal systems, particularly in corporate and other commercial law, would be needed. In addition, the government needs to design a way to make large business group companies transform themselves into socially more responsible entities. A similar problem would apply to the privatization process in the SOE sector. For such purposes, a well-functioning financial system would need to be developed since it is sure to play a key role in building a decent corporate system.

7 Appendix

The Foreign Exchange Transaction in the Private Sector before the Reform

Under the repressed foreign exchange market system, the private sector seemed highly exploited. In practice, however, the private sector might have adjusted itself well to the regulations to overcome the unfavorable conditions. In order to see the behavior of private firms in the black market for foreign exchange, we conducted a survey of private importers in Yangon Division[14] between August and November of 2009.

The sample of firms surveyed was selected from the 294 largest private importers whose imports exceeded US$1 million in 2008 according to Myanmar customs records. Out of 100 firms surveyed, 95 provided answers (firms were not selected at random, but based on their consent and availability for interviews).

Among the different categories of foreign exchange transactions in the black market, this survey focused on export-tax-deducted export-earning transactions. It

[14]This survey was commissioned by the Myanmar Survey Research (MSR) Co., Ltd., with the assistance of the Japan International Cooperation Agency (JICA), Yangon Office.

Table 3.7 Sources of export-earning foreign currency

Amount of imports in 2008	Only own export earnings	Purchased directly from other companies	Purchased via brokers	Subtotal
US$1 Mil.–US$2 Mil.	7	33	6	46
US$2 Mil.–US$5 Mil.	5	19	5	29
>US$5 Mil.	5	14	1	20
Subtotal	17	66	12	95

Source: 2009 JICA Survey

was legal at the period of the survey for private exporters to hold export earnings as foreign currency deposits (FCDs) and sell them to importers through account transfers. Transactions in the black market included illicitly held foreign currency in the form of cash and deposits in foreign countries. Because the firms interviewed would not disclose information on illicit foreign exchange transactions, these were eliminated from the survey. As will be shown, "export-earning foreign currencies" are mostly traded through direct negotiations between buyers and suppliers.

Firstly, Table 3.7 summarizes the sources of "export-earning foreign currencies" for the private importers surveyed. Only 17 out of 95 firms acquired "export-earning foreign currencies" through their own or related firms.[15] The remainder (78 firms) acquired them either through brokers or directly from exporters. This indicates that 80 % of the firms surveyed depended on the black market as a source of "export-earning foreign currencies." While smaller firms appeared to be more dependent on the black market, 75 % of import firms whose imports exceeded US$5 million in 2008 also acquired "export-earning foreign currencies" from the market. Regarding the number of suppliers from which an importer acquired "export-earning foreign currencies" in 2008, the median number is 4.

Secondly, for 78 of the firms who purchased "export-earning foreign currencies," the survey asked what sources of information they would use to find an alternative supplier of export earnings. Table 3.8 summarizes the results. Companies with whom they had an existing business relationship were more popular as a source of information than brokers. In this regard, there is no notable difference between large and small importers.

Compared with actual sources of "export-earning foreign currencies" (Table 3.7), the proportion of brokers as a source of information for alternative suppliers is higher in Table 3.8. This suggests that an importer and an exporter enter into a transaction for the first time using a broker as an intermediary and then engage in a direct transaction subsequently.

Brokers play various roles in foreign exchange transactions. Introducing a supplier to a buyer (and vice versa) is one of their functions. Another is providing price information. Brokers also often guarantee the enforcement of contracts: As both suppliers and buyers run the risk that their counterparty will default on the contract,

[15] "Related firms" include firms owned by the same company.

Table 3.8 Sources of information on alternative suppliers of export-earning foreign currency

Amount of imports in 2008	Companies in business relationships	Brokers	Others (relatives, etc)
US$1 Mil.–US$2 Mil.	25	19	6
US$2 Mil.–US$5 Mil.	18	7	0
>US$5 Mil.	10	7	0
Subtotal	53	33	6

Source: 2009 JICA Survey

Table 3.9 Time necessary to find alternative supplier of export-earning foreign currency

Amount of imports in 2008	Within several hours	Within 1 day	Within 1 week	Subtotal
US$1 Mil.–US$2 Mil.	31	8	0	39
US$2 Mil.–US$5 Mil.	19	5	0	24
>US$5 Mil.	11	3	1	15
Subtotal	61	16	1	78

Source: JICA Survey

brokers provide a guarantee by taking advantage of the information they have on each supplier and buyer. This guarantee might be the reason why some firms surveyed regularly use brokers rather than engage in direct transactions with suppliers.

Third, the survey asked how long it took for the firms surveyed to find alternative suppliers. The results are summarized in Table 3.9. Among the 78 surveyed firms that acquired "export-earning foreign currencies" outside their company, all firms except one answered that they could find an alternative supplier within 1 day; meanwhile, 61 surveyed firms answered that they could find one within several hours. This implies that transactions of export earnings in the black market were smooth.[16]

The fact that the majority of the firms surveyed could immediately find alternative suppliers implies that they did not have to depend on a long-term relationship with a fixed supplier. This suggests that the price of "export-earning foreign currencies" (the black market exchange rate) was determined competitively. The fact may suggest that the foreign exchange black market achieved efficient functioning to a degree.

[16] It should be taken into account that when this survey was conducted in 2009, conditions in the black market were favorable for buyers of "export-earning foreign currencies." As growth in private exports was robust, this made it easier for buyers to find suppliers of export earnings.

References

Asian Development Bank. (2012). *Myanmar in transition: Opportunities and challengers*. Manila: Asian Development Bank.

Corden, W. M. (1984). Booming sector and Dutch disease economics: Survey and consolidation. *Oxford Economic Papers, 36*, 359–380.

Davis, G. (1995). Learning to love the Dutch disease: Evidence from the mineral economies. *World Development, 23*(10), 1765–1779.

Fujita, K., & Okamoto, I. (2009). Overview of agricultural policies and the development in Myanmar. In K. Fujita, F. Mieno, & I. Okamoto (Eds.), *Economic transition in Myanmar after 1988: Market economy versus state control* (pp. 169–215). Singapore: NUS Press/Kyoto University Press.

Fujita, K., Mieno, F., & Okamoto, I. (Eds.). (2009). *Economic transition in Myanmar after 1988: Market economy versus state control*. Singapore: NUS Press/CSEAS of Kyoto University.

Ito, T., & Kumamoto, M. (2004). The relationship among currency, inflation, and the exchange rate. In K. Fujita (Ed.), *Myanmar's economy in transition: Market versus control*. Chiba: Institute of Developing Economy (in Japanese).

Katz, M., et al. (Eds.). (2004). *Lifting the oil curse*. Washington, DC: IMF.

Kiryu, N., & Nishizawa, N. (1996). *Basics of Myanmar economy*. Tokyo: Nihonhyoronsha (in Japanese).

Kubo, K. (2007). Determinants of parallel exchange rate in Myanmar. *ASEAN Economic Bulletin, 24*(3), 289–304.

Kubo, K., Fukui, R., & Mieno, F. (2009). The financial sector during the transition to a market economy in Myanmar. In K. Fujita, F. Mieno, & I. Okamoto (Eds.), *Economic transition in Myanmar after 1988: Market economy versus state control* (pp. 128–165). Singapore: NUS Press/Kyoto University Press.

Kudo, T., & Mieno, F. (2009). Trade, foreign investment and Myanmar's economic development in the transition to an open economy. In K. Fujita, F. Mieno, & I. Okamoto (Eds.), *Economic transition in Myanmar after 1988: Market economy versus state control* (pp. 103–127). Singapore: NUS Press/Kyoto University Press.

Mieno, F. (2009). Characteristics of capital accumulation in Myanmar, 1988–2003. In K. Fujita, F. Mieno, & I. Okamoto (Eds.), *Economic transition in Myanmar after 1988: Market economy versus state control* (pp. 23–65). Singapore: NUS Press/CSEAS of Kyoto University.

Mieno, F. (2013). Toward Myanmar's new stage of development: Transition from military rule to the market. *Asian Economic Policy Review, 8*(1), 94–117.

Mya Than & Myat Thein. (2000). *Financial resources for development in Myanmar: Lessons from Asia*. Singapore: Institute of Southeast Asian Studies.

Mya Than. (2004). *Economic development of Myanmar*. Singapore: Institute of Southeast Asian Studies.

Tanzi, V., & Zee, H. H. (2000). *Tax policy for emerging market: Developing countries* (IMF Working Paper WP/00/35). Washington, DC: International Monetary Fund.

Taylor, R. (2008). *The state in Myanmar*. Honolulu: University of Hawaii.

Turnell, S. (2009). *Fiery dragons: Banks, moneylenders and microfinance in Burma*. Copenhagen: Niras Press.

Turnell, S. (2011). Fundamentals of Myanmar's macroeconomy: A political economy perspective. *Asian Economic Policy Review, 6*(1), 136–153.

Wang, S. (2004). Private banks in Myanmar (1990–2003). In K. Fujita (Ed.), *Myanmar under transition to market economy* (pp. 265–310). Chiba: Institute of Development Economies.

Chapter 4
Physical Social Overhead Capital (SOC)

Konosuke Odaka

1 Introduction

Of highly important preconditions for modern economic growth (MEG) are the supply of energy and the formation and geographical growth of the market economy, assuming that the basic biological needs, that is, measures to ensure a sound water supply and sewage, are satisfied.

Electricity and gas have been commonly and widely employed as energy sources, while the improvement and expansion of communication and transportation means have been indispensable for the successful growth of the market economy. In all these activities, improvement in the quality and the geographical expansion of the respective services are required. Energy production is characteristically related to the economies of scale and the usefulness of the communication and transportation means related to the coverage of their geographical areas. Consequently, often of crucial importance with respect to these social overhead activities are queries as to whether or not, and to what extent, public financing could be, and should be, utilised for their support. One may also ask: in which one's hands would it be best to entrust their management: public or private?

An urgent need for Myanmar at the beginning of the twenty-first century was the drastic improvement in the conditions of its physical social overhead capital (SOC). This chapter will review specifically the conditions of the country's electricity and transportation services. It will, at the end, also briefly touch upon the issues of water supply, sewage, and waste disposal in the representative big cities.

The author is indebted to Drs. Asuka Mizuno and Koichi Fujita for having supplied a portion of reference materials needed for the preparation of this chapter. However, the present author is wholly responsible for the manner of implementing it.

K. Odaka (✉)
Institute of Economic Research, Hitotsubashi University, Tokyo, Japan

Hosei University, Tokyo, Japan
e-mail: k-odaka@ier.hit-u.ac.jp

K. Odaka (ed.), *The Myanmar Economy*, DOI 10.1007/978-4-431-55735-7_4

2 Electric Energy

Indispensable for modern industrialisation is the availability of and ample use of electricity. With the progress of economic development, its use is bound to increase not only in production sites but also in private households. In fact, the realisation of MEG would be unimaginable without the smooth supply of electric power.

In the history of Western Europe and North America, MEG preceded the arrival of an electricity supply. The sources of energy were limited and often faced unavoidable, geographical constraints and were thus confined to selected, narrow regions: a reason, in part, as to why the early industrialisation process in these areas proceeded at a relatively moderate pace.

The arrival of electricity as the industrial source of energy brought about a drastic change in the premodern conditions for economic development. Also greatly affected was the structure of industries. A notable example of the change, for example, was the use of electric motors, which not only made possible separate, independent operation of production facilities but also the introduction of prime power into small-scale enterprises. Electrification also resulted in a drastic transformation in the patterns of consumption and other daily behaviour of private households as well as the living style of citizens. Farmers also, in villages with electricity, experienced changes in work environment, for instance, the shortening, etc., of their working hours. More recently, the arrival of new information technology and digitalisation in the wide areas of daily life, including artistic activities, so-called globalised business activities, and so on, are all closely related to the extensive and increased use of electricity. The supplies of other social overhead capital such as water and gas are often seriously hampered when electric supplies are suddenly taken away.

The origin of the electricity supply in Myanmar (then known as Burma) goes back as far as 1905 when the Rangoon Electric Tramway and Supply was established in the city of Rangoon (now called Yangon). Prior to the Second World War, approximately 180 plants were operating, most of which were

> small or moderate-sized diesel and steam installations, with no more than 10 hydroelectric plants. At least thirty of these were destroyed [during the War], and much work remain[ed] to be done to restore prewar facilities and production. (Economic and Social Board 1954: 74, brackets added)[1]

Especially when industrialisation was renewed in the late 1980s, the inadequacy of the electricity supply was keenly felt in many aspects of national life, most nota-

[1] A report in 1939 listed 102 public and 77 commercial and industrial undertakings. "Of the former all were small diesel plants, 10–500 kW, except for the 24,000 kW Rangoon Steam Station and nine minor hydro and steam stations. Of the industrial undertakings, six were hydro stations ranging from 300 to 10,000 kW; 24 were diesel plants up to 1,300 kW; and the remainder were steam stations up to 20,000 kW capacity" (KTAM 1953: 561). According to the same report, the total electricity generated by public undertakings in 1939 amounted to 47 MW, and out of 102 public stations that generated electricity in 1939, 47 were still in operating condition in 1952 with a total output of 55 MW (of which 5 were diesel powered, 3 hydro powered, and 47 team powered) (ibid. 562–564).

Table 4.1 Capacity undersupply and the shortage of electricity (estimates), 2000–2008

Year	(a) Capacity of grid system (MW)	(b) Power available year-round (MW)	(c) Power demand year-round (MW)	(d) Power undersupply (%)	(e) Power shortage (%)
2000	976.2	724.0	785.0	25.8	7.8
2001	1,008.7	724.0	860.0	28.2	15.8
2002	1,038.7	744.0	860.0	28.4	13.5
2003	1,038.7	744.0	880.0	28.4	15.5
2004	1,072.1	895.0	900.0	16.5	0.6
2005	1,472.1	962.0	1,050.0	34.7	8.4
2006	1,472.1	996.0	1,150.0	32.3	13.4
2007	1,497.1	1,050.0	1,275.0	29.9	17.6
2008	1,527.1	1,060.9	1,300.0	30.5	18.4

Sources: (a) Odaka's estimates (see footnote to Fig. 4.1); (b) and (c) Myanmar Electric Power Enterprise (MEPE) data as cited by Thein Tun (2011: 7)
(d) = {(a) – (b)}/(a) *100, and (e) = {(c) – (b)}/(c)*100

bly in the sphere of industrial production. Table 4.1 illustrates the demand and supply condition of electricity in Myanmar from the end of the twentieth century through the beginning decade of the twenty-first century.

Inasmuch as the essential need of electricity was obvious ever since early MEG efforts in Myanmar, inadequate investment, especially during the decades of socialist rule, was probably a major reason for the inadequacy in the provision of electricity in subsequent years and even through the first decades of the twenty-first century. In addition, one suspects that the electricity supply system had been constructed with insufficient engineering expertise. Figure 4.1 illustrates the sum of potential supply capacities of major electricity generating stations, which remained at fairly low levels through the beginning years of the 1990s. Needless to say, the shortage of foreign exchange during the Burmese Way to Socialism must have made it quite difficult for the authorities at the time to facilitate the provision of the needed financial resources for constructing a generating system. Even after the end of the socialist era, the lack of financial resources, due partly to economic sanctions, made it hard to improve the system (JICA and PwC 2013: 4-1). One may also suspect, as a reason for the low potential of electricity generation, that a certain number of the state-operating economic enterprises (SOEs) during the socialist period had their own electricity generating facilities.[2] Perhaps, for military, security, financial, or other reasons, they had to start operations within the shortest time span possible; they could not wait until the construction of large-scale generating stations was

[2] For instance, Thayet Cement Factory in Thayet Township had installed seven generators by 1967, with a total generating capacity of approximately 6,000 KW. As for other examples, a paper factory at Kyaikto in Mon State had a diesel-powered generator, and a slate factory at Loikaw in Kayah State attempted hydro generation at a small nearby river. Needless to say, there were state factories that purchased their electric energy from the Public Electric Corporation (Ministry of Industry 1 1991: 162, 190, 196, 200–201).

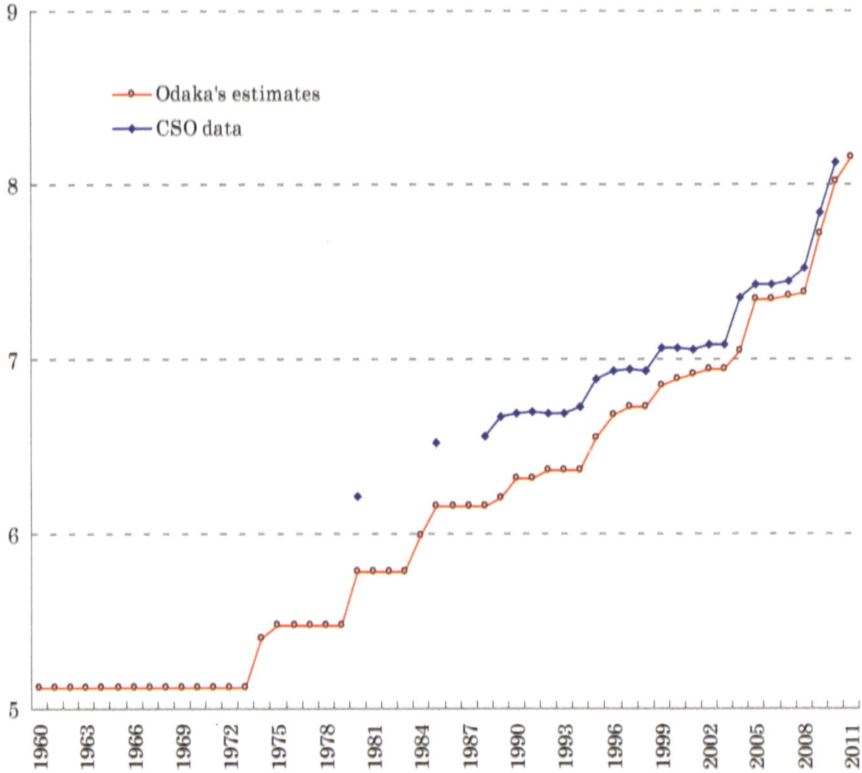

Fig. 4.1 Electricity generating capacity of stations in grid system (natural log of MW) (*Sources*: *CSO* (Central Statistical Organisation) data have been taken from its *Statistical Yearbook*, versions 1998: 161–163, 2002: 161–164, 2007: 165–168, and 2011: 239–240. Odaka's estimates are based on the data listed in ADB, "Myanmar energy sector initial assessment", 2012, cited by JICA and PwC (2013: 4-1), and Ministry of Electric Power (2) data as cited by Thein Tun (2011: 31–33). Note: Based on the information listed in the sources above, the total generating capacities of the stations were obtained by adding up the capacity figures of all the stations in operation in the respective years, assuming that the capacities were maintained throughout the entire period

completed. The higher supply price of self-generated electricity, as compared with the service charge of a specialised power plant, was probably of little concern for the operation of state enterprises. The setting up of water-powered electricity generating systems not only called for huge sums of money but also took a long time to complete, whereas energy supply for production must start right away.

The low-electricity generating capabilities notwithstanding, considerable effort was made after the 1990s to increase them, as evidenced in Fig. 4.1. Nonetheless, the effort failed to quickly and smoothly yield the anticipated results as had been expected, since water-powered generating stations required a substantially long gestation period before they started functioning. Needless to say, various ways and means for increasing electricity supply through oil, coal, gas, etc., were eagerly sought and explored by the administrators concerned. Despite the effort being made, the majority of electricity generating stations—all state owned and operated—were water operated as of 2013.

The shortcomings notwithstanding, the energy supply potential of the grid system in the country in 2012 reached 3,495 MW, which was far above the peak demand for electric power in 2011, which was 1,535 MW. In fact, total electricity generated in the year 2012 (17,814 GWh) far surpassed actual demand in the same year (6,321 GWh). These facts lead one to conclude that the frequent blackouts in the country were due not to the absolute deficiency (or lack) of generating capability but to the unreliable nature of the electricity supply system, a large portion of which might be attributable to some engineering-related factors. The underutilisation of the generating capacity was due to unavoidable reasons as well as to the technical loss of electricity before it reached its final place of demand. In other words, what lay behind the frequent electricity supply stoppages were:

1. Serious water shortages in the dammed reservoirs, especially during the dry season when electricity generation competes with the high demand for water from farming
2. Electric current voltage being too low while up on the grid system
3. Little or no alternative grid routes in case of sudden damage to the grid circulation route
4. The shortage of automatic devices that could guard the grid system against unexpected, long shutdowns
5. An electricity distribution system at the gateway to final demand being too old-fashioned and characterised by its essential components such as electricity measuring metres being outdated, as well as being subject to illegal rerouting of electric currents and so on, the majority of which could be resolved by way of engineering measures (cf. JICA and PwC 2013: 4-1 and Thein Tun 2011: 15–16)

In past years, electricity suppliers increasingly made efforts (under the grid system) to remedy all these system defects, thanks to which the loss of produced electricity was said to have gone down from as high as 40 % in the latter half of the 1990s to approximately 16 % by 2010.

In addition to the loss of product (i.e. electricity), consideration should be taken of the nonengineering aspects of electricity generation, such as business organisation, production control, and accounting system. Ever since the revised Electricity Law of 1990, the Myanmar government has welcomed private capital owners, both domestic and overseas, to participate in the country's electricity generating industry (JICA and PwC 2013: 10–12). The related public laws invited them to participate in the venture under the following conditions:

1. Ten percent or more of the output be provided for free to the government of Myanmar (in lieu of royalty payments).
2. The unit price of the product (electricity) be negotiated with the government agency concerned each year.

3. The duration of the concession period be 30 years, after which all the production equipment and facilities be transferred to the government of Myanmar in good, workable condition, except that a 5-year extension of the tenure be granted once and only once (if requested).
4. Myanmar Power Generating Enterprise shall participate in the joint venture by bearing a third of the annual costs for operation and for the maintenance activities of electricity power generation (JICA and PwC 2013: 4–14).

As of the beginning of the twenty-first century, however, extremely low rates of service charge were applied to public electricity. For this reason, considerable gaps emerged between the production cost and the sales prices of the electricity, although the latter was raised several times after 1988 (for instance, 1988, 1994, 1999, 2006, and 2012) (JICA and PwC 2013: 12–13; Thein Tun 2011: 11–13, 27–28). Naturally, interested private concerns were attracted to the direct sales or exportation of the product. Those interested in the joint venture were limited (at least through 2011) either to home enterprises, which were in direct contract with domestic end consumers, or foreign companies from neighbouring countries (e.g. China and Thailand, but mostly China), which would supply the product back to their home countries. In any event, it is an extremely important matter how and on what economic principles the electricity charges are determined.

3 Domestic Transportation Networks

3.1 Water Transport

Myanmar is blessed with a rich natural environment, including the mountains that run along its northern, national border areas and its four main rivers: the Chindwin, Irrawaddy (or Ayeyarwady), Salween, and Sittang, which flow from north to south. Of the total length of the rivers, and the Irrawaddy Delta waterways, about 6,626 km has historically been utilised for commercial transportation, for both cargo and people (Aung Myint 2011: 12).[3] The domestic shipping network has formed a very convenient, frequently used, and economical means of physical communication for a multitude of purposes.

The major rivers are subdivided into many sub-branches in the delta area of the country, hindering physical movements in east-west directions, but constituting an essential reason for the importance of transportation by water. Ships going across the rivers played an especially important role as the biggest and most convenient means of physical movement until the arrival of automobiles.

Hydraulic conditions such as depths and widths of streams, as well as current intensity, are important factors that determined the development of the original

[3] Of the total length, about 22 % is attributable to the Irrawaddy River and about 56 % to waterways in the Irrawaddy Delta.

Table 4.2 Age distribution of the ships owned and operated by MIWT (around 2010)

Age (years)	Number	%
1–20	100	23.8
21–40	74	17.6
41–60	134	31.8
61–	113	26.8
Total	421	100.0

Source: JICA and PwC 2013: 4–63

types and structures of ships used. The depth of the Irrawaddy River, for instance, is about 1–2 m during the dry season, while it increases up to 5–6 m in the wet season. In pre-Second World War days, powered craft were already employed, together with barges and launches.[4] On the Irrawaddy River, in the 1950s, fairly large, cargo-passenger-type steamers were in use, that is, vessels 310–360 ft in length and 46 ft in width equipped with stern (or side) paddle wheels (KTAM 1953: 338). On the other hand, the widespread use of wooden vessels (barges) must have resulted in the constant demand for the services of shipwrights (cf. Cheng 1968: 63–64), while not necessarily creating much demand for machinists or metal-working artisans. The historical as well as geophysical circumstances surrounding the early modern use or absence of indigenous machines, it seems, present a striking contrast to the initial conditions for industrialisation between Thailand and Myanmar, respectively.

Myanmar Inland Water Transport (MIWT) is a state-owned concern with a long history of cargo handling and passenger transportation, whose origins go back to 1860 (JICA and PwC 2013: 4–63), owning six dockyards, some of which were originally built in the latter half of the nineteenth century, although none were equipped with modern production facilities until the twenty-first century (see Table 4.2). Yet the substantive marine repair services, available since the pre-Second World War days, with sufficiently spacious dry docking facilities, have provided the necessary conditions for the smooth and safe operation of both overseas and inland waterway transportation (KTAM 1953: 294–296, 309–312). The active operation of dockyards implied the existence of properly trained, skilled workmen.

The existence of demand for skilled artisans and/or workmanship, as suggested above, provided the opportunity for nurturing the country's own manufacturing capacity, however unsophisticated it may have been. The very slow pace of industrialisation in the country after the 1950s, in spite of the presence of such appropriate initial conditions for eventual take-off, might be ascribed to the closing of the nation to the international community after 1963, especially with respect to exchanges of technological information and personnel.

Be that as it may, even the planning-minded post-independence government administrations have imposed few restrictions on entries into the market by private

[4] One of the waterway operators, Irrawaddy Flotilla Company, operated 246 powered craft and 372 barges prior to the War. The company introduced diesel-powered craft in 1930 (KTAM 1953: 339–340).

enterprises, recognising the popularity of waterways that have served as the essential means of inland transportation. The private vessel carriers have been just as equally (or even more) active as the public enterprise ones. In fact, many private shipping companies have owned their high-speed, motor-driven boats, which have moved around freely and independently according to their own schedules and fare settings. According to a report in 2011, the number of privately owned vessels was about 20 times more than that managed by MIWT (JICA and PwC 2013: 4–63). In fact, privately owned and managed port facilities have operated at Yangon Port all through this period.

The easy access to, and convenience offered by the inland water transport system, may have had the effect of slowing down the development of a land highway system, except for a few especially important routes such as the one that connects Mandalay and Yangon. Adding to this fact must have been the small number of long bridges crossing the rivers, necessitating the frequent use of ferries. Surprisingly, up to the end of the 1990s, there was only one long bridge crossing the Irrawaddy River—a structure built by the British at the beginning of the twentieth century (Japan Infrastructure Partners 2012: 1). During the colonial period, the colonial governor was in charge of setting up and maintaining the physical social structure, including long bridges across the big rivers, thus leaving little room for developing a local skill set for long bridge construction. A Myanmar engineer, who participated in the training course for bridge engineering held in 1979 by JICA, recollected

> whereas there are probably over half a million bridges in Myanmar, none of us local bridge engineers were capable of constructing big, long bridges ourselves if their total length extended over a hundred meters. (JICA 2012: 1)

Such recollection notwithstanding, there was an increase after 1988, according to a national survey taken in 2007, in the building of long bridges. That is to say, of 405 long bridges in use in the survey year that extended over 54 m in length, 198 had been completed prior to 1988, leaving 207 which were built between 1988 and 2006 (Japan Infrastructure Partners 2012: 3–4).[5]

It should be noted that most of the modern, long bridges in the country during the post-independence period have been constructed with the country's own funding and engineering resources. In other words, basic designing and bridge structure making have been entrusted to the Public Works (a subordinate organ of the Ministry of Construction), whereas foreign assistance, if any, has been confined mainly to overhead steel structures[6] (ibid.).

[5] Of the 77 long bridges inspected in the Yangon and Irrawaddy districts in 2009, 56 % were concrete, 17 % steel truss, 16 % Bailey, and 12 % suspension or cable-stayed bridges (Japan Infrastructure Partners 2012: 4).

[6] However, in view of the discovery by bridge inspections, conducted in fiscal year 2010–2011, of the need for improvement in engineering practices (such as the combined use of seawater while preparing concrete materials—a serious offence in the basic principle of concrete making), measures were duly taken for retraining and on-the-job training (OJT) of the local staff (Japan Infrastructure Partners 2012: 11, 13, 19–20, 29, 43, 53, 62).

3.2 Inland Highways

Land transportation is made up of two components: transportation by highways (motor vehicles) or by railways. The development of a super highway system in Myanmar lagged behind that of inland waterways until the arrival of the age of the automobile (cf. KTAM 1953: 356).

An important factor to recognise here, however, is that the country's land transportation is closely interwoven with its social, economic, and political relations with Myanmar's neighbouring countries due primarily to its close geographical proximity. In other words, its national borders directly face Bangladesh, China, India, Laos, and Thailand. Myanmar constitutes a hub where international social and economic transactions take place between and among these countries, including itself. This fact has been long recognised by the countries concerned, so they came to agree in September 1999, first, to jointly construct a super express road (Trans-Asian Railway) and, second, in 1960, to establish an international railway ("the Asian Express"). Myanmar was of course prepared to take part in realising this plan.

Despite the strong will and wishes, however, Myanmar's pace in making the plan reality has been sluggish mainly due to the shortage of necessary funding. Moreover, the express roads it constructed were not of the top quality (called class 1 roads) expected. Regarding the international railway, on the other hand, Myanmar's socialist regime simply did nothing because of its basic policy stance, namely, seclusion from the international community.[7]

In the area of domestic highways, by contrast, the decades towards the end of the twentieth century saw clear signs of new development. That is to say, the total length of the domestic major highways increased drastically from 23,458 km in 1988 to 29,992 km in 2004 and further to 32,178 km by 2008: an increase of approximately 37 % (Fig. 4.2). The drastic improvements must have been closely related to the circumstances surrounding domestic sociopolitical conditions. One notes, in this connection, that the main superhighways run, in principle, from north to south, parallel to the four big rivers.

3.3 Railways

The origin of the modern railroad system in the country goes back to 1877,[8] which is prior to the British annexation of the nation in 1886. Transportation services between Rangoon and Mandalay (1,028 km or 385 miles) began in 1889. By the

[7] Incidentally, in order for the Myanmar national railways to be connected directly with the international express (the Asian Express), some engineering aspects such as double tracking would be needed, since the national railways of the country have adopted, in accordance with the old policy of the British colonial governor, the metre gauge system.

[8] The metre gauge line of 258 km (161 miles) between Rangoon (now Yangon) and Prome.

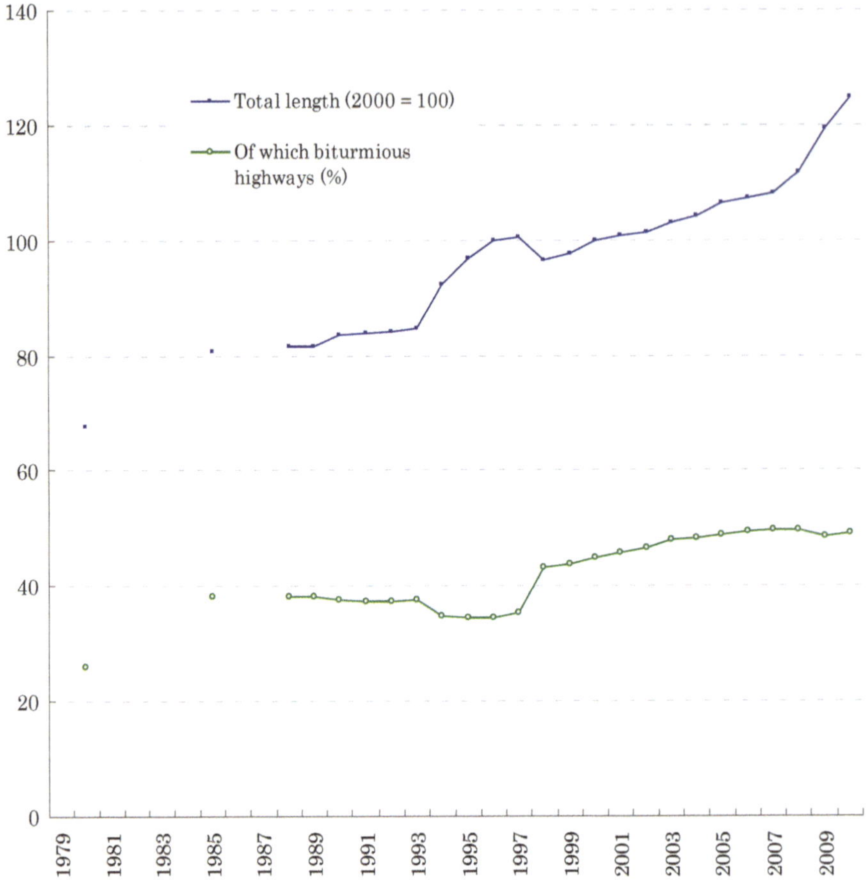

Fig. 4.2 Index of the length of arterial highways (*Sources*: CSO, *Statistical Yearbook*, versions 1998: 284–286; 2002: 295; 2007: 304, and 2011: 389). Note: The total length of arterial highways in 2000 was 28,759 km

beginning of the Second World War, the total length of the railroad system had reached 4,938 km or 2,058 miles.[9] In fact,

> [t]he monumental 3,760 ft. [1,128 m] high-level Ava Bridge, constructed in 1934, closed the water gap between Rangoon and Myitkyina. The pre-war freight and passenger services ranked high in physical performance among the meter gauge railways of the world. (KTAM 1953: 256)

The system suffered severe damage during the Second World War. For instance, 285 out of 350 locomotives, 7,000 out of 9,500 goods wagons, and 956 out of 1,156

[9]The system was initiated by the Irrawaddy State Railway, which was succeeded in 1896 under a lease arrangement with a private corporation, the Burma Railway Company, Ltd., of London. Its control was transferred again in 1928 to the Indian Railway Board (KTAM 1953: 256).

passenger carriages were destroyed (KTAM 1953: 256). Strenuous efforts began after independence to restore the system to its prewar level, when the train service was noted for its efficiency. According to the records of 1953, the railway owned 307 steam locomotives, of which 187 had been manufactured between 1946 and 1950, whereas the remainder (120) had been manufactured between 1901 and 1932 (KTAM 1953: 259–260).

Nonetheless, the system was not fortunate enough to receive the sufficient care it needed in terms of such areas as continued investment in restoration, replacement, renewals, and new additions. Even during the post-1988 era, it seems the national railroads (totally state owned and state operated) failed to improve much in physical terms until the 1990s. A consultant report in 2013 remarked that

> acutely needed are investment in basic infrastructure for upgrading rails and passenger cars especially sleepers, ballast, etc., and the replacement of the operation system in general but especially the signals and trans-communication. (JICA and PwC 2013: 4–46)

Even after the introduction of market liberalisation in the 1990s, improvements and/or extensions to the domestic railway services remained quite slow. If anything, relevant statistical records reveal that the capacity of Myanmar Railways to carry cargo as well as passengers showed clear signs of a long, downward slide. The same report as cited above observed that most of the newly opened railway routes went through the northern mountainous areas in which it was costly to lay new railroads. The high cost implied shorter extensions to the needed lines of the new services. While transportation demand was bound to increase, the funds that could be allocated decreased. In 1993, the nation's railway system accounted for approximately 20 % of the nation's total demand for cargo transportation (three million tons altogether).[10] The size of the equivalent services remained more or less on the same level in 2011 (JICA 2013: 4–46). One may safely surmise that a substantial portion of the newly constructed railways must have been carried out in close connection with the national objective of strengthening the political integrity of the nation, by way of improving the means of long distance domestic transportation.

The extension of the railroad is a clear improvement in land transportation. However, its service to the public as measured by way of its total truck mileage still remained much smaller than that in (say) Thailand. Figure 4.3 indicates that, whereas there has been a clear sign of historic improvement in the motive capacity of train engines, the railway's performance has actually degenerated when measured by actual quantities of cargo transported. And yet the rates of cargo-carrying efficiency of both engines and of carriages showed remarkable improvement over time, implying that a great (human) effort must have been made by the railroad and its employees during the period concerned to raise the organisation's productive efficiency, given the deteriorating state of all the production equipment and facilities. In other words, a tremendous effort was made to improve productivity, given the quality and quantity of the present capital stock (see Fig. 4.4).

[10] More or less the same quantity of cargo was transported in 2011 (JICA and PwC 2013: 4–46).

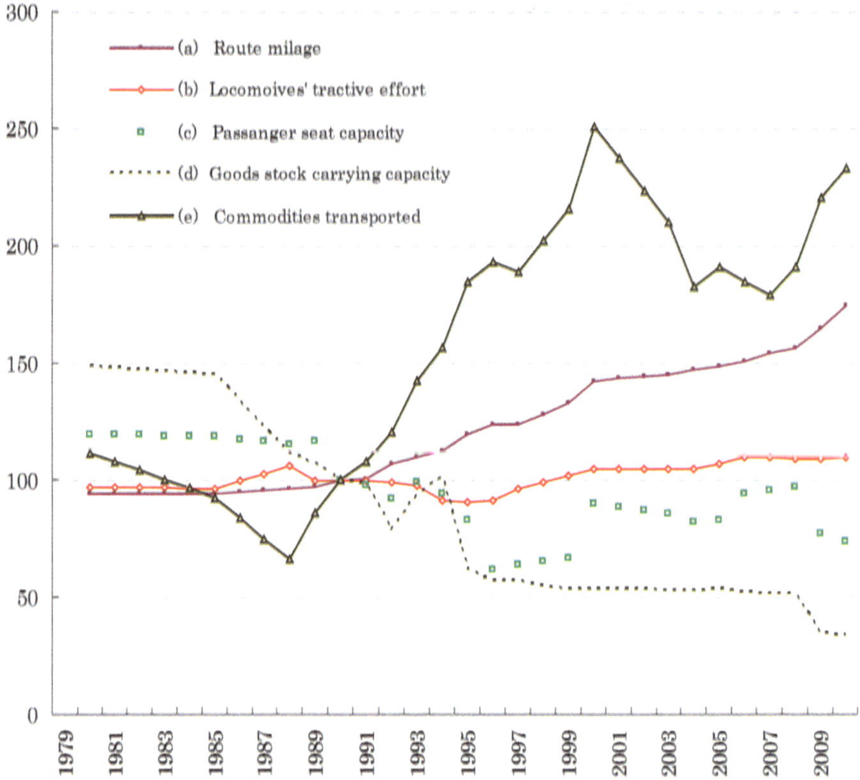

Fig. 4.3 Indices of railway's economic capacity and performance (year 1990 = 100) (*Sources*: Myanmar Railways as recorded by CSO, *Statistical Yearbook*, versions 1998: 259–267; 2002: 267–275; 2007: 275, 281; and 2011: 359). Note: 1990 means the 1990–1991 fiscal year and similarly for other years

As was pointed out long time ago by foreign experts, most of the locomotive engines, passenger carriages and cargo containers were getting quite old, having certainly been used beyond their normal depreciation limit. It was clear, beyond any discussion, that renewed capital investment was urgently called for by way of introducing new facilities and/or by repairing the present stock, so that the capacity, efficiency, and safety bc immediately improved and guaranteed.[11]

[11] During the years 1983 and 1986, the Myanmar government executed a pilot project, in anticipation of the future electrification of its railroad system, by applying for an ODA loan of 2,580 million yen from Japan. An inside-the-factory transport system of about 20 km in length at Kyangin Cement Mill, approximately 240 km north of Yangon, was chosen as the project site, where rolling stock was renewed, railway electrification facilities inclusive of a transformer station and telecommunication and signal systems were introduced, and four electric locomotive engines and 47 open freight wagons were imported. Ten staff from the factory and the National Railway received training in Japan, and about ten Japanese experts worked together with them at the factory site to set up

Fig. 4.4 A railway engine at Mandalay Station (Drawn in spring 2013)

In order to improve the economic efficiency of the railroad, it would be desirable to invite private capital to participate in the railroad venture.[12] For that purpose, a system of efficient, yield-earning transportation charges must be developed along with the renovation (perhaps) in management control. With regard to the appropriate setting of service charges, similar consideration is appropriate, just as in other areas of social overhead cost (e.g. energy charges). One may safely argue for the introduction of a system, for instance, where the railroad trucks are owned by the public, whereas the railway operations are executed privately. At any rate, the service charges might directly reflect the managerial cost of production, while long-

the renovation. The project was duly completed, and the railroad system, since then, has been administered with proper care.

The project was a dream come true for the old Burma Railway Corporation (now Myanmar Railways), which had long wanted to electrify its circular line in the city of Rangoon (now Yangon). However, it has turned out that the simultaneous use of diesel and electric locomotives was necessary in order to cope with untimely electricity blackouts (JICA 2002).

[12] One would recognise, in passing, that the extent of privatisation of the railroads is subject to sensitive checking from the viewpoint of military strategies.

term cost (the cost of capital) could be entitled to receive public subsidies. Accompanying such revisions in transportation fees, it would be appropriate to introduce travel charge assistance provisions for the economically depressed.

3.4 Changing Labour Division in Inland Transportation

Figure 4.5 illustrates historical changes in the volume of transported cargo via waterways as compared with that via railroads. Clearly, the overall volume of cargo transported increased markedly since the beginning of the twenty-first century. Note, however, that the proportions of rice transported by means of these two methods have declined sharply during the period, reflecting notable changes that must have taken place in the market transactions of rice dealers (Fig. 4.6). One may deduce that the liberalisation of the market dealings of rice has promoted regional,

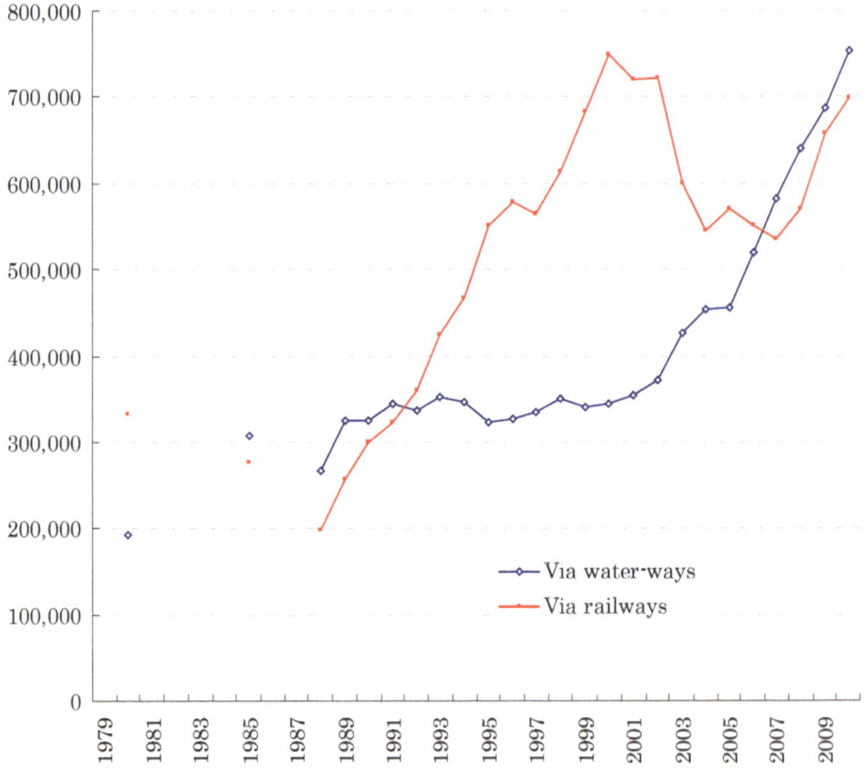

Fig. 4.5 Commodities transported via waterways and railways (in 1,000 ton-miles) (*Sources*: CSO, *Statistical Yearbook*, versions 1998: 259–267, 270; 2002: 267–275, 278; 2007: 279–281, 278–281; and 2011: 359–365, 371)

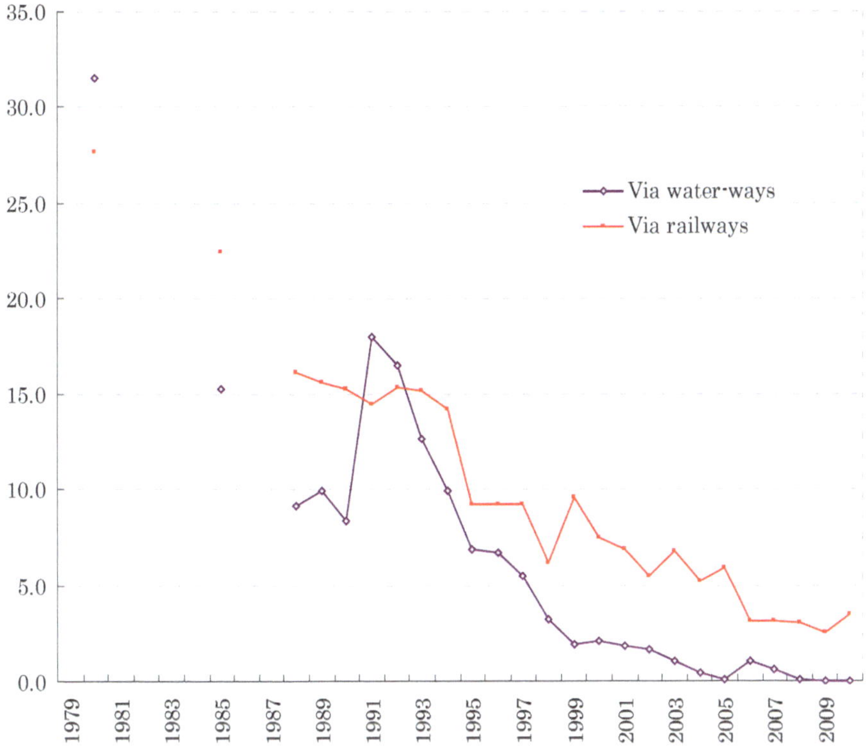

Fig. 4.6 Proportion (percentage) of rice transported via waterways and railways (*Sources*: Same as Fig. 4.5)

local transactions on the one hand while encouraging quicker and less cumbersome transaction methods on the other (cf. Okamoto 2004: 173, 190).

As the experiences of modern economic history in the United States and Japan indicate, the two means of transportation, railroads and highways, are complementary in some aspects but highly competitive (substitutable) with one another in other aspects (cf. Tsuru 1969). Railroad services in many areas have often lost in the competition since its economic viability requires exceptionally large sums of money as well as public consent by way of special procurement, public subsidies, environmental protection, etc., whereas road transportation via motor vehicles is handy and more convenient by offering door-to-door services.

Nonetheless, one should be reminded that railroads have various advantages over motor vehicles, especially in terms of much bigger (heavier, more voluminous, etc.) transportation capability per space: they do not increase urban congestion, they are less likely to increase environmental pollution, and they are much less prone to transportation accidents. These considerations lead one to the conclusion that a balance is required between the two means of transportation. It is also possible that inland water transportation by way of certain vessels may share the same problems with that of railroads. It would be against the public interest to let the power of market transactions dominate in the decision-making process regarding the choice of transportation.

4 Water Supply and Sewage[13]

The water supply and sewage systems in the cities of Yangon and Mandalay are concisely reviewed in this section. The very important issue of garbage disposal will be touched upon very briefly at the end.

The modern water supply system in Yangon was started when Myanmar was part of British India. The British carefully designed the city (then called Rangoon) in order to help maintain their own living standards. Until the beginning of the twentieth century, the city's water demand was easily satisfied by groundwater and the reservoirs of Kandawgyi and Inya Lay lakes, as the city was geographically located in a water-rich delta area. The underground distributing pipes then installed have been used through the entire twentieth century.

According to the Yangon City Development Committee, a large-scale water supply plant was built in 2005 to meet the demand of the city's growing population, which had by then exceeded five million. Whereas the supply capacity had continuously increased, it could meet only about 60 % of the required quantity. In Mandalay, on the other hand, a water-purifying plant was under construction at that time, which, however, would meet only 73 % of the city's daily demand.

The conditions of the sewage system have been much poorer than those of the water supply system. The first sewage facility in the nation was installed in 1888, having been designed to cover the needs of the residents of Yangon (Rangoon), with the design such that the sewage water flowed, by gravity, to the final disposal plant through ground pipes, into which compressed air was pumped to prevent the water stagnating in flat areas. As many as 39 such air compressors, installed in the bottom of manholes in selected zones, have been kept in good working condition, thanks to careful maintenance. Surprisingly, the facility has kept working continuously for more than a century with no renovation.[14]

Until December 2004, unprocessed sewage water was pumped directly into the nearby river or lakes, causing bad smells and water pollution. But a high-level government decision changed this. A new sewage processing plant, which processes 3.25 million gallons per day, was planned and completed with domestic funds and technologies.

---

[13] This section is based on information collected from a field survey made by Mr. Haruyuki Shimada. However, the present writer alone is responsible for the views expressed herein.

[14] According to the staff of Yangon City Development Committee, suspension of the facility occurred only once when an antigovernment riot took place in 1988.

Regarding the very touchy issue of garbage collection, the city of Yangon collected, in August 2009, 1,480 tons of garbage per day with 4,000 staff.[15] With regard to the most critical issue, final disposal measures, there was no other option than open dumping. In addition, industrial and medical waste was dumped without any special pretreatment. Even though city committees realised the problems, they could not take any effective measures due to budget constraints, the shortage of staff, and the lack of technical skill. Under such conditions, the mayor of Mandalay advocated the "No Plastic Bag" campaign, which encouraged big supermarkets to not provide plastic bags to their customers. The initiative had an unexpectedly large impact, and in Naypyidaw and Yangon, the use of bags made of lotus and banana leaves, instead of plastic, was promoted by the city authorities.

The issues of water supply and of waste disposal are of high importance in view of not only the convenience of daily life for the citizens but also for maintaining and improving the health of the general public. The experiences of big cities like Yangon and Mandalay are of critical significance, as they provide salutary lessons for other cities and communities to learn from.

5 Concluding Remarks: Funding for SOC

A notable characteristic of SOC building in contemporary Myanmar since the end of the twentieth century has been that it plans to make use of as much private funding as possible. This is in striking contrast to the experiences of a country like Japan, which had no clear alternative but to rely on overseas countries in lending long-term financing, by publicly issuing foreign bonds. The establishment of public-private joint ventures, for instance, has been encouraged by the Myanmar government, a trend which has been made possible by the relative abundance of global financial capacity: a unique global trend beginning in the latter half of the twentieth century. Intentionally or not, the trend in Myanmar since the end of the twentieth century followed this global tendency.

The recent worldwide trend notwithstanding, one should note the obvious fact that the financing of SOC, regardless of the specific areas of its concentration, normally requires exceptional strength in financial funding capabilities. This implies that the private organisations, which participate in constructing physical social overhead capital, would be large sized, especially with regard to their paid-in capital. It would be important to come up with a proper institutional (especially legal) setup in such a way that the huge capital requirement in these ventures will not create any disturbing factors in fair market performance. Also from this consideration, it would be appropriate to proceed with the early establishment of a stock market, so that common citizens and private organisations, both big and small, may actively participate in public ventures inclusive of SOC. For the same reason, it is highly desirable for the Myanmar economy to encourage private capital formation.

[15] The figure was for August 2009; 1,480 tons were said to be roughly equivalent to 90 % of the total amount of daily garbage.

References

Aung Myint. (2011). *Transport sector development issues and strategies, Myanmar (watertransport)*. Background paper for development policy options. Yangon: ARDC (Agribusiness and Rural Development Consultants).

Cheng, S.-H. (1968). *The rice industry of Burma: 1852–1940*. Kuala Lumpur: The University of Malaya Press.

Economic and Social Board, Government of the Union of Burma. (1954). *Pyidawtha, the New Burma*. Printed and bound in London: Hazell, Watson and Viney.

Japan Infrastructure Partners. (2012). *Current situation and issues of Myanmar's bridge work*. http://www.infrajip.or.jp/H23BridgeMaintenanceReportengl:sh.pdf. Accessed 7 Mar 2014.

JICA (Japan International Cooperation Agency). (2002). *Kyangin cement mill transportation reinforcement project*. http://ww.jica.go.jp/english/our_work/evaluation/oda_loan/post/2002/pdf/071_full.pdf. Accessed 17 Mar 2014.

JICA (Japan International Cooperation Agency). (2012). Roads, bridges, power lines, ferries. *Focus on Myanmar*. http://www.jica.go.jp/english/news/focus_on/myanmar2012/myanmar_09.html. Accessed 7 Mar 2014.

JICA (Japan International Cooperation Agency) & PwC (Pricewaterhouse Coopers). (2013). *Myanmar renpō kyōwakoku tōshi kankyō seibi jōhō shūshū kakuho chōsa hókokusho* [Investment environment in the Union of Myanmar Republic: A report on the information collected and confirmed]. Tokyo (in Japanese).

Ministry of Industry I. (1991). *Myanma naingan sethmu lethmu loutngan thamaing* (A History of Manufacturing Industry in Myanmar, Vol. 4). Yangon: Ministry of Industry I.

Okamoto, Ikuko. (2004). Myanmar ni okeru kome ryūtsū shisutemu [The rice distribution system in Myanmar]. In Koichi Fujita (Ed.), *Shijō keizai ikō ka no Myanmar, sono hatten katei oyobi genjō* [Myanmar under transition to a market economy, its development process and current condition], ch. 5. Chiba City: Institute of Developing Economies, Japan Export Trade Research Organization. (in Japanese)

Thein Tun. (2011). *Power sector development issues and strategies, Myanmar*. Background paper for the development of policy options. Yangon: ADRC (Agribusiness and Rural Development Consultants).

KTAM (Knappen Tippetts Abbett McCarthy Engineers, in association with Pierce Management Inc. and Robert R. Nathan Associated, Inc.). (1953). *Economic and engineering development of Burma, comprehensive report prepared for the government of the Union of Burma*, 2 vols. Printed and bound in Aylesbury/London: Hazell, Watson and Viney.

Tsuru, S. (1969). Dōro tai tetsudō mondai no keizaigaku-teki kōsatsu, iwayuru rōkal sen haishi mondai ni kanren shite' (Highway vs. railway: An economic comparison). *Keizai kenkyū (Economic Review), 20*(1), 1–9 (in Japanese).

Chapter 5
Agriculture and Rural Development Strategy in Myanmar: With a Focus on the Rice Sector

Koichi Fujita

1 Introduction

Agriculture (including livestock, forestry and fisheries) in Myanmar in 2011 still produced 45 % of the GDP and absorbed roughly 60 % of the labour force (CSO 2010). It is common in the modern world that the share of the agricultural sector in the national economy decreases in the process of economic development, in which nonagricultural sectors such as manufacturing and services grow rapidly, dramatically raising the living standard of the population. Hence, industrialization has been regarded as vital for developing countries that suffer from low income and poverty.

However, history tells us that if a country impetuously promotes industrialization, it often fails. Theoretically, if a country quickens industrialization while neglecting agriculture, firstly, since agriculture stagnates and food prices surge, industrialists have to raise wages (because in the early stage of economic development, labourers have to spend a large share of their expenditure on food, according to Engel's law), which reduces their profit margins. Or, if food is imported in large volumes to prevent wage hikes, the country faces a shortage in foreign exchange, which is necessary to import materials, intermediate goods, and capital equipment for industrialization.[1] Secondly, if a country quickens industrialization in a situation in which most people depend on agriculture for their livelihood, the income of the masses remains low, which prevents the formation of outlet markets for industries and ultimately holds back industrialization. In summary, if a country desires to hurry industrialization, it should develop agriculture beforehand or at least at the same time.

An industrialization strategy negligent towards agriculture had typically been adopted by socialist countries. They were the latecomers in economic development

[1] It is known as the 'Ricardian trap'. See Hayami (1997).

K. Fujita (✉)
Division of Economic and Political Dynamics, Center for Southeast Asian Studies, Kyoto University, Kyoto, Japan
e-mail: kfujita@cseas.kyoto-u.ac.jp

K. Odaka (ed.), *The Myanmar Economy*, DOI 10.1007/978-4-431-55735-7_5

and in order to show the 'superiority' of the socialist system vis-à-vis the capitalist system, they adopted a speeded-up industrialization strategy. Meanwhile, they collectivized agriculture, through which they intended to achieve efficiency in production by enjoying the economies of scale and investing the agricultural surplus in industrialization. However, in reality, the economies of scale did not work well in the agricultural sector, and agriculture stagnated due to the inefficiencies caused by collectivization, which dragged down whole economies. China (followed by Vietnam), beginning in the late 1970s, decided to break up the collective farms and restore family farms, which resulted in rapid agricultural recovery and growth,[2] and industrialization followed. Experiences in China and Vietnam were in sharp contrast with those of the Soviet Union and Eastern Europe, where a total collapse of the socialist regime was experienced.

In the case of Myanmar, a special type of socialist system (called the 'Burmese Way to Socialism') was adopted in 1962 when General Ne Win took power. Under the military regime, agriculture was not collectivized, but agricultural surplus was extracted by introducing a state procurement system at very low prices. Marketing channels through private traders were negated, and the export of agricultural produce (mainly rice) was monopolized by a state marketing agency. However, the inefficiency of the system drastically reduced rice exports by the mid-1970s.[3] After the late 1970s, although the economy recovered for a time by utilizing foreign aid (mainly from Japan), the inefficiency inherent in the economic system itself could not be overcome, and by the mid-1980s the economic situation worsened significantly. In 1987, the government finally had to abandon the agricultural procurement system and also the 'Burmese Way to Socialism' itself. The decontrol of agricultural marketing, however, resulted in a surge in agricultural prices, especially rice, which triggered the outbreak of the 'Democratic Movement' in 1988.

After quelling the movement by force, a new military government (SPDC, State Peace and Development Council) started in 1988.[4] The SPDC government took the bold step to liberalize and open the economy and achieved economic recovery and development at least until the mid-1990s. However, the economic growth rate slowed down thereafter, basically because the government took only halfway measures in economic reforms. The most important fields where the government postponed reforms until very recently were the foreign exchange market and state-owned enterprises. The rice procurement system, which was reintroduced soon after 1988, was also not abolished until 2003.

---

[2] Note, however, that the success was not achieved only by the reorganization in the agricultural production system. It should be emphasized that both in China and Vietnam, rural infrastructure such as irrigation, drainage and rural road networks were dramatically improved by utilizing a cheap labour force under the collectivization regime, which contributed more decisively to long-term agricultural development, once economic incentives for farmers to work hard recovered under the family farm system.

[3] In the prewar period, by the late 1930s, Myanmar had become the largest rice exporter in the world. Rice exports reached more than 3 million tons at its peak.

[4] It was called SLORC (State Law and Order Restoration Council) until 1997 when a reorganization was undertaken and it was renamed SPDC.

In summary, if we compare the case of Myanmar with other socialist countries, Myanmar overcame its regime's crisis in the mid-1970s by accepting foreign aid, but the recovery was only temporary; the economy ultimately collapsed in the late 1980s but not the (military) regime itself.[5] After quelling the 'Democratic Movement' in 1988, the new military government started economic liberalization and reforms, but since the reforms were a halfway measure, the economic development was not sustainable (unlike China and Vietnam), although it avoided total collapse.[6] Since the mid-2000s, however, the Myanmar economy has again started to grow rapidly, mainly led by natural gas exports. In 2006, the transfer of its capital city from Yangon to Nay Pyi Taw was completed. And finally, a general election was held in November 2010 and a civil government was established. It started a series of bold political and economic reforms.

It should be noted that the above-mentioned 'fundamental' reforms in Myanmar only started more than 20 years after those in Vietnam and Laos. The international economic environment changed drastically during these 20 years or so. For instance, the rice export market was largely transformed after Vietnam's resurgence and India's participation in the market. Myanmar lost the chance for increasing rice exports during this period. Another example is the Bangladesh economy, which has grown rapidly during the last 20 years due at least in part to the success of garment exports, in which Myanmar also had a huge potential to develop by utilizing its cheap and plentiful labour force. Myanmar tried to start 'genuine' economic development after 2011 by utilizing foreign aid from Western countries, but in an international economic environment completely different from that faced by other transitional Asian economies. In this context, how can Myanmar agriculture exploit its opportunities and how should agricultural policies lead it?

As discussed later in this chapter, Myanmar is blessed with abundant and diverse natural resources. Agricultural development potential seems to be very large. However, up to the beginning of the twenty-first century, Myanmar failed to fully utilize the resources for agricultural development. The major reason, in my view, was the failure in its rice (staple food) policy, which had started in the socialist period and continued more or less until 2010. It should be noted here that Myanmar experienced outbreaks of large-scale social unrest three times in the socialist period; all three outbreaks were triggered by sharp increases in rice prices.[7]

My hypothesis is that such bitter experiences remained in the memory of the Myanmar government, so it continued to stick to the policy of increasing rice production. Unfortunately, the government physically forced farmers to produce more rice, instead of giving them economic incentives to do so. The 'silent' struggles between the government and the farmers who pretended to obey the government but actually tried to circumvent its policies whenever possible resulted in large-scale

---

[5] It should be noted that the military regime itself was 'democratized' in 1974 when the BSPP (Burma Socialist Program Party) governed the country under a unique party system. But Ne Win continued to control the nation until the late 1980s, which was a de facto military government.

[6] See Chap. 3 of this volume by Fumiharu Mieno and Koji Kubo.

[7] They occurred in 1967, 1974 and 1988. See Okamoto (2008a) for detail.

resource wastages in terms of land, labour and capital. Hence, only when the Myanmar government finally escapes from the 'rice trauma' will the principle of comparative advantage carry through in resource use in agriculture, and thereby the huge development potential of Myanmar agriculture will begin to be realized. This is a major reason why I focus on the rice sector in this chapter.[8]

The major purpose of this chapter is to show the 'basic structure' in which the rice sector in Myanmar is located and to consider the way how the government can escape from the 'rice trauma'. The more fundamental issues related to the agricultural sector, that is, the land tenure system and the agricultural financial system, will also be examined before concluding the chapter, since the reforms in these two vital spheres should never be overlooked when considering rice sector reforms.

The remaining part of the chapter is organized as follows: in Sect. 2, some basic conditions of Myanmar agriculture, which were historically formulated based on its ecological conditions, will be presented. This is followed by Sect. 3 which focuses on major policy issues related to the rice sector in Myanmar. Section 4 discusses the issues of the land tenure system and the agricultural/rural financial system in Myanmar, before concluding the chapter in the last section.

2 Basic Conditions of Myanmar Agriculture

2.1 Formation and Transformation of the Rice-Exporting Economy in the Colonial Period

Large-scale reclamation started in the Ayeyarwady Delta after Lower Myanmar was annexed by the British in 1852.[9] The reclamation process accelerated after the 1870s when the rice price started to rise rapidly in the world market. The progress of flood control by constructing artificial levees facilitated the process. A large number of farmers migrated from Upper Myanmar and started rice cultivation. Indian labourers also flowed in, mainly from the Madras Presidency, and worked as coolies in rice mills and ports. They were also hired for rice harvesting. In addition, the business caste people (mainly *Chettiers*) migrated from south India and engaged in trade and money lending. The British controlled the most lucrative economic activities such as rice milling, rice export, finance and insurance, and shipping.

Thus, Myanmar achieved rapid economic growth, and by the 1930s, it became the biggest rice-exporting country in the world. Development was stimulated by the increased demand for rice overseas, mainly in India and Malaysia (Malaya), and was achieved by utilizing the hitherto 'idle' land and labour resources. Myanmar

[8] For a more comprehensive analysis on Myanmar agriculture since 1988, see Fujita and Okamoto (2009).

[9] See Adas (1974) for comprehensive descriptions on the reclamation and development process of the Ayeyarwady Delta.

economist Hla Myint characterized this pattern of development as 'vent for surplus' (Hla Myint 1980).[10]

At first, economic development ran relatively smoothly. When there still remained un-reclaimed land, the different groups of people (the British, *Chettiers*; Myanmar farmers; and Indian labourers) were segmented and everyone earned reasonable profits. Such a harmonious relationship, however, started to change after the twentieth century as land frontiers disappeared. Before, even if Myanmar farmers failed, they could move to other frontiers for new settlement, but gradually it became difficult, and some of them fell into perpetual debt to the *Chettiers* and ultimately lost their land to become tenants or agricultural labourers. A scramble for jobs between Myanmar farmers and Indian labourers also gradually developed.

The Great Depression, which began in 1929, impacted heavily such a vulnerable economy. Rice prices collapsed, and many Myanmar farmers failed to repay their debts, finally losing their land. The *Chettiers* moved quickly to accumulate farmland. The formation of an agrarian society in which many Myanmar farmers worked as tenants/agricultural labourers under Indian (*Chettiers*) landlords or, at least, the formation of such a (rather stereotyped[11]) notion widely shared among the Myanmar people (especially political leaders) strongly affected economic policies after the independence of Myanmar.

2.2 Emergence and Persistence of Rural Landlessness

One of the notable features of the Myanmar agricultural sector has been the existence of a large number of landless agricultural labourers. After farmland was nationalized in 1953 (Agricultural Land Law), there have been no farmers who 'own' farmland in Myanmar. However, farmers were given land use rights which were inheritable. Land use rights were quite strong: they were de facto ownership rights for the land. In this sense, the difference between farmer households with land use rights and landless households without such rights has been apparent and significant. Because of the scarcity of nonfarm job opportunities in rural Myanmar in general, the landless households have depended mainly on agricultural wage work. In other words, rural Myanmar has been comprised of two classes: farmers and landless agricultural labourers.[12] At the end of the twentieth century, one estimate indicates that 30–50 % of rural households in Myanmar are landless, of whom 20–30 % can be classified as agricultural labour households, with the definition of more than 50 % of income coming from agricultural wages alone (Fujita 2009a).

Many of the *Chettiers* returned to India after the independence of Myanmar in 1948, and when General Ne Win took power in 1962, the remaining *Chettiers* also

[10] Also see Chap. 2 by Asuka Mizuno of this volume.

[11] See Chap. 2 by Asuka Mizuno of this volume.

[12] It should be noted here, however, that unlike India, this has been basically the economic class, not the social class.

fled Myanmar. Farmers who worked as tenants of the *Chettiers* became de facto owner-farmers through this process. The Myanmar government implemented a land reform programme in the 1950s, in which land larger than the ceiling area[13] was taken by the government for redistribution. However, since the priority for redistribution was given to (1) tenants, (2) owner-farmers with land less than *da doun htun*,[14] (3) permanent/seasonal agricultural labourers, and (4) others, most of the landless (agricultural labour) households were not given land. Landless agricultural labour households were thereby largely neglected, because the government feared that if land were distributed to them, agricultural production would decline since they had no bullocks and farm implements such as ploughs, harrows and bullock carts.

The 1953 Agricultural Land Act not only nationalized farmland but also prohibited its sale, transfer, mortgage and rental. The formation of a land tenancy market has been strongly impeded. Thus, the landless agricultural labourers in Myanmar could not be tenant farmers and continued to work as permanent/seasonal or casual agricultural labourers.

2.3 *Abundant Land and Natural Resources*

In 2008/2009, of the 677,000 km^2 (67.66 million ha) of land in Myanmar, the net sown area accounted for only 11.88 million ha (18 %), in contrast with the quite large forest area accounting for 33.26 million ha (reserved forest 16.84 million ha and other forest 16.42 million ha) (CSO 2010).

Since the 1870s, Thailand developed as another major rice-exporting economy through large-scale reclamation of the Chao Phraya Delta. After World War II, the area used for upland crops (such as maize and cassava) and also for rice cultivation expanded rapidly (Fig. 5.1), causing large-scale deforestation. By contrast, forest areas have been relatively well conserved in Myanmar. As shown in the figure, the net sown area of rice in Myanmar (reached its peak in the 1930s at around 5 million ha) had been stable until the early 1990s.[15]

In contrast with other Asian countries with a high population density, Myanmar is relatively blessed with a favourable land/man ratio. The distribution of farmland among farm households in 2010 is shown in Table 5.1. The land area per household is 6.34 acres (=2.57 ha) on average and is quite large by the standards of contemporary

---

[13] The ceiling area per household was stipulated depending on type of land. In the case of paddy field, for example, it was 50 acres.

[14] *Da doun htun* in Myanmar means land area that can be cultivated by a pair of bullocks and sufficient for a household to make a living (Takahashi 1992: 73).

[15] The net sown area of rice started to increase again after 1992/1993 when the 'Summer Paddy Program' was introduced. But the program mainly encouraged double cropping of rice in the existing land and not outward expansion of the rice area.

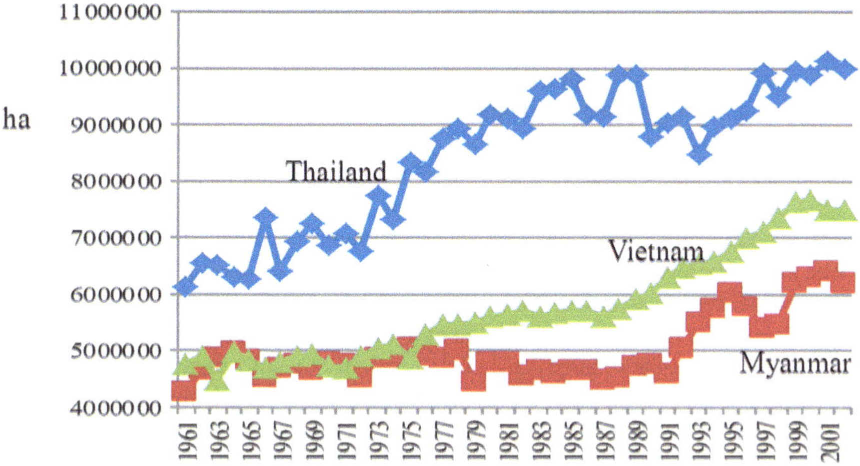

Fig. 5.1 Rice sown area in the major rice-exporting countries in Southeast Asia (*Source*: FAO)

Table 5.1 Distribution of farmland in Myanmar

	2010				
Size category	No. of farm households	Share of households (%)	Land area (acre)	Share of land (%)	Average land size (acre)
Less than 1 acre	247,584	5.0	111,711	0.4	0.45
1–3 acre	1,345,024	27.0	2,338,996	7.4	1.74
3–5 acre	1,102,363	22.1	3,959,043	12.5	3.59
5–10 acre	1,336,222	26.8	8,805,156	27.9	6.59
10–20 acre	727,458	14.6	9,488,066	30.0	13.04
20–50 acre	212,231	4.3	5,750,299	18.2	27.09
50 acre and over	15,789	0.3	1,161,824	3.7	73.58
Total	4,986,671	100.0	31,615,095	100.0	6.34

Source: Ministry of Agriculture and Irrigation, Report on Myanmar Census of Agriculture 2010

Asia (albeit we must take into account the existence of a large number of rural landless households, as mentioned above).

In addition, in 2008/2009, Myanmar still had a large area of 'cultivable waste' land, which accounted for 5.70 million ha (nearly half of the net sown area). As argued later, 'The Vacant, Fallow and Virgin Lands Management Law' was enacted in March 2012, yielding the expectation that the reclamation of the vast 'cultivable waste' land would be accelerated in the near future. How to balance the development vis-à-vis environmental protection will be much more important for Myanmar, because Myanmar has so far conserved its natural resources (albeit not intentionally) but now is about to accelerate their 'development'. Besides preventing large-scale deforestation and promoting environmentally friendly farming systems (see Chap. 6 by Masahiko Matsuda in this volume), how to 'develop' the vast 'cultivable waste' land is another important policy issue in the country.

Myanmar is also blessed with abundant water resources. However, the net irrigated area in 2008/2009 was only 2.27 million ha (19 % of the net sown area), comprising of canals (0.63 million ha, 28 % of total net irrigated area), tanks (0.32 million ha, 14 %), wells (0.14 million ha, 6 %), and others (1.15 million ha, 51 %) (CSO 2010). Note that the 'others' includes surface water pump irrigation in the Ayeyarwady Delta and other areas. The potential for water resources development, especially the groundwater resources in the Ayeyarwady Delta (so far largely unexploited), seems to be large.[16] The development potential of hydroelectric power generation is also sizable. The development of large-scale duck husbandry by utilizing the abundant water resources in the lower Sittaung River basin is also worth mentioning here.

Table 5.2 shows the changes in the major export items from Myanmar since the mid-1980s up to 2009. It is evident that except for garments, which increased from the late 1990s to the early 2000s, Myanmar depended mainly on primary products such as wood, agricultural crops (mainly rice and pulses), marine products, and natural gas. In the early twenty-first century, natural gas, teak (and other wood) and marine products accounted for roughly 50 % of total exports. The dependency of exports on natural resources was still high and even increasing.

The Myanmar government has promoted large-scale deforestation through providing private sectors (including joint-venture companies) with concessions. In addition to cutting teak and other wood in forests, the government has encouraged large-scale oil palm plantation development in the southern part of Tanintharyi Region since the mid-1990s in order to reduce palm oil imports. Several big private companies in Myanmar participated in oil palm plantation development and destroyed large forest areas.

The government also promoted offshore marine fisheries by providing Thai fishing companies with fishery rights. Fishery rights have been sold off piecemeal through a Thai private company (Siam Jonathan) as an intermediary since 2003. The depletion of fishery resources, however, was already noticeable by the late 2000s, considering that since 2009, Siam Jonathan company was obliged to reduce the commission rate collected from Thai boats (Fujita et al. 2010).

Myanmar had long been suffering from a trade deficit and therefore an acute shortage of foreign exchange, but after the mid-2000s, the trade balance became a surplus due to the start of natural gas exports (Table 5.2). Now it seems possible and necessary for the Myanmar government to re-examine the hitherto 'piecemeal natural resources sell off' policy and switch to more environmentally friendly development strategies.

---

[16] It is well known that Bangladesh and West Bengal of India achieved rice double cropping by tapping groundwater resources by tubewells. However, the quick survey conducted by the author in February 2014 shows that under the current economic environments (mainly due to the need of high frequency of irrigation according to land conditions, which results in too much costs incurred), there is no major room for large-scale groundwater irrigation development in Ayeyarwady Delta at present.

Table 5.2 Major export items of Myanmar (million kyats)

	Export																
	Total	Teak and hard wood	%	Rice and rice products	%	Pulses	%	Marine products	%	Garments	%	Natural gas	%	Others	%	Import	Trade balance
1985/1986	2566.1	1046.0	40.8	763.0	29.7	238.0	9.3	94.0	3.7	6.0	0.2			419.1	16.3	4802.0	−2235.9
1990/1991	2952.6	999.0	33.8	172.0	5.8	515.0	17.4	165.0	5.6	8.0	0.3			1093.6	37.0	5522.8	−2570.2
1992/1993	3590.0	949.0	26.4	249.0	6.9	667.0	18.6	259.0	7.2	97.0	2.7			1369.0	38.1	5365.3	−1775.3
1993/1994	4227.8	1241.0	29.4	268.0	6.3	724.0	17.1	368.0	8.7	220.0	5.2			1406.8	33.3	7923.3	−3695.5
1994/1995	5405.2	1061.0	19.6	1166.0	21.6	799.0	14.8	617.0	11.4	343.0	6.3			1419.2	26.3	8332.3	−2927.1
1995/1996	5032.7	1048.0	20.8	440.0	8.7	1358.0	27.0	615.0	12.2	300.0	6.0			1271.7	25.3	10301.6	−5268.9
1996/1997	5487.7	985.0	17.9	126.0	2.3	1272.0	23.2	887.0	16.2	402.0	7.3			1815.7	33.1	11778.8	−6291.1
1997/1998	6446.8	853.0	13.2	38.0	0.6	1403.0	21.8	945.0	14.7	436.0	6.8			2771.8	43.0	14366.1	−7919.3
1998/1999	6755.8	789.0	11.7	167.0	2.5	1135.0	16.8	941.0	13.9	471.0	7.0	5.0	0.1	3247.8	48.1	16871.7	−10,115.9
1999/2000	8947.3	925.0	10.3	65.0	0.7	1179.0	13.2	807.0	9.0	2722.0	30.4	31.0	0.3	3218.3	36.0	16264.8	−7317.5
2000/2001	12,736.0	803.0	6.3	208.0	1.6	1658.0	13.0	934.0	7.3	3785.0	29.7	1110.0	8.7	4238.0	33.3	15073.1	−2337.1
2001/2002	17,130.7	1880.0	11.0	754.0	4.4	1898.0	11.1	861.0	5.0	2985.0	17.4	4247.0	24.8	4505.7	26.3	18377.7	−1247.0
2002/2003	19,955.1	1871.0	9.4	633.0	3.2	1760.0	8.8	1116.0	5.6	2976.0	14.9	5919.0	29.7	5680.1	28.5	14910.0	5045.1
2003/2004	14,119.2	2049.0	14.5	131.0	0.9	1731.0	12.3	966.0	6.8	1965.0	13.9	3478.0	24.6	3799.2	26.9	13397.5	721.7
2004/2005	16,697.3	2242.0	13.4	180.0	1.1	1283.0	7.7	1036.0	6.2	1238.0	7.4	5812.0	34.8	4906.3	29.4	11338.6	5358.7
2005/2006	20,646.6	2750.0	13.3	214.0	1.0	1876.0	9.1	1147.0	5.6	1586.0	7.7	6235.0	30.2	6838.6	33.1	11514.2	9132.4
2006/2007	30,026.1	2939.0	9.8	18.0	0.1	3498.0	11.6	1357.0	4.5	1602.0	5.3	11676.0	38.9	8936.1	29.8	16835.0	13,191.1
2007/2008	35,296.8	2964.0	8.4	552.0	1.6	3463.0	9.8	1653.0	4.7	1555.0	4.4	13938.0	39.5	11171.8	31.7	18418.9	16,877.9
2008/2009	37,027.8	2212.0	6.0	1112.0	3.0	4069.0	11.0	1503.0	4.1	1594.0	4.3	12996.0	35.1	13541.8	36.6	24873.8	12,154.0

Source: CSO (2010)

3 Pricing and Marketing Policies of Rice in Myanmar

3.1 Rice Procurement and Rationing System

As mentioned before, under the 'Burmese Way to Socialism', which started in 1962, Myanmar agriculture was not collectivized, but a state procurement and rationing system was introduced for almost all agricultural products. Since the procurement price was depressed at a very low level, the system functioned as a harshly exploitative measure for famers. In addition, the export of agricultural products was monopolized by state agencies.

The most important crop, needless to say, has been rice, the staple food of Myanmar. Rice has been cultivated by most farmers as a subsistence crop and also as an important cash crop. Some ethnic minorities used to eat maize or other coarse cereals as a staple food, but the introduction of a rice rationing system in the socialist period substituted their non-rice staple food for rice. As of 2013, a part of Chin State was the only exception where people still eat maize as a staple food.

Since rice is a 'wage good' (a basic commodity which has a large share in household expenditure and thereby its price strongly affects the level of real wages of the people) in the regions where rice is the staple food, it is desirable for a government that quickens industrialization to depress rice prices to a low level. However, such a low rice price policy gives serious disincentives to the rice farmers, and rice production will be stagnated or reduced, and in the medium to long term, the government will face a situation in which the rice price surges, or in order to prevent this, the government has to import a large volume of rice. Therefore, the rice price should not be too low (for producers) and at the same time should not be too high (for consumers and for industrialization), which is a big challenge for the government.

Such a problem tends to be more serious and complicated for rice-exporting countries like Myanmar. Because rice is an important source of foreign exchange, rice export needs to be promoted for industrialization. However, when rice export increases (with other things being equal), domestic rice prices will rise, which will hold back industrialization through the aforementioned mechanism.[17]

In reality, the introduction of the state procurement and rationing system in Myanmar, which exploited the rice farmers, resulted in the stagnation of rice production and the decline of rice exports. Thus, the path to industrialization by utilizing the economic surplus from the rice sector had been walled off by the mid-1970s. After the mid-1980s, because almost all the surplus rice (after keeping rice for self-consumption and seed for the next season for farmers) was procured by the state and also because the gap between the procurement price and the market

[17] Edible oil is another indispensable food in the diet of Myanmar people. For a long period, the major oil crops had been sesame and groundnut, although more diversification occurred in the 1990s by adding mustard, sunflower, niger, etc. But the major problem for Myanmar is that the country has virtually no international comparative advantage in producing these oilseed crops (except for sesame, which is exported) and that after 1988, a lot of edible oil (mainly palm oil) started to be imported and Myanmar has been obliged to spend a lot of precious foreign exchange. See Fujita and Okamoto (2009).

(black market) price became very large, the frustration among the farmers was aggravated (Takahashi 1992). In 1987, when the state procurement system stopped functioning due to resistance by the farmers, the government finally liberalized the agricultural markets; however, this induced a surge in agricultural prices (especially rice) and resulted in the outbreak of the 'Democratic Movement' in 1988.

After the movement was quelled by force, a new military government (SLORC/SPDC) started in 1988. As the government realized that the core of the problem was the rice price hike, they reintroduced the rice procurement and rationing system (while abolishing it for other agricultural products), but in a reduced volume: only 10 baskets[18] per acre (out of approximately 60 baskets per acre of average yield), and beneficiaries from the rationing were limited to government staff (including the military) and some other disadvantaged people (such as patients in hospitals). Besides, the summer paddy was precluded from state procurement in order to give farmers incentives to participate in the 'Summer Paddy Program', which started in 1992/1993 to promote double cropping of rice, especially in the Ayeyarwady Delta. Farmers started to sell their surplus rice to private traders who had been working unofficially in the socialist period. The rice price was basically determined by supply and demand conditions in the domestic market, because the rice export volume remained small under the government monopoly.

Nonetheless, the rice procurement and rationing system continued to be unpopular.[19] The procurement price remained well-below market prices, and farmers were harassed by the government staff of the Mynma Agricultural Produce Trading (MAPT), which actually procured rice. Farmers were also often prevented from selling rice to private traders until they had met their obligations (for the state procurement). Large rice mill owners had to make a contract for polishing government paddy (since MAPT did not have enough rice mills to polish the entire procured paddy), but received a significantly lower milling charge compared to the market rate. Lastly, government staff who received the rationed rice usually sold it immediately to animal feed traders, as the rice was of very bad quality. This rice procurement and rationing system was not abolished until 2003.[20]

Finally, an important but largely unknown fact should be noted here. After 1988, the beneficiaries of the rice rationing system were limited mainly to government staff, which implied that not only urban citizens but also a large number of rural landless people (as well as marginal farmers without marketable surplus) were excluded. In the socialist period, the rice rationing system, although it had many problems, had been functioning as a safety net that ensured food entitlement for the people. But it was suddenly abolished without any compensation. Furthermore, after 1988, rice prices continued to rise more than the general inflation rate.[21] Such

---

[18] Basket is a unit of capacity. One basket is equivalent to 20.9 kg of paddy.

[19] The descriptions below are mainly from Okamoto (2009).

[20] When the system was abolished, the salaries of the government staff were raised to compensate. After the abolishment of the system, MAPT was not dissolved but reorganized into a new organization with drastically reduced staff.

[21] See Fujita and Okamoto (2009). Compared to the consumer price index (=100), rice prices surged especially in 1989 (177) and 1993 (175).

a rice price surge, it seems, hit the landless agricultural labourers in particular because the rise of the wage rate failed to catch up with the rice price increase and real wages declined substantially.[22] Besides, the large fluctuation in rice prices after 1988 (to be explained later) also must have hit vulnerable agricultural labourers. It can be concluded that the poverty situation of the rural landless labourers worsened after 1988, since they lost the safety net of rationed rice and they also started to be exposed to high and fluctuating rice prices in the market. Note also that after 1988, the income disparity between farmers and agricultural labourers has widened.[23]

3.2 Rice Export Policy and Rice Price Management

For many years after the independence of Myanmar, rice exports were under the monopoly of the government. Because rice was exported only if the procured rice remained after fulfilling the demand for rationing, it was not a system that encouraged rice export. Rice export reduced sharply after the 1970s and declined to nearly zero at the end of the socialist period. It remained at low levels even after 1988, except in 1995 when 1 million tons were exported, mainly owing to the success of the 'Summer Paddy Program' starting in 1992/1993.

Although it seems that a substantial volume of rice was smuggled, the rice price in Myanmar, up to 2009, was determined basically by the supply and demand conditions in the domestic market. According to the estimate of Fujita and Okamoto (2009), the domestic rice price in Myanmar during the period was considerably (40–60 %) lower than the international price, especially compared to the Thai export price (Fig. 5.2). Besides, with the lack of policies to mitigate price fluctuations (such as keeping a buffer stock of rice or adopting the 'Rice Premium' system like Thailand later argued), the domestic rice price kept fluctuating significantly.

As shown in Fig. 5.2, the export prices of rice from Myanmar up to 2009 were at around 70 % of the Thai export prices. This was mainly attributed to the fact that firstly, Myanmar exported mainly lower-quality rice, 25 % broken rice vis-à-vis 5 % broken rice in Thailand, and secondly, Myanmar had weaker bargaining power in the determination of price vis-à-vis the buyers, because it was a marginal supplier of rice in the international market (Table 5.3). Furthermore, the inadequate transport infrastructure including the poor port facilities worked against rice export from Myanmar.

[22] The real wages of the agricultural daily labourer (male) in terms of 'rice wage' (rice which can be purchased with the daily wage), for instance, declined sharply from 9 kg in the late 1970s to 4–5 kg in the late 1990s and the early 2000s (Fujita 2009a).

[23] See Takahashi (2000). The widened income disparity can be attributed not only to the decline of agricultural wages but also (1) to the increase of farmers' income due to the export boom of pulses and beans and the increase of vegetables and fruit production for the domestic market and (2) to the profit earned by farmers who invested their increased agricultural surplus in various nonagricultural business activities.

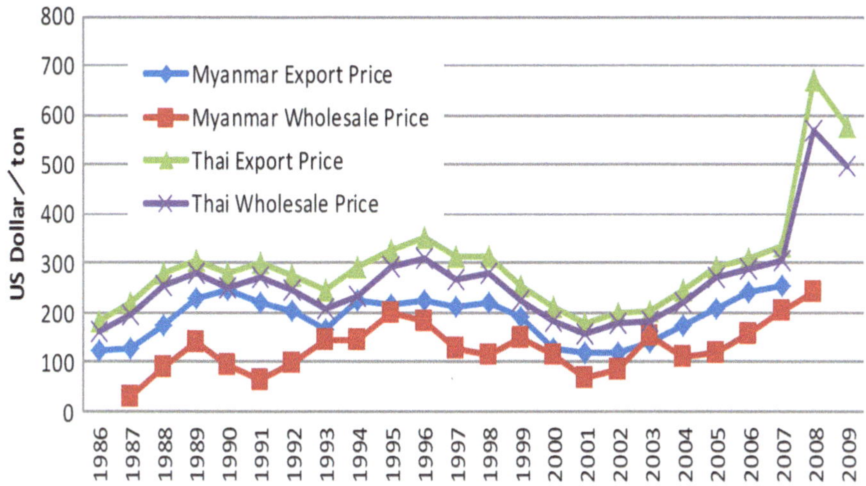

Fig. 5.2 Rice price in Myanmar and in the international market (Note: The Myanmar export price was estimated from the statistics of export values and amounts by FAO (the quality of rice is unknown). The Myanmar wholesale price was estimated by converting the Yangon wholesale market price (Emata 35 % broken) to US dollars by the market exchange rates. The Bangkok FOB price of 100 % Grade B and Bangkok wholesale market price (5 % broken) was used for the Thai export price and wholesale market price, respectively. *Source*: Prepared by Mr. Koji Kubo (Institute of Developing Economies, Chiba, Japan) by utilizing the materials from the United States Department of Agriculture, *Rice Outlook*, Bank of Thailand, *Key Economic Indicators*, FAO, FAOSTAT website (http://faostat.fao.org/ accessed on March 26, 2010), Central Statistical Office (Myanmar), *Statistical Yearbook*, and material for the market exchange rate in Myanmar)

Figure 5.3 illustrates the determination mechanism of the domestic rice price in Myanmar during the period under consideration. Under the assumption of minor influences of rice procurement and rice export by the government on domestic rice prices, the domestic rice price was determined to a slightly higher level than the equilibrium price in the domestic market because of the existence of smuggling (mainly to China and Bangladesh). Farmers had to deliver a part of the production to the government at the official procurement price (part of the procured rice was exported). Therefore, if the rice consumed by farmers was neglected for simplification, the farmers' revenue would be

$$[\text{procured volume}]\times[\text{procurement price}]+[\text{production}-\text{procured volume}]$$
$$\times[\text{domestic market price}].$$

The implications are as follows: first, the farmers lost from the state procurement system at below-market prices. Second, since the domestic market price was well below the equilibrium price under the free market regime (international price), they also lost from the government's rice export monopoly (restriction) policy. Furthermore, the withdrawal of government subsidies from major inputs such as

Table 5.3 Destinations of export of rice from Myanmar

	Indonesia	Philippines	Malaysia	Singapore	Bangladesh	Sri Lanka	China	Vietnam	Middle East	Africa	Others	Total
1985/1986			40		29	40	73	131		210	81	604
1990/1991			10	5		56			3	40	20	134
1992/1993						65			6	114	14	199
1993/1994		2				35			3	174	47	261
1994/1995	613				33	59				276	60	1,041
1995/1996	169	92			20		18			23	32	354
1996/1997	12	23								25	33	93
1997/1998					12	11					5	28
1998/1999	52				11					31	26	120
1999/2000	12				17						26	55
2000/2001	33		7	6	174					25	6	251
2001/2002	201	11	48	94	47		1		367		170	939
2002/2003	203		58	40	29			12	350		101	793
2003/2004	18		27	32	39			1	33		18	168
2004/2005	1		3	24	39				66		49	182
2005/2006	1		31	17	12				90	9	20	180
2006/2007				3					12		0	15
2007/2008				55	193				44	58	8	358
2008/2009			17	24	202	8	4		12	377	22	666

Source: CSO (2010)

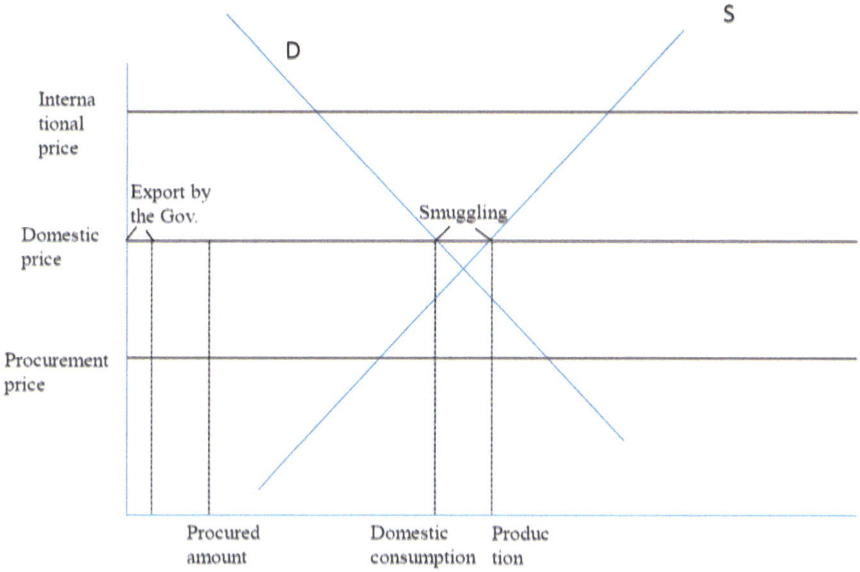

Fig. 5.3 Rice price determination mechanism in Myanmar (*Source*: Prepared by the author)

chemical fertilizers and diesel oil after 1988 compelled the farmers to face quite unfavourable terms of trade for rice production, because they had to pay international prices for such inputs, whereas they received roughly only half of the international price for their product, that is, rice. Third, rice mill owners also incurred losses. If private rice export had been allowed, they could have modernized their rice mills, or at least they could have purchased imported spare parts to maintain the quality of rice. However, in reality, there was no way for the millers to earn foreign exchange. Besides, as mentioned above, they had been forced to mill the government paddy at cheap rates.

Finally, in 2003, the rice procurement system was completely abolished. It was an epoch-making moment. The MAPT, which had long procured rice from farmers, stopped functioning. At the same time, it was announced that the government would allow the private sector to export rice, because MAPT would also stop rice exports. The private sector was delighted to hear the news, although it was planned that a system would be introduced in which rice exporters could retain only a half of the earned foreign exchange in the form of the local currency, kyat. The remaining 50 % of foreign exchange earnings would be collected by the government. Unfortunately, however, the domestic rice price in Myanmar was surging at that time, and finally, the government suspended its decision on liberalization of rice export.[24]

[24] Since private traders visited several overseas buyers for negotiations to prepare for export, they were hugely disappointed when they heard of the suspension.

In 2007, the government finally allowed private rice export. An export quota system was introduced, where only a 10 % export tax (the same as other export items) was imposed. In 2007 and 2008, after the harvest of summer rice, 800,000 tons of export quota was announced for each year, which was allocated to several large rice wholesalers. In 2009, the announcement of a yearly quota was stopped and the government announced monthly quotas while monitoring the supply and demand conditions in the domestic market.[25]

As argued before in this chapter, how to manage rice prices is an extremely important issue in Asia where rice is the staple food. The problem is more serious and complicated for rice-exporting countries. Even Thailand, the biggest and the most competitive rice exporter in the world after World War II, had to depress the domestic rice price at around 60 % of its export price through an export system called ‘Rice Premium’ for a long period of time (Choeun et al. 2006). It was not until the mid-1980s when the Thai government at last abolished the ‘Rice Premium’ system that the domestic price climbed to around 90 % of its export price thereafter. The mid-1980s was the turning point for the Thai economy, when the Japanese yen rapidly appreciated after the Plaza Accord and a large amount of foreign direct investment (FDI) flowed into Thailand from Japan, followed by the other Asian countries (such as Korea, Hong Kong and Singapore), and thereby heavy industrialization in Thailand accelerated. By the mid-1980s, Thailand had already achieved industrialization to some extent, although the major industries were light industries such as textile and food processing, but it still had to keep the ‘Rice Premium’ system so as to prevent rice price hikes to protect the urban poor. In the case of Myanmar, which has a large number of poor people in rural areas (mainly landless agricultural labourers) besides the urban poor, it can be easily imagined that the problem is much more serious.

However, it is doubtful how seriously the Myanmar government thought about the poor rice net buyers such as the landless agricultural labourers. The world food market started to be tightened after late 2006 and peaked in April/May 2008 (its effect lasted more than 2 years thereafter), but surprisingly, Myanmar aggressively exported rice amidst the food crisis (Fig. 5.4). Such behaviour of the Myanmar government was in sharp contrast with India, which banned rice export in early 2008 and did not lift it for more than 3 years for the sake of national food security.

After that, sometime in 2011, the Myanmar government decided to abolish the export quota system and completely liberalized rice export.[26] This policy initiative seems to be a decision in the context of the narrowed price differentials after 2008 between the export price from Myanmar and the domestic price in Myanmar. In other words, even if rice export had been completely liberalized, there would not have been much incentive for private traders to export rice from Myanmar.

[25] Based on private communications with Mr. Koji Kubo, Institute of Developing Economies, Chiba, Japan.

[26] When the government made the decision was not clear, but it was at the latest by February 2012 when we interviewed the Minister of Commerce.

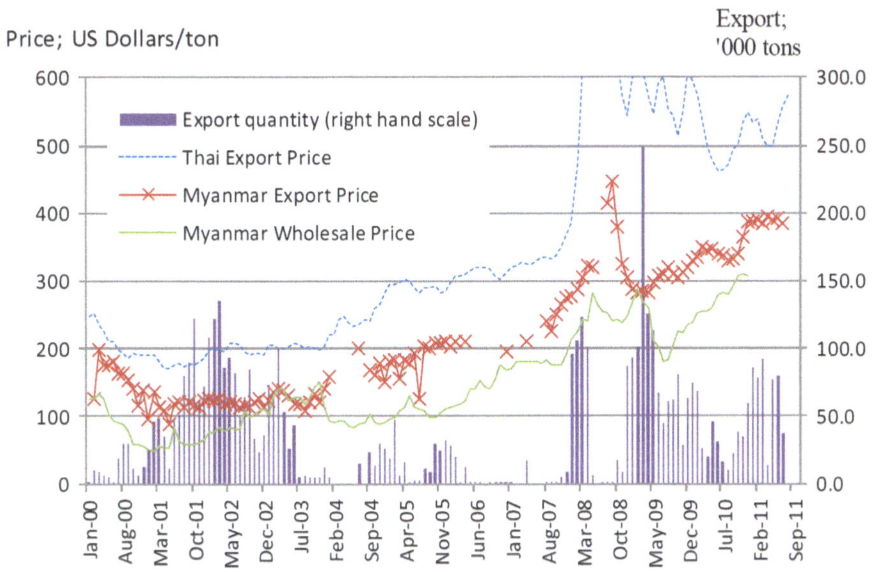

Fig. 5.4 Rice export and export price from Myanmar in years 2000–2011 (Note: The Myanmar export price was estimated from the statistics of export value and amount by the Central Statistical Office (CSO) of Myanmar (quality of rice is unknown). The export price was adjusted by the market exchange rates as the CSO's data are based on the official exchange rates. The Myanmar wholesale price was estimated by converting the Yangon wholesale market price (Emata 35 % broken) to US dollars by the market exchange rates. The Bangkok FOB price of 100 % Grade B was used for the Thai export price. *Source*: Prepared by Mr. Koji Kubo (Institute of Developing Economies) by utilizing the materials from the Ministry of Agriculture and Irrigation, *Market Information Service Price Bulletin*; CSO, *Selected Monthly Economic Indicators*; United States Department of Agriculture, *Rice Outlook*; and material for market exchange rates in Myanmar)

Note here that in Fig. 5.4 we can see that in 2005 the export price from Myanmar was almost double its domestic price. This was a 'normal' situation for Myanmar and had been maintained for a long period of time. But by the end of 2008, the gap became very small. Then, why did the differentials of the two prices suddenly become almost nil during such a short period of time? The conclusion was that it was mainly attributed to the rapid appreciation of the kyat (especially vis-à-vis the US dollar). The real value of the kyat (after considering the differences in inflation rates between Myanmar and the USA) became two to three times higher vis-à-vis the US dollar during the 5-year period from 2006 to 2011 (Fig. 5.5).[27]

Needless to say, the appreciation of the local currency (kyat) affected every sphere of the Myanmar economy. Exporters (not only for rice but also all the commodities including pulses and fishery products, for instance) experienced more difficulties, whereas the prices of imported commodities declined for the benefit of consumers. The surge in labour wages in terms of foreign currency gave disincentives

[27] See also Chap. 3 of this volume.

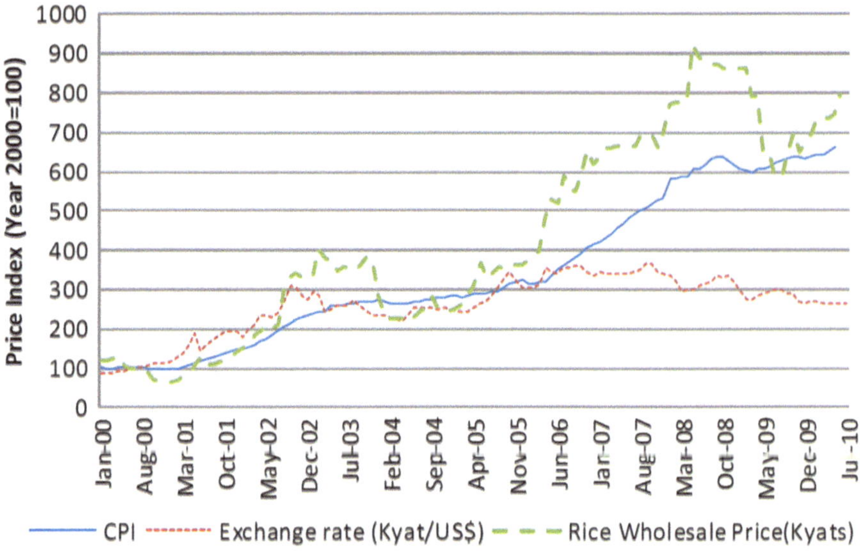

Fig. 5.5 Exchange rate and rice price (Note: Price index is based on the price in July 2000 (=100). *Source*: Prepared by Mr. Koji Kubo (Institute of Developing Economies))

for labour-intensive export-oriented manufacturers such as those in the garment industry. We should realize that the difficulties faced by the rice exporters (and farmers) in those years was nothing but a phenomenon in the context of much larger issues arising from a drastic change in the macro-economy (real exchange rates) in Myanmar.

It cannot be foreseen how exchange rates will move in the future. It is possible that the real value of the kyat will remain high, but it is also possible that it will decline again to the former level. And if, in the future, the rice export price from Myanmar becomes much higher (say, double) than the domestic price, it is possible that the government will be obliged to revise again the rice export policy.

But to revive the export quota system seems to be unwise. It has many deficiencies. The 'Rice Premium' system once adopted by Thailand has various advantages in this regard. It is a kind of variable export levy system, in which the government sets an export price ('reference export price') substantially lower than the international price, and the difference between the two prices is collected from the exporters as an export tax (Fig. 5.6). Under this system, the domestic price of rice is prevented from surging more than the 'reference export price'. It should be noted here that the tax revenue of the government under the 'Rice Premium' system is taken by private traders (as a 'rent') under the export quota system.

The 'Rice Premium' system had long been criticized as an instrument for exploiting Thai farmers, but in a sense, it can be appreciated as a rather well-institutionalized system. The advantages of the 'Rice Premium' system are as follows: first, the domestic rice market can be kept separate from the volatile world market, and price

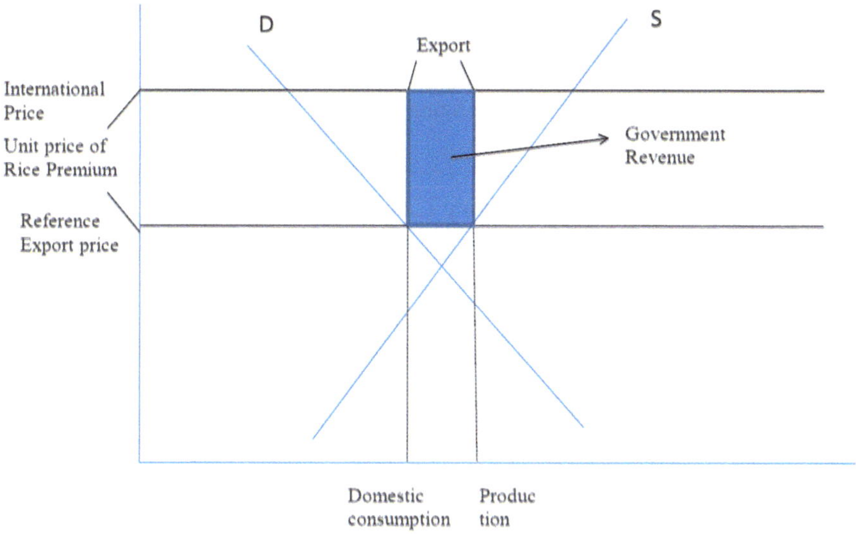

Fig. 5.6 Rice export under the 'Rice Premium' system (*Source*: Prepared by the present author)

hikes of more than the 'reference export price' can be prevented. Second, under the export quota system, the exporters who obtain quotas can get 'rent', and corruption easily occurs among government officials and/or politicians in the process of quota allocation. The 'Rice Premium' system is free from such a problem. Third, the government can get tax revenue and spend the revenue for mitigating the adverse effects on rice farmers. This includes investment for irrigation and other rural infrastructure, provision of credit to rice farmers with concessional terms and conditions, and income compensation for rice farmers, etc. Fourth, the government can save on administrative costs, as it is much easier and less time-consuming to set the 'reference export price' than to determine the amount of export quotas and allocate that to private traders.

Lastly, we should mention the policy initiative in 2012 of the Myanmar government on the rice buffer stock. The National Buffer Stock Committee, which was established in January 2012 through an initiative of the Myanmar Rice Federation (MRF) and Ministry of Commerce, organized township-level subcommittees in the major rice-producing areas and purchased paddy/rice to keep it as a buffer stock. They had already purchased paddy/rice four times: the 2011/2012 monsoon season, 2012 summer season, 2012/2013 monsoon season and 2013 summer season,[28] but at limited amounts—a maximum 50,000 tons—because of budget constraints.[29]

[28] At first they purchased paddy directly from farmers, but faced lots of logistic problems; therefore, later, they purchased rice from rice millers and finally from Yangon and Mandalay wholesale markets. The procurement prices were decided based on a production cost survey conducted by MRF.

[29] The total budget was only 14.53 billion kyat (10 billion from the government, 3.53 billion from MRF and 1 billion from cooperatives).

Apparently, such a small-scale buffer stock was far from sufficient for stabilizing domestic rice prices. The recent trial on rice buffer stock, however, should basically be appreciated because it was the first time in the history of the Myanmar government to take actual measures for stabilizing domestic rice prices.[30]

3.3 The System of Compulsory Cropping

A ‘sophisticated’ system for collecting land revenue was introduced in Myanmar in the British colonial period, the same as in India. Land was classified into paddy fields (*le*), upland fields (*yar*), orchard (*uyin-chan*), riverine land (*kaing-kyun*), nipa land (*dahni*) and swidden land (*taungya*) (Takahashi 2000), and every plot was measured, and detailed information such as area, shape, soil condition, owner, cultivator, crops grown, yield and tax rate was recorded in the cadastral books. In each agricultural season, crops and yields (with other information, if necessary) were recorded for all plots of land. After independence, the task was succeeded by the Department of Settlement and Land Record (SLRD) of the Ministry of Agriculture and Irrigation, but since the tax rate was never revised in accordance with inflation, the importance of the system as taxation for land disappeared long ago in spite of its high administration costs.

However, since the Myanmar government can continuously obtain detailed information on every plot of land, the system has been utilized as a tool for the government to control farmers’ cropping behaviour, a kind of system of compulsory cropping (Takahashi 2000). In particular, the government has historically utilized the system for monitoring rice cultivation.[31] Farmers have had an obligation to grow rice in the rainy season in land classified as paddy fields (*le*). And if the paddy field is irrigable, summer paddy in the dry season must also be grown there.[32] Even when the rice price collapsed to an extremely low level under the rice export monopoly by the government, the farmers had to grow rice at a huge loss.[33] On the other hand, the

[30] How the rice buffer stock issue is related to the enactment of the ‘Protecting Rights and Enhancing Economic Welfare of Farmers Law’ is unknown, but if the government purchases rice from farmers, the price should not be too high compared to the production cost. More sophisticated and scientific concepts and methodology need to be introduced in the survey of production costs.

[31] The compulsory cropping system had also been applied to industrial crops such as sugarcane, cotton, jute and rubber until the mid-2000s. The state-owned enterprises had procured the crops (at low prices) for processing. Besides, the system has been applied occasionally to other crops such as sunflower, mustard and niger.

[32] The compulsory cropping of summer paddy has been applied not only in the irrigated area by government canals or pumping systems but also in the irrigable land by private pumping systems mainly in the Ayeyarwady Delta.

[33] As members of the Agriculture and Rural Development Working Group of the Myanmar Economic Structural Adjustment Program of JICA (Japan International Cooperation Agency) during 2001–2002, we participated in the village surveys selected from different agro-ecological zones of Myanmar. In 2000, the rice price remained at a very low level even in the preharvest season of the monsoon paddy and farmers incurred a loss. The extreme low rice price persisted

Myanmar government has implemented the 'Regional Rice Self-sufficiency Promoting Policy' since the late 1990s, under which rice cultivation was strongly encouraged even in unsuitable lands such as in the Central Dry Zone and mountainous areas like Shan State and Kachin State.[34,35]

Under the low rice price policy in Myanmar in which the rice procurement system and the rice export monopoly were combined, a strange phenomenon (never seen in other Asian countries) was often observed: farmers in mountainous upland areas enjoyed a higher living standard than their counterparts in lowland areas.[36] Such a phenomenon, it seems, persisted even after 2003 when the rice procurement system was finally abolished, since the government continued the compulsory cropping of rice under depressed rice prices by restricting private rice export.

In upland areas, agricultural income increased sharply, not only in the vegetable-producing areas (such as for chilli) but also in areas where pulses and beans were cultivated for export. In lowland areas, however, agricultural income stagnated due to the adverse terms of trade in rice production. The rain-fed lowland areas were relatively better because farmers introduced some lucrative crops like pulses and beans in the summer season after harvesting rice. However, farmers in irrigated lowland areas had no choice but to continue double cropping of rice. This is the reason why farmers in Myanmar do not welcome (rather they are afraid of) an introduction of government irrigation projects to their villages.

Although compulsory cropping is an irrational policy running against the principle of comparative advantage, why has it been adopted for so long in Myanmar? We can point out a habit for 'achieving quantitative targets' in Myanmar since the socialist period, which is considered to still persist in the market transitional economy. An attitude of neglecting the price factor can also be noted. A more serious problem is that the farmers' income and livelihood have been inadequately considered by the government.[37]

---

thereafter also and farmers were reluctant to grow summer paddy, because they had to irrigate land with their private pumps using imported (and so expensive) diesel oil and chemical fertilizers. However, they were forced to grow summer paddy under the compulsory cropping system. In June 2001, we conducted a survey in Myaungmya, one of the major rice-producing areas in the Ayeyarwady Delta, and found that farmers had to borrow money for summer paddy cultivation from informal sources, including pawn shops, at high interest rates. We found in a storehouse of a pawn shop a lot of pawned items such as diesel engines (for pump irrigation), bullock carts (only wheels were deposited due to the shortage of space), bicycles, etc. See Kurita et al. (2004).

[34] In 2001, we visited various parts of Myanmar and observed in the Central Dry Zone and mountainous areas that many government staff (in the Ministry of Agriculture and Irrigation) made a desperate effort to expand rice cultivation to lands unsuitable for rice.

[35] See also Chap. 6 by Masahiko Matsuda in this volume, which explains a case in Shan State where the government encouraged rice cultivation by constructing rice terraces, although the local farmers had historically developed a refined system of irrigated upland farming, suitable to local ecological conditions.

[36] For instance, we encountered several such cases when we toured a wide rural area in Kyaukse Township in 2001 for selecting study villages.

[37] See Tin Htut Oo (2012) for more systematic diagnosis on fundamental problems included in the Myanmar's agricultural policy.

On the other hand, the land management system by SLRD, which supported compulsory cropping, can be a good base for maintaining accurate agricultural statistics. But in reality, under strong pressure by the government to achieve production targets, overreporting by SLRD field staff became pervasive. The most typical example is the rice production statistics.[38]

Figure 5.7 shows the rice production statistics of Myanmar with a comparison between two sources: the Food and Agriculture Organization (FAO) (based on Myanmar government official statistics) and the United States Department of Agriculture (USDA) (independent estimates). A large discrepancy is observed between the two sources. The discrepancy started emerging in the late 1970s when the Myanmar government launched the 'All Township Special Rice High-Yielding Varieties Production Program' with the help of Official Development Assistance (2 KR[39]) granted by the Japanese government.

Since the mid-1960s, the rice Green Revolution, the introduction of high-yielding varieties (HYVs), was mainly started in parts of Southeast Asia such as the Philippines, Indonesia and Sri Lanka. Since water control was indispensable to introduce HYVs, the large river deltas where land was extensively flooded in the monsoon season usually faced difficulties. This is the major reason why Thailand lagged behind in accepting Green Revolution technology. It was common for such large river deltas that after introducing irrigation in the dry season through pump irrigation, etc., summer paddy cultivation started with HYVs first, with a substantial delay in the monsoon paddy.[40]

However, according to the FAO statistics in Fig. 5.7, the average rice yield in Myanmar increased rapidly from 2 to 3 tons/ha in several years between the late 1970s to the early 1980s. Considering that the major rice-producing area of Myanmar is in the Ayeyarwady Delta, it is apparently impossible. The overreporting of rice production data seems to have started in this period. The estimates of USDA are more reliable.

The second big campaign by the Myanmar government for increasing rice production started in 1992/1993 (when the 'Summer Paddy Program' was launched). The intention of the programme was to expand the summer paddy cultivation area with HYVs and promote the double cropping of rice.[41] Figure 5.7 illustrates that the gross cropped area of rice increased rapidly from 5 to 6 million ha in a few years after 1992/1993. However, in this period, the two sets of statistics show almost the same trend, indicating that such a rapid increase in rice area actually happened under rising rice prices. It can be said that the farmers voluntarily responded to the

[38] The overreporting of agricultural production statistics became more serious after the mid-2000s, including non-rice crops.

[39] 2 KR (Kennedy Round) means a type of ODA by the Japanese government for increasing food production through providing inputs such as chemical fertilizers and agricultural machinery.

[40] In Bangladesh (located in the Bengal Delta), for example, rice sector development typically followed such a path (Fujita 2010).

[41] See Fujita and Okamoto (2000), a case study of a village that experienced rice double cropping in this period.

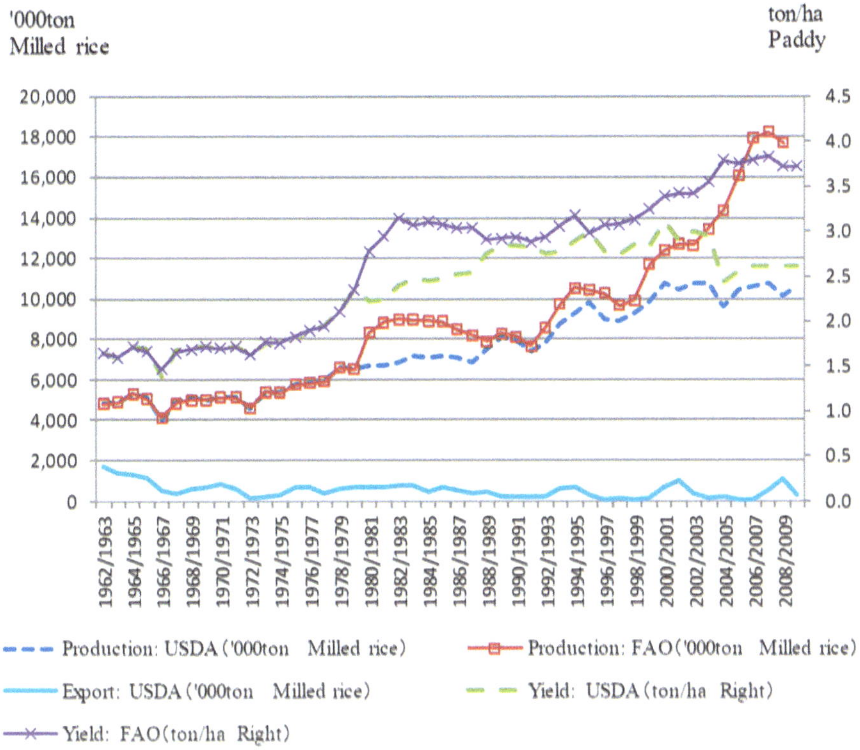

Fig. 5.7 Rice production data in Myanmar (Note: Paddy is converted to milled rice by using the conversion rate of the United States Department of Agriculture (USDA). *Source*: Prepared by Mr. Koji Kubo (Institute of Developing Economies) by utilizing the materials from the USDA, Production, Supply and Distribution online website (http://www.fas.usda.gov/psdonline/ Accessed on September 6, 2010), FAO, FAOSTAT website (http://faostat.fao.org/ Accessed on September 6, 2010))

government's campaign. The success of the programme resulted in rice exports of 1 million tons in 1995. Soon after that, however, the rice double cropping movement stagnated, mainly because of the adverse terms of trade for rice production due to the price hike of diesel oil and chemical fertilizers.[42]

The Myanmar government started a programme for promoting rice self-sufficiency at each region/state level since the late 1990s, as mentioned earlier. The major strategy was to expand the rice cultivation area towards land frontiers. However, it was apparent that such a movement had limitations. Consequently, the field staff of the Ministry of Agriculture and Irrigation had to achieve certain targets, so they started overreporting again, resulting in the rapid increased discrepancy between the two sets of statistics: rice production reached 18 million tons according to FAO in the late 2000s, whereas it remained at around 10 million tons in the

[42] The disappearance of suitable areas for the double cropping of rice was the other major reason.

estimates of USDA. If the aggressive rice export policy adopted by the Myanmar government in the late 2000s (Fig. 5.4) was based on such overreported rice production statistics, the overreported statistics should be blamed.

4 Towards Improvement in the Agricultural Production Structure in Myanmar

Myanmar is blessed with rich natural resources for agricultural production, especially a large room for diversification to non-rice crops. The largest constraint that hampers such potential to flourish, in my opinion, has been a kind of adherence by the Myanmar government to increase rice production. It was more unfortunate that the government tried to physically force the farmers to increase rice production, instead of giving economic incentives to them to do so. In the process of a fierce (but silent) struggle between the government and farmers, who pretended to obey the government but resisted whenever possible, significant economic resources (land, labour and capital) were wasted. This was the essence of the problem.

After abolishing the rice procurement system in 2003 and the recent liberalization of rice export since 2008, it seems that there is no institutional barrier at present to rice sector development in Myanmar, but a big gap still seems to exist in policy stance among different ministries, especially between the Ministry of Agriculture and Irrigation and the Ministry of Commerce. Until the Ministry of Agriculture and Irrigation removes the compulsory cropping system, the problem in the rice sector will persist. As discussed later, the compulsory cropping system, which hitherto has been only informally executed, is clearly stated in the new Farmland Law enacted in March 2012.

The key to solving the problem is how to release the Myanmar government from the 'rice trauma'. It can be accomplished only when the government finally sweeps away their fear that social upheavals will reoccur when the rice price surges. There is a need for comprehensive measures, including those for raising the productivity of rice, stabilizing rice prices, promoting economic development with the increased income of the people, and construction of a social safety net.

Finally, let us look at the most fundamental issues that affect the whole agricultural sector in Myanmar, that is, the land tenure system and the rural financial system, which will be discussed below.

4.1 Land Tenure Reforms

The former Farmland Law was enacted in 1953. Under the law, the ownership of all agricultural land belonged to the nation, and farmers had only the users' rights. The users' rights could be inherited, but the sale, transfer, lease and mortgage of the land were prohibited.[43] Farmers seldom felt the real meaning of nationalized land in everyday life, but sometimes when, for instance, the government needed to expropriate land for some public works projects, forced expropriation of farmland was undertaken without sufficient (sometimes nil) compensation, based on the 'fact' that the land belonged to the nation.[44] In addition, when there was the rice procurement system, as in the last invocation of the state power, the government grabbed land from farmers who strongly resisted the procurement and transferred it to other more 'cooperative' farmers.

The other weakness in the land tenure system in Myanmar was that farmers could not borrow money from banks by providing land as collateral. As will be discussed below, historically, rural institutional credit in Myanmar has been highly underdeveloped, hampering the agricultural/rural development of the country. One of the major obstacles has been the lack of bank loans using land as collateral.

A new epoch-making movement happened recently in this regard: the new Farmland Law was at last enacted in March 2012. The 'Vacant, Fallow and Virgin Lands Management Law' was also enacted at the same time. The major points of these laws are as follows:

1. The Farmland Law

   (a) The Farmland Management Bodies are organized at nation, region/state, district, township and village tract/ward levels.
   (b) The Union Minister of Agriculture and Irrigation is appointed as the Chairman of the Central Farmland Management Body, with the Deputy Minister as the Vice Chairman and Director General for the Settlement and Land Records Department (SLRD) as Secretary.
   (c) A person or an organization with the permission of right to use farmland has to apply for a Land Use Certificate to the Township SLRD office, which passes it through the relevant Ward/Village Tract Farmland Management Body. And the Township Farmland Management Body issues the Land Use Certificate.
   (d) The land use right can be sold, mortgaged, leased, exchanged or donated.
   (e) 'Mortgages' are permitted only to acquire funds for investment for agricultural production, by means of mortgaging farmland with the government or authorized banks.
   (f) Farmland is prohibited for use for nonagricultural purposes without permission.

[43] Note here that, however, sales of the users' rights have commonly been observed in Myanmar by transferring the name in land registrars with informal consent among the seller, buyer, Village Tract chairman and SLRD field staff. Because of this, if we asked for the 'land price' in villages, we could get the answer immediately. By contrast, lease (tenancy) or mortgage of the users' rights could rarely be observed except in a few cases among close relatives.

[44] An example was the agricultural research/education district in Yezin. It was built by expropriating a large land area, and many farmers became landless in the process (although some people got a job in the agricultural university or research institutes). The construction of the new capital, Nay Pyi Taw, was another major case.

(g) Farmland is prohibited for growing other than regular crops without permission (the Central Farmland Management Body gives permission to grow other crops on paddy fields after checking the prescribed conditions so as not to diminish rice sufficiency; and the Region/State Farmland Management Body gives permission to grow other crops on farmland other than paddy fields, after checking the prescribed conditions).

2. The Vacant, Fallow and Virgin Lands Management Law

   (a) The Central Committee for the Management of Vacant, Fallow and Virgin Lands is organized, with the Union Minister for Agriculture and Irrigation as Chairman, the Director General of SLRD as the Secretary and suitable persons of the concerned government departments and organizations, and other suitable persons as Members.
   (b) The Central Committee permits the right to utilize vacant, fallow and virgin land for the purposes of (a) agriculture, (b) animal husbandry and aquaculture, (c) mining and (d) others that the government allows in line with the law.
   (c) The following persons and organizations have the right to make an application to the Central Committee: (a) Myanmar citizen investors, (b) government department/organization and nongovernment organizations, (c) exempted persons who are eligible in accordance with Section 4 of the Transfer of Immovable Property Restriction Law (1987), (d) joint-venture of investors who have the right to carry out an application with the government department/organization in accordance with the Foreign Investment Law and (e) joint-venture of investors who have the right to carry out an application with Myanmar citizen investors in accordance with the Foreign Investment Law.
   (d) The maximum area and the period permitting utilization rights are determined according to the purposes.[45]

These new laws have far-reaching implications for Myanmar agriculture,[46] but here we focus only on the plausible effects of the Farmland Law on the landless agricultural labourers in Myanmar, especially on the possibility for them to be tenant farmers.

---

[45] In the case of perennial crops, for example, not more than 5,000 acres at a time and whenever cultivation is completed on 75 % of the permitted acreage, an additional area of not more than 5,000 acres at a time up to a total of 50,000 acres shall be permitted. (However, in the case of farmers and families that want to run manageable farms, they shall be allowed to use an area not exceeding 50 acres with the permission of one of the respective local organizations.) Actual cultivable land of more than 5,000 acres at a time shall be permitted for the state interest with the agreement of the Cabinet of the Union Government. The duration for rights to use the land cannot exceed 30 years from the year of the grant.

[46] The major problems to be raised are as follows: (1) there is no restriction written in the law on the ceiling of land area a person or an organization can hold (thereby accumulation of land in the hands of a few private companies may become a serious social problem in the future) and (2) compulsory cropping, hitherto only informally enforced, is clearly stipulated in the new Farmland Law, which is very problematic.

As already mentioned, the landless agricultural labourers are the major group of poverty-stricken people in Myanmar, and income disparity vis-à-vis farm households has widened since 1988. Furthermore, the disparity in asset holdings has been much larger than income disparity.[47] They do not have farmland, livestock, agricultural machinery or farm implements. They usually lack almost all consumer durables (including tables and beds), and sometimes they do not even own the houses in which they live. The fact that they are poor not only in income but also in asset holdings implies that they are vulnerable to risks (such as drought and flood) and shocks (such as sickness and injury). How they can escape poverty is a big challenge for the government as well as the international community.

It can never be expected that many landless agricultural labourers would become tenant farmers, although tenancy is allowed by the new law and the land tenancy market would be developed in the near future. But at least if some of them become tenants, it is altogether meaningful because, firstly, agricultural productivity would be enhanced in family labour-based small-scale tenant farms vis-à-vis hired labour-based large-scale farms.[48] Secondly, the landless labourers could accumulate assets by doing tenant farming, which would open the path for upward mobility in their socioeconomic status.

However, it should be noted that the development of a rental market for power tillers/tractors is indispensable for promoting landless tenants, since most of them do not have the necessary production means such as draft animals and farm implements (bullock carts, ploughs, harrows, etc.), which is the most serious obstacle for them to be tenants.[49]

At the beginning of this chapter, I emphasized the importance of agricultural development for a country before it achieves industrialization, mainly because the outlet market for industries must be developed by increasing the purchasing power (income) of the people in rural areas. Considering the fact that in Myanmar roughly 30 % of rural households were landless agricultural labour households as of 2014, raising their incomes is indispensable for increasing rural purchasing power. In this sense, if at least some of the labourers could be tenant farmers, it would have a significant impact on national economic development.[50]

[47] See Kurita et al. (2004). Saito (1980) already pointed out the large disparity in terms of asset holding in the socialist period.

[48] It is well known that in traditional agriculture, family labour-based small-scale farming is more efficient and productive in terms of land productivity. The major reason is the higher expenditure for supervising labourers for hired labour-based large-scale farms, whereas there is no advantage in large-scale farms as the 'economies of scale' do not work in traditional agriculture. See Fujita (2009b), for example, in the case of Bangladesh agriculture.

[49] It is usually argued that the rental market for draft animals is difficult to function, since owners of animals cannot prevent borrowers from misusing the animals (Ohno 1988). Note, however, that Fujita (2009) observed in rural Bangladesh the development of such markets, albeit insufficiently.

[50] Given the fact that there are many large landowners in Myanmar with more than several hundred or even several thousand acres, the Myanmar government should examine the possibility of a radical land reform program to redistribute farmland to needy people.

4.2 Development of a Rural Financial System

The lack of a sufficient amount of institutional credit, which farmers can utilize, has long been a serious constraint for the development of agriculture in Myanmar. The Mynma Agricultural Development Bank (MADB) provided farmers with seasonal crop loans, but until 2008, they were too small, less than 10 % of the production cost. MADB also extended medium-term loans of usually 3 years for purchasing farm machinery, etc., but with a very limited total amount. The other financial institutions to which farmers had access included the Mynma Economic Bank (MEB) and the Mynma Small Loan Enterprises (MSLE). Farmers could get loans through the Cooperative Bank, but the number of cooperatives especially in pure rural areas has been very small.

A number of private commercial banks flourished after 1988, but most of the branches were concentrated in urban areas, and many private banks were badly hit (some had to be closed) by the nationwide bank run that happened in 2003. Pawn shops are the other major private financial institutions, which are classified either as authorized or unauthorized shops. Pawn shops usually lend 70 % of the market value of pawns (usually gold) with a monthly interest rate of 3–5 % for a period of 3–6 months. Interest should be paid every month. In the case of failure to pay interest for several months, the pawns would be taken by the shops. The above-mentioned MSLE are public pawn shops, which are soundly managed and have never suffered losses.[51]

However, the development of MADB in the early 2010s, especially in terms of the amounts of seasonal loans for rice cultivation, was remarkable: the per acre loan amount for rice was raised from 8,000 kyat in 2008/2009 to 10,000 kyat in 2009/2010, 20,000 kyat in 2010/2011, 40,000 kyat in 2011/2012, 50,000/80,000 kyat in 2012/2013 and finally 100,000 kyat in 2013/2014. In the case of non-rice crops, it was also raised from 3,000/4,000 kyat in 2008/2009 to 6,000 kyat in 2009/2010, 10,000 kyat in 2010/2011–2012/2013 and 20,000 kyat in 2013/2014. The major problem of MADB's seasonal loans for crop production had long been its extremely small size, but such a problem was largely reduced in recent years. In particular, the

[51] According to a survey by the author in a branch office of MSLE at Waw Township, Bago, on September 21 2001, MSLE had its head office in Yangon, with 9 regional offices and 178 township offices. The outstanding lending amount in 2000/2001 for the Waw Township branch office was 11.7 million kyat (to a total of 1,201 customers). They borrowed money from the Mynma Economic Bank at an annual interest rate of 11 %, which is lent by keeping gold as collateral, at a rate of 42,000 kyat per one tickle of gold (which was valued at more than 100,000 kyat at that time) with a monthly interest rate of 3 % for a period of 5 months. The number of staff of the branch office was seven, including a branch manager. According to them, there was one authorized private pawn shop and roughly 50 unauthorized ones in the township. Compared with the MSLE, the interest rate charged by the private pawn shops was lower but with a shorter lending period. When customers cannot repay the loan from the MSLE, they usually borrow money from others (mainly private pawn shops) and repay with that. Therefore, the cases in which pawn agreements are taken up by the MSLE are rare.

Table 5.4 Major financial indicators of MADB (million kyat)

	Capital	Deposits	Loan Seasonal	Term	Total	Deposit/loan	Net profit
2000/2001	1,000	NA	12,124	63	12,187	NA	322
2001/2002	1,000	3,730	12,741	277	13,018	0.287	263
2002/2003	1,000	4,617	12,015	1,088	13,103	0.352	225
2003/2004	1,000	6,271	20,416	1,606	22,022	0.285	300
2004/2005	1,000	7,586	27,382	5,712	33,094	0.229	467
2005/2006	2,000	11,132	34,390	3,261	37,651	0.296	933
2006/2007	2,000	16,902	44,876	7,945	52,821	0.320	400
2007/2008	2,000	24,055	59,628	9,057	68,685	0.350	1,211
2008/2009	2,000	31,018	68,970	3,010	71,980	0.431	1,053
2009/2010	5,000	39,676	93,489	3,780	97,269	0.408	821
2010/2011	5,000	57,604	190,660	8,897	199,557	0.289	2,670
2011/2012	5,000	85,807	312,113	7,105	319,218	0.269	8,485
2012/2013	5,000	15,192	557,847	13,207	571,054	0.027	9,335

Source: MADB

seasonal loan for rice cultivation would cover roughly half of the production cost (in the case of monsoon paddy), which seems to be satisfactory.

However, a bias to rice crops in MADB loans was furthermore strengthened because of such a development in seasonal loans; the share of rice seasonal loans in total seasonal loan disbursement was already 81.4 % in 2009/2010, which increased further to 90.9 % in 2012/2013. Note here that in 2012/2013, the share of seasonal loans in the total of MADB's loans reached 97.7 %. The remaining 2.3 % was disbursed as term loans mainly for purchasing agricultural machinery such as power tillers and water pumps. Such a very strong bias towards rice crops in MADB's loan disbursement is apparently contradictory to the needs for agricultural diversification in Myanmar.

The most fundamental problem of MADB in the early part of the twenty-first century was its insufficient mobilization of savings from farmers (Table 5.4). As the table shows, the deposit/loans ratio increased from 0.287 in 2001/2002 to 0.431 in 2008/2009, but after that it declined rapidly, mainly because of the rapid increase in the amount of seasonal loans mentioned above. The sharp decrease in deposits in 2012/2013 was a result of returning deposits to farmers in accordance with the request by parliament as one of the relief measures following the devastating flood in the monsoon season of 2011. The shortage of funds was met by borrowing from the Mynma Economic Bank (MEB) at an interest rate of 4 % per annum. Note that MADB pays 8 % (per annum) interest to depositors and the lending interest rate was 8.5 % (per annum) for both seasonal loans and term loans as of 2013. Considering that the MEB's major source of funds was also deposits from the general public at 8 % of interest rate, MADB made a large profit at the expense of MEB.

The deposits in MADB shown in Table 5.4, however, were basically various kinds of obligatory deposits. In this sense, so far, MADB could hardly be called a 'real' bank to intermediate on financial resources between depositors and borrowers. Such a fundamental problem could be solved by transforming MADB into a real bank that would mobilize more savings from farmers.[52]

In summary, the formal financial institutions (either public or private) to which rural people have easy access were historically limited in Myanmar. Microfinance was also quite underdeveloped up to the early 2010s. As a result, rural people were obliged to borrow from informal sources, which included relatives, friends, rich farmers, traders, pawn shops and moneylenders. The interest rates usually charged by such informal lenders were 10–15 % per month without collateral and 5 % with collateral (in many cases gold); interest-free loans were rare even among relatives and close friends (Okamoto 2008b). In the case of standing crop sales, the effective interest rate reached to more than 20 % per month.

The situation landless agricultural labourers faced was much more serious. As they eked out a living, and with no major assets other than their labour, no one would usually be willing to lend money even at very high interest. As a last resort, they would have to borrow money from employers as a wage advance. The estimated effective interest rates for such cases were 20–30 % per month (Okamoto 2008b). As argued earlier, since 1988, the real wage (especially the 'rice wage') for unskilled labourers in Myanmar has declined rapidly. In case workers could get a wage advance, the actual payment they receive would be further reduced.

The underdevelopment of institutional finances (including microfinance) and the high dependency on informal sources with exorbitantly high interest rates in rural Myanmar would, therefore, entail not only underdevelopment of the agricultural sector in general but also the low income and living standard for both farmers and landless agricultural labourers.

Rural Myanmar has never experienced a 'healthy' development of its financial market (Turnell 2009). As mentioned earlier, the rapid development of private banks in the 1990s also largely bypassed the rural areas.

In order to develop a strong and healthy institutional financial market in rural Myanmar, the infusion of money from above is far from sufficient. A financial intermediary system should be developed, in which savings are mobilized and circulated within the rural areas. The MADB, in particular, should be reformed so as to mobilize savings from rural areas. It should not be forgotten here that microfinance is not a panacea.[53]

---

[52] A branch office of MADB is usually located in a major town in each township. As of 2013, the total number of MADB branch offices was 206. Therefore, the major problem for farmers when depositing money in MADB is the long distance from villages to the branch office, resulting in a very high transaction cost for depositors. In order to solve this problem, the reintroduction of the village banking system, which worked very well until 1993, can be considered.

[53] The Myanmar government's expectations of microfinance for poverty alleviation seem large. Note here also that, with fund aid from the United Nations Development Program (UNDP), a microfinance project has been conducted for many years in the three areas of the Ayeyarwady Delta, Central Dry Zone and Shan Plateau by PACT (Kubo et al. 2009).

5 Concluding Remarks

In this chapter, from the viewpoint of historical path dependency, we have conducted an analysis on a set of contemporary issues relating to the agriculture and rural sector of Myanmar, with a focus on the rice sector. It is based on our hypothesis that the biggest obstacle limiting the huge development potential of Myanmar agriculture from flourishing is that the Myanmar government has been caught by the 'rice trauma' trap. The trauma was formed through the bitter experience of social unrest, which occurred three times during the socialist period, and all of which were triggered by rice price hikes. The government therefore wanted to depress the domestic rice price to low levels by means of various policy measures, including the rice procurement/rationing system, and the monopoly of rice export by the state. However, because of such policies, rice became an unprofitable crop for farmers, and they were reluctant to produce it. But the government forced farmers to produce it by the compulsory cropping system of rice in paddy fields. In the fierce (but silent) struggle between the government and farmers who tried to escape from the policy whenever possible while pretending to obey the government on the surface, a lot of economic resources including land, labour and capital have been wasted.

There are two fundamental problems in Myanmar agriculture: firstly, the problem in agrarian structure in which a large number of poverty-struck landless agricultural labourers have been working under an unequal land distribution system and, secondly, the problem of underdeveloped institutional finance in rural areas has been aggravating the problems in the rice sector.

The agricultural policies of the Myanmar government, especially for the rice sector, have been characterized by 'authoritarianism' and 'irrationality' as exemplified in the compulsory cropping system, the 'Regional Rice Self-sufficiency Promoting Policy' and the forced milling of procured paddy by the private rice mills, on the one hand, and 'inflexibility' as exemplified in the rice export policy, on the other. The agricultural policies of the government have had many deficiencies, and much more sophisticated and fine-tuned policies were necessary because of the extreme difficulty the country faced: the existence of a large number of poor people in rural areas (landless agricultural labourers).

One would expect and welcome an acceleration of economic reforms in Myanmar. Regarding the rice policy, the government should, firstly, look at the reality[54] and the seriousness of their problems and, secondly, based on that recognition, should formulate and implement a more cool-headed (and warm-hearted), rational and flexible set of policies. The government should be reminded again that even Thailand, for a long period until the mid-1980s, continued to adopt a low rice price policy with the 'Rice Premium' system. How to deal with the rice sector has been difficult for all Asian governments. Once the Myanmar government is released from the 'rice trauma', the huge development potential of its agricultural sector (as well as agro-based industries) is expected to fully flourish.

---

[54] The development of accurate and detailed statistics is very important in this sense.

References

Adas, M. (1974). *The Burma delta: Economic development and social change on an Asian rice frontier, 1952–1941*. Madison: The University of Wisconsin Press.

Central Statistical Organization (CSO), Government of the Union of Myanmar. (2010). *Statistical Yearbook 2009*. Nay Pyi Taw: Central Statistical Organization.

Choeun, H., Godo, Y., & Hayami, Y. (2006). The economics and policies of rice export taxation in Thailand: A historical simulation analysis, 1950–1985. *Journal of Asian Economics, 17*(1), 103–125.

Fujita, K. (2009a). Agricultural laborers in Myanmar during the economic transition: views from the study of selected villages. In K. Fujita, F. Mieno, & I. Okamoto (Ed.), *The economic transition in Myanmar after 1988: Market economy versus state control* (pp. 246–280). Singapore: NUS Press in association with Kyoto University Press.

Fujita, K. (2009b). Worlds apart: Peasants in Japan and agricultural laborers in Japan. *International Journal of South Asian Studies, 2*, 87–104.

Fujita, K. (2010). *Re-thinking economic development: The green revolution, agrarian structure and transformation in Bangladesh*. Kyoto/Melbourne: Kyoto University Press/Trans Pacific Press.

Fujita, K., & Okamoto, I. (2000). An economic study on irrigated summer rice production in Myanmar: The case of a village near Yangon" (in Japanese). *Southeast Asian Studies, 38*(1), 22–49.

Fujita, K., & Okamoto I. (2009). Overview of agricultural policies and development in Myanmar, In K. Fujita, F. Mieno, & I. Okamoto (Ed.), *The economic transition in Myanmar after 1988: Market economy versus state control* (pp.169–215). Singapore: NUS Press in association with Kyoto University Press.

Fujita, K., Endo T., Okamoto I., Nakanishi Y. & Yamada M. (2010). *Myanmar migrant labourers in Ranong, Thailand*. Chiba: (IDE Discussion Paper No. 257).

Hayami, Y. (1997). *Development economics: From the poverty to the wealth of nations*. Oxford: Oxford University Press.

Hla Myint. (1980). *Economics of the developing countries* (5th ed.). London: Hunchington & Co. Ltd.

Kubo, K., Fukui, R., & Mieno, F. (2009). The financial sector during the transition to a market economy in Myanmar. In K. Fujita, F. Mieno, & I. Okamoto (Eds.), *The economic transition in Myanmar after 1988: Market economy versus state control* (pp. 128–165). Singapore: NUS Press in association with Kyoto University Press.

Kurita, K., Okamoto, I., Kurosaki, T., & Fujita, K. (2004). The rice production increase supremacist policy and rural economy in Myanmar: Focusing on income analysis based on household-level data collected in eight villages (in Japanese). *Ajia Keizai, 45*(8), 2–37.

Ohno, A. (1988). Agricultural development and land rental market in Haryana, India. In Y. Hayami (Ed.), *Re-investigation of market mechanism in agricultural development* (pp. 59–96). Tokyo: Institute of Developing Economies (IDE-JETRO).

Okamoto, I. (2008a). Food problems in Myanmar: Regime conservation and rice policy (in Japanese). In T. Kudo (Ed.). *The real image of the Myanmar economy: Why the military government survived* (pp. 89–116). Chiba: Institute of Developing Economies (IDE-JETRO).

Okamoto, I. (2008b). *Economic disparity in rural Myanmar: Transformation under market liberalization*. Singapore: NUS Press/IDE-JETRO.

Okamoto, I. (2009). Transformation of the rice marketing system after market liberalization in Myanmar. In K. Fujita, F. Mieno, & I. Okamoto (Eds.), *The economic transition in Myanmar after 1988: Market economy versus state control* (pp. 216–245). Singapore: NUS Press in association with Kyoto University Press.

Saito, T. (1980). The agricultural labourers in lower Burma rice villages: Case of the Kyungalay Village (in Japanese). *Ajia Keizai, 21*(11), 76–91.

Takahashi, A. (1992). *A rice village in the Burma delta: Village economy under the rule of 'Socialism'* (in Japanese). Tokyo: Institute of Developing Economies (IDE-JETRO).

Takahashi, A. (2000). *Myanmar's village economy in transition: Peasants' lives under the market-oriented economy*. Tokyo: University of Tokyo Press.

Tin Htut Oo. (2012). Devising a new agricultural strategy to enhance Myanmar's rural economy. In N. Cheesman et al. (Eds.), *Myanmar's transition: Opening, obstacles and opportunities* (pp. 156–181). Singapore: Institute of Southeast Asian Studies.

Turnell, S. (2009). *Fiery dragons: Banks, moneylenders and microfinance in Burma* (Nordic Institute of Asian Studies, Monograph series No. 114). Copenhagen: NIAS Press.

Chapter 6
Sustainable Farming Systems in Myanmar: The Implications of Findings from Field Surveys in the 2000s

Masahiko Matsuda

1 Introduction

After the country's first general election in 20 years in 2010, Myanmar moved from being ruled by a military junta to being ruled by an elected government and began to develop relations with the international community. The new government has sought to steadily accelerate the economic and social development of the country with the assistance of the international community. The development of agriculture and the rural sector is important in order to improve the welfare of Myanmar's people, because the majority live in rural areas and are engaged in agriculture.

To formulate an effective development policy, it is essential to understand the agricultural and rural livelihood situation in the country. Additionally, to realise sustainable development in the sector, it is necessary to consider people's local practices and their site-specific knowledge, which has been accumulated over a long period. From many case studies in developing countries, for example, in Africa, it has been recognised that traditional farming systems and their livelihood strategies can often be rational (Shimada 2007). There have also been trials to find better regional approaches to agriculture and rural development through analysing local practices and drawing lessons from them (Brookfield et al. 2003; Scoones et al. 2005).

The present agricultural and rural livelihood situation in Myanmar is, however, not sufficiently well understood. The government has been reluctant to permit field surveys by foreigners in rural areas, so the available information is limited. However, there have been some research outputs, which have been discussed mainly from an agro-economic viewpoint (Takahashi 2000; Kurita et al. 2004; Fujita et al. 2009); additionally, statistical reports have been published periodically by the government.

M. Matsuda (✉)
College of International Relations, Ritsumeikan University, Kyoto, Japan
e-mail: matsu@ir.ritsumei.ac.jp

K. Odaka (ed.), *The Myanmar Economy*, DOI 10.1007/978-4-431-55735-7_6

This chapter[1] aims to portray the recent, actual situation regarding agriculture and rural livelihoods in Myanmar in the light of findings obtained from in-depth field surveys conducted in the 2000s. Local farming systems and people's practices in natural resource management are considered as indigenous knowledge, mainly from an agro-ecological viewpoint. These may indicate some of the potential of Myanmar's agricultural sector and an alternative strategy for sustainable rural development, even if the knowledge seems to be fragmentary.

The following sections deal with three topics that are relevant to different agro-ecological zones (Fig. 6.1). Section 2 focuses on rice farming in the lowlands, mainly in the delta zone. The present status of chemical fertiliser use in rice production in Myanmar will be evaluated from field-level data, and its sustainability and autonomy will be assessed in comparison with other Asian countries. Section 3 examines upland farming systems in the central dry zone to consider area-specific forms of development. This examination will clarify whether the systems can contribute to stabilising annual agricultural production and farmers' incomes in a harsh natural environment. Finally, Sect. 4 considers a case study in the southern part of Shan Plateau, in the mountainous zone, which reveals the historical changes in mountain agriculture. The background of recent farming systems that have sprung up with the disappearance of traditional shifting cultivation and of forest management will be discussed.

2 Lowland Rice Farming in Myanmar: The Reality of Intensification Levels and Implications for Its Sustainable Development

2.1 A Brief History of Rice Production in Myanmar[2]

Lowland rice farming has long been practised in monsoon Asia, and its high productivity provides a strong economic backbone for the dense populations of East and Southeast Asia. In Mainland Southeast Asia, commercial rice production was boosted after the nineteenth century, when substantial wild deltas were reclaimed as production bases to grow rice for export (Takaya 1985). The Ayeyarwady Delta of Lower Myanmar was transformed into paddy fields from the middle of the nineteenth century (Takaya 1985).

During the British colonial era, which might be considered a dark period in Myanmar's history, Myanmar's development of rice production was distinguished internationally. In spite of the negative aspects of reclamation in the delta under colonial rule, some of whose attendant socioeconomic issues are mentioned in Chaps. 2 and 5, Myanmar fulfilled its natural resource potential during that era. The

[1] A previous version of this chapter was published as Matsuda (2012) in Japanese.

[2] This section is largely adapted from Matsuda (2011) and Tanaka and Matsuda (2010). Details of the research methods, results and discussions are presented in the articles.

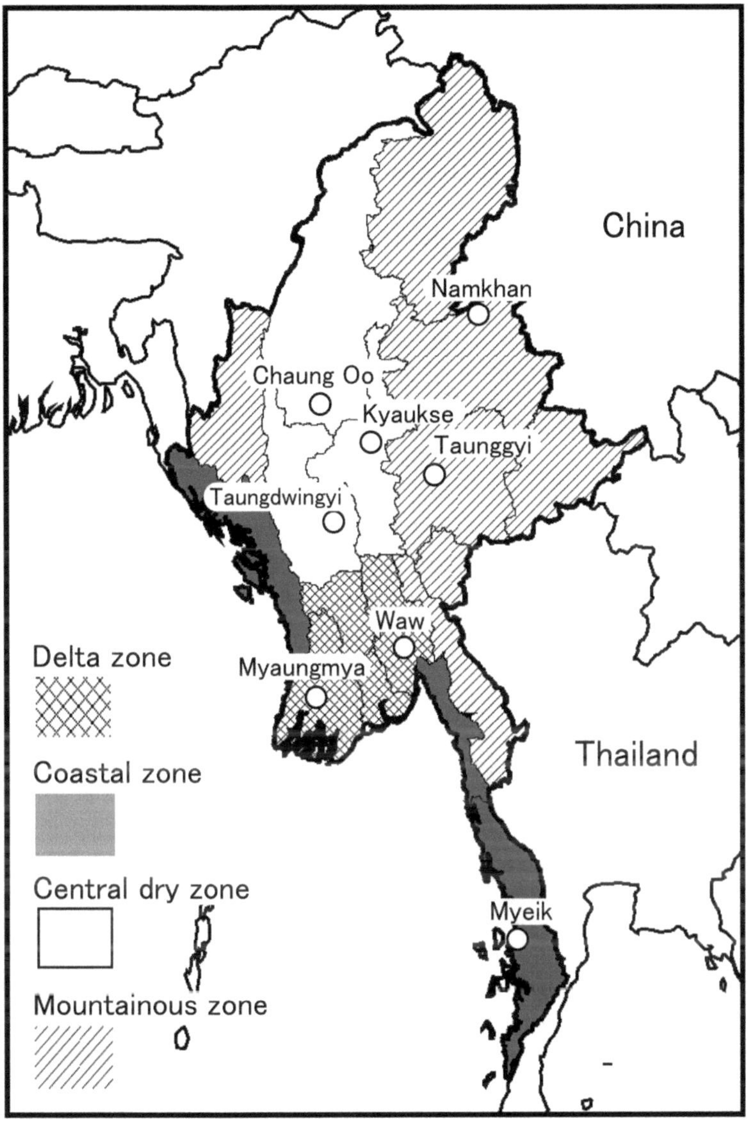

Fig. 6.1 The agro-ecological setting of Myanmar and sites mentioned in the text. The base map shows the agro-ecological zones of Myanmar (From Matsuda 2009)

colonial rulers built horseshoe embankments in the Ayeyarwady Delta, which was sparsely populated at that time, and significantly expanded the rain-fed paddy fields (Matsuda 2009). In the late nineteenth and the early twentieth century, rice produced in the Ayeyarwady Delta could satisfy the international market together with Thai rice from the Chao Phraya Delta and Vietnamese rice from the Mekong Delta (Takaya 1985). Rice exports from Myanmar reached a peak of 3 million metric tonnes per year in the 1930s, at which time Myanmar was the world's leading producer (Matsuda 2009).

From the Second World War until recently, however, Myanmar's rice exports declined (Matsuda 2009). During the socialist era, the government strictly controlled the export and domestic market for rice (see Chap. 5). Vietnam also decreased its rice exports under a planned economic policy. Vietnam, however, boosted its rice production and exports after the economic liberalisation called *Doi Moi* in the mid-1980s, and it then became the world's second largest exporter of rice after Thailand. The increase of rice production in Vietnam can be attributed to technological change in the farming systems, similar to the 'Green Revolution' that had occurred in other Asian countries after the 1960s. Traditional varieties of rice were replaced by modern high-yielding varieties, and the input of agrochemicals, such as chemical fertiliser and pesticides, increased sharply. After the mid-1970s, the socialist government in Myanmar was eager to expand the use of technology by subsidising input materials (Matsuda 2009). Consequently, during the 1990s, the military junta invested heavily in the construction of irrigation and drainage systems (Matsuda 2009).

2.2 Rice Production in Myanmar Based on Statistical Data

According to the statistical data published by the government of Myanmar and the Food and Agriculture Organization of the United Nations (FAO), the national average paddy yield in Myanmar reached 3.6 metric tonnes/ha in 2005 (FAO 2009). This yield level is not low relative to that of neighbouring countries, considering that only about 30 % of the rice cultivation area in Myanmar benefits from irrigation. Some researchers, however, have pointed out that the rice production figures in the official statistics could be overestimated and might also perhaps have been biased towards achieving the high targets set by the government (Saito 1987; Thawnghmung 2004; Fujita et al. 2009; Matsuda 2009). The United States Department of Agriculture (USDA) estimated the national average paddy yield in Myanmar to be lower than the official statistics or approximately 2.6 metric tonnes/ha in 2005 (IRRI 2009).

On the other hand, some statistical data suggest that the input of chemical fertiliser for rice production in Myanmar, which is an indicator of intensification in rice farming, was very low. From the socialist era to the early 2000s, the estimated nutrient input of chemical fertiliser in the rice production fields of Myanmar has ranged from 15 to 30 kg NPK/ha (nitrogen, N; phosphate, P_2O_5; and potash, K_2O) (CSO 2006; IRRI 2009). Even in Thailand, where rain-fed lowlands are dominant and only about 20 % of the rice-sown area is irrigated, the nutrient input is estimated to be three to six times as much as that in Myanmar (IRRI 2009).

2.3 The Reality of the Intensification of Rice Production in Myanmar

The above subsection has suggested that there might be an inconsistency between the relatively high yield and the very low nutrient input in Myanmar's rice farming in the 2000s, in the light of official macro-statistics. The actual situation of rice farming technology should be evaluated on the basis of data obtained from field surveys. In other words, the intensification of rice farming in Myanmar, which is represented by paddy yield and the input of chemical fertiliser, should be estimated by using farm-level data.

Farm-level data were obtained from a field survey in 2001. This survey was conducted under a joint Myanmar–Japan research project, and interviews at the household level were conducted in villages selected from different agro-ecological zones (for details see Kurita et al. 2004). Rice was widely cultivated in five survey villages, which are located in townships (TS) covering three different agro-ecological zones: the delta zone (Myaungmya TS and Waw TS), the coastal zone (Myeik TS) and the central dry zone (Kyaukse TS and Taungdwingyi TS) (Fig. 6.1). The total sample size of farm households was 257, and they included both farming types (rain-fed and irrigated lowland) and both cropping seasons: monsoon (rainy) and summer (dry) seasons. Data relating to rice farming technology in 2000 (e.g. rice variety, yield, chemical fertiliser use etc.) were picked up and analysed for this purpose.

Rice farming in irrigated lowland areas was generally found in parts of the central dry zone, and it was dominant in the summer cropping season in the delta zone. In most cases, the high-yielding varieties of rice were grown in the irrigated lowlands. According to the results of this field survey, farmers applied more chemical fertilisers to the irrigated rice fields and achieved higher paddy yields than in the case of the rain-fed fields. In a survey village of Kyaukse TS, which was well known for its weir irrigation system, the farmers applied 120 kg NPK/ha of nutrient through chemical fertiliser and harvested 3.6 metric tonnes/ha of paddy in the summer season on average. In the summer season in Myaungmya TS, the use of chemical fertiliser was 160 kg NPK/ha and the yield of paddy was 3.5 metric tonnes/ha on average. As indicated above, recent rice farming in the irrigated lowlands of Myanmar has been of a relatively high-input type, and the input–output balance can be roughly estimated as 120 kg NPK/ha of chemical fertiliser input and 3.3 metric tonnes/ha of paddy yield, according to the field data of 2000 (plotted in Fig. 6.2).

In contrast, rice farming in the rain-fed lowlands, such as the monsoon crop in the delta and coastal zones, was low input using local varieties of rice. Although the farmers applied chemical fertilisers in the rain-fed paddy fields, they used only a little. According to data from the field survey, 35 kg NPK/ha of chemical fertiliser was used and 2.1 metric tonnes/ha of paddy rice was harvested on average in the low-input type of rice farming (plotted in Fig. 6.2). Because it is difficult to completely manage water conditions in the delta and coastal zones, farmers might have adopted the low-input type of rice farming during the monsoon season there.

Approximately 30 % of the rice-producing area of the country was found to be in the irrigated lowlands and 60 % in the rain-fed lowlands, according to the Ministry of Agriculture and Irrigation. The rest, about 10 %, was in deepwater and upland areas. Assuming that the yield in deepwater and upland areas is about 1 metric tonne/ha without the use of chemical fertiliser, the recent national average can be roughly calculated as 2.4 metric tonnes/ha and 60 kg NPK/ha, using the above estimates for high-input and low-input types. There is a gap between these calculated values and the official statistics presented in the last subsection; however, the value of paddy yield is relatively close to that estimated by the USDA (IRRI 2009).

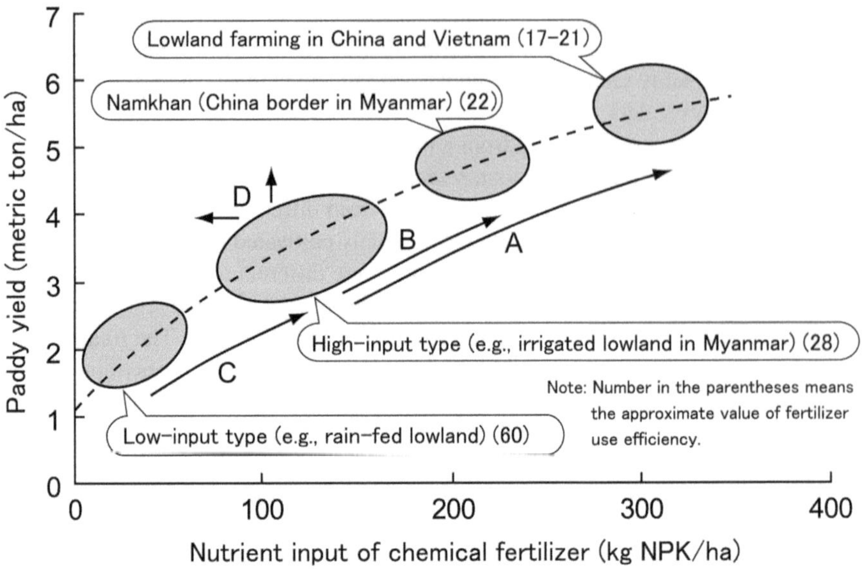

Fig. 6.2 Nutrient input of chemical fertiliser, paddy yield and fertiliser use efficiency in Myanmar, China and Vietnam. Lower values indicate less efficient use of chemical fertiliser in rice production. *Arrows* (*A*, *B*, *C* and *D*) indicate shifts of the input–output status induced by actual and possible changes in rice farming technology mentioned in the text. *Source*: This is a schematically modified version of the figure found in Matsuda (2011). Data for Myanmar come from field surveys in 2001 (five survey sites) and 2004 (Namkhan) (The data for China and Vietnam, around 2000, are from Tan et al. (2007), Tong et al. (2003), IRRI (2009) and Yanagisawa (2000))

2.4 The Implications of Intensification from the Viewpoint of Sustainability and Autonomy

To evaluate the level of intensification in recent rice farming in Myanmar and discuss future strategies for its development, rice farming in neighbouring countries, namely, China and Vietnam, was investigated on the basis of previous studies. Rice cultivation in China and Vietnam has intensified a great deal more than in Myanmar. The input–output balance was estimated at about 300 kg NPK/ha and 5–6 metric tonnes/ha around 2000 (plotted in Fig. 6.2). This suggests that high-input rice farming in Myanmar has the potential for increased production through greater intensification (shift of the input–output status indicated by arrow A in Fig. 6.2). This technological change could be encouraged in suitable areas, such as the irrigated lowlands, by stronger incentives for farmers to increase rice production and without further investment in agricultural infrastructure. For example, if the domestic price of rice is pushed up by the new government's recent export liberalisation, rice farming could easily become more intensive. Vietnam experienced such a process of intensification in the 1990s, and in Myanmar a similar case was found in an area bordering China. The Chinese hybrid variety of rice was found growing widely in a township in this area, Namkhan TS, in 2004. The average yield of paddy rice reached 4.7 metric tonnes/ha and the average nutrient input was 210 kg NPK/ha (plotted in Fig. 6.2). This intensive rice farming using hybrid varieties was possible only under the unique economic conditions of the border area in Myanmar at that time. Although rice exports from Myanmar were considerably restricted in the 2000s, it was not difficult for local people living in that area to access the Chinese market. Because farmers in the border area could produce and sell hybrid rice under almost the same economic conditions as those found in China, they could intensify their rice farming to a greater degree than in other parts of Myanmar (shift of the input–output status indicated by arrow B in Fig. 6.2).

Technological intensification, involving the enhancement of high-input rice farming, would be an effective way of increasing productivity in Myanmar, where there may not be sufficient land left to expand the agricultural acreage. However, the negative impact on ecosystems caused by modern agricultural practices, such as water eutrophication and soil degradation resulting from the heavy application of agrochemicals, should be considered carefully in the interests of sustainability (Tilman et al. 2002). The consumption of chemical fertilisers for rice production in East and Southeast Asian countries has increased, so that it is more important to monitor the intensification level and its possible negative impact (Ko et al. 1998; Hossain and Singh 2000; Nawata 2008). China has achieved a high yield of rice per unit of land; however, the overuse of agrochemicals has been pointed out and possible ways of improving the situation have been extensively discussed (Tong et al. 2003; Peng et al. 2006; Ma et al. 2009).

Additionally, although low energy efficiency and heavy dependence on fossil fuels for food production in modern agriculture were pointed out at a distinct stage of the Green Revolution (Pimentel et al. 1973), these issues have still not been attenuated (Ko et al. 1998; Tilman et al. 2002). Ko et al. (1998) suggested that the efficiency rate for cereal production, which is one major component of sustainability, has generally decreased to around 20 in fertiliser use efficiency rate and stagnated there since intensive cultivation was promoted. The efficiency of fertiliser use in rice farming in Myanmar, China and Vietnam around 2000 is shown in Fig. 6.2. Efficiency of fertiliser use in China and Vietnam had already decreased to the lowest level and had reached saturation point. On the other hand, efficiency of fertiliser use in Myanmar in the 2000s had not fallen to such disappointing levels.

When Myanmar seeks to increase its rice production, it should avoid excessive intensification of farming technology. Taking into account the natural environment and energy resource issues, the country needs to pay attention to sustainability and autonomy, not solely to productivity per area. 'Advanced' rice farming, such as that in China, Vietnam and Namkhan TS, may not be a good model or a desirable goal from the viewpoint of sustainability. Further, the extensive use of intensive technology for food production would not be economically viable and would reduce the country's economic autonomy, because it would largely depend on imported materials or fossil fuels whose supply and price are not reliable in the long term (MacLeod and Moller 2006).

One of the options for the sustainable development of rice production is to move from the low-input type to the controlled high-input type by improving water management conditions, for example, the construction of embankments and sluice gates as well as irrigation and drainage systems (change indicated by arrow C in Fig. 6.2). This could be a possible sector for public investment, although the people and the government of Myanmar have made efforts to upgrade the hydrological control of agricultural fields throughout the country for a number of years (Matsuda 2009). Monsoon cropping in the Ayeyarwady Delta still has the potential for such modification, but it may require enormous amounts of capital. Myanmar should learn from the various experiences of delta development in other Asian countries, such as the Bengal Delta, developed in recent decades, the Red River Delta, which underwent modification over many centuries, and the Mekong Delta, where local farmers are modifying on their own initiative. The ecological characteristics of the Ayeyarwady Delta, for example, a high tide level and a naturally developed canal network (Kaida 1997), should also be taken into consideration when the feasibility of further development is investigated.

The other option is to encourage research and the extension of environmentally friendly food-production technologies (change indicated by arrows D in Fig. 6.2). Because such technological change is not generally either dramatic or short term, many effective practices need to be assembled step by step. The government should support research on the breeding of a new rice variety that has higher nutrient use efficiency and on integrated pest and nutrient management. As pioneers in this field, in the 2000s some private companies began to produce organic fertiliser made, for example, from water hyacinths, which grow abundantly on the surface of canals in the delta. Agricultural products produced by environmentally friendly technologies may be traded extensively at a higher price. On the other hand, a high-quality variety of rice will be accepted by farmers if the market values it highly. Cultivation of *Paw San Hmwe*, a fragrant rice variety, has expanded to Upper Myanmar since the middle 2000s. Myanmar can learn from Thailand's experience of fragrant rice production (Miyata 2008) and also refer to Vietnam's strategy. The government agency for agricultural research, the Department of Agricultural Research of the Ministry of Agriculture and Irrigation, has already carried out some research in this area, and it should determine the future direction of such research.

As discussed above, Myanmar may need to start controlling the appropriate level of fertiliser use efficiency in rice farming by designing long-term strategies, before it reaches saturation level. This can mitigate negative impacts on the ecosystem (ensuring ecological sustainability) and reduce vulnerability to unstable international prices for fertiliser and fossil fuels (ensuring economic autonomy), which in turn can result in profits to its people on a long-term basis.

3 Rain-Fed Upland Farming in the Central Dry Zone: Indigenous Knowledge of Cropping Systems and Future Strategies for Rural Development

3.1 Ancient Prosperity and Recent Poverty in the Central Dry Zone[3]

A wide plain of the Ayeyarwady River Basin runs through the centre of Myanmar, and approximately a quarter of the national population lives there. The area is called the central dry zone, because it has rainfall of less than 1,000 mm per year. It is drier than northeast Thailand and has a semiarid climate, which is exceptional in Southeast Asia, which is generally humid.

During the country's long history, dynasties flourished in the central dry zone. The Pagan Kingdom of Anawrahta, a Burmese kingdom, was established there in the eleventh century, and before that the Pyu Kingdom was also founded there. Rice production probably formed the economic basis of the kingdoms (Ito 1979). Large-scale weirs, canal systems and ponds for irrigation, for example, those in Kyaukse and Meiktila, were constructed by the rulers before the British colonial era (Saito 1974). Additionally, farmers grew rice in alluvial fields and conducted irrigated farming of rice using small-scale weirs (Ito 1979; Kono 2009). On the other hand, in upland fields, which constituted most of the central dry zone, rain-fed commercial farming might have been developed for quite some time, according to documents from the colonial era (Takaya 1985). Thus, sometimes people modified their natural environment and sometimes people adapted their farming style.

At the time of present writing (Jan. 2015), the central dry zone still has been viewed as a less economically developed area than other areas in Myanmar. In the official statistics on household expenditure by region/state in Myanmar in the 2000, the figures for Magwe and Mandalay Region, which are in the central dry zone, tend to be lower (Tanaka and Matsuda 2010). One reason, as Kurita et al. (2004) suggest, may be that the government's policy on national agriculture has retarded economic development, especially in the central parts of Myanmar. Further, low agricultural productivity and occasional poor harvests due to the unreliability of rainfall might account for rural poverty in this area (although there is no direct evidence). Sometimes the domestic media sensationally report crop failures in this region, and such images might have become imprinted on people's minds.

The government has invested in this region's agriculture and rural development. For example, it spent a large amount on the construction of a dam and on pump irrigation to draw water from a large river. The beneficiaries of the irrigation project, however, were limited because it depended on the availability of water resources and could be implemented only under suitable ecological conditions. Hence, rain-fed upland farming has been targeted for agricultural development, and outsiders retained by the development project have tried to 'improve' and 'change' the existing farming systems.

[3] This section is largely adapted from Matsuda (2008, 2013).

However, traditional upland farming in the central dry zone has been developed over a long time by farmers and reflects their strategies for mitigating the risk of complete crop failure. The gazetteer in the colonial era reported that farmers anticipated a bad harvest once every 3 years and carried out mixed cropping to avoid total failure (Scott and Hardiman 1900). Ito (1979) and Ando et al. (2010) pointed out that farmers' flexibility in choosing crops could reduce this risk. Although the expected effects of such risk-reduction strategies in local farming practices have not been adequately examined as yet, they should be carefully considered when outsiders intervene in local livelihoods.

3.2 Cropping Systems as Indigenous Knowledge: How to Cope with Uncertain Rainfall

This subsection will use the results of field surveys to evaluate the stability of crop production by means of existing cropping systems in the rain-fed upland fields of the central dry zone. Findings over several years in the 2000s reveal the extent to which uncertain rainfall has made crop production and rural livelihoods unstable and show how local practices and knowledge mitigate the negative effects.

The survey site was a village on the east bank of the Chindwin River located in Chaung Oo TS, Sagaing Region (Fig. 6.1). A rain-fed upland field, called *Ya* in Myanmar, occupied most of the agricultural area in this village. Over 30 households lived in this village and all of them were interviewed about their crop production and livelihoods over the previous several years. The village is located in the lowest rainfall area of the dry zone, with an average annual rainfall of 558 mm during 1994–2008 (Fig. 6.3). Like other semiarid regions in the tropics, the annual rainfall variation was large, with more than 1,100 mm of rain in the wettest year and less than 300 mm in the driest year during this period. The pattern of monthly rainfall also varied year by year. Although the average showed a bimodal shape with a clear rainy period from May to October, the patterns of each year were, in fact, irregular (Fig. 6.3).

Even under such uncertain rainfall conditions, most of the households in the survey village grew crops. Major crops were pigeon pea, cotton, sesame, sorghum and other pulses (e.g. butter beans, green gram etc.). They were cultivated mainly for commercial use. People sold the harvest and bought rice, their staple food and other necessities. Pigeon pea and cotton were sown in June, at the beginning of the rainy season, and they were often intercropped. Sesame and pulses were usually grown from early September as winter cropping. A farm household in the village would have about 5 acres and grew more than three kinds of crops on average.

Regarding the four major crops in the village, Table 6.1 shows the annual yield changes for 5 years from 2002 to 2008 based on the interviews. This is presented as an index which is the ratio of each year's yield to the maximum yield during the 7 years. As is to be expected, the yield of all the major crops fluctuated widely. For each crop, the farmers experienced poor harvests about three times during the 7 years, when the yield was about half of a good harvest or even less. However, total failure of the major crops seldom happened. Some poor crop harvests were compen-

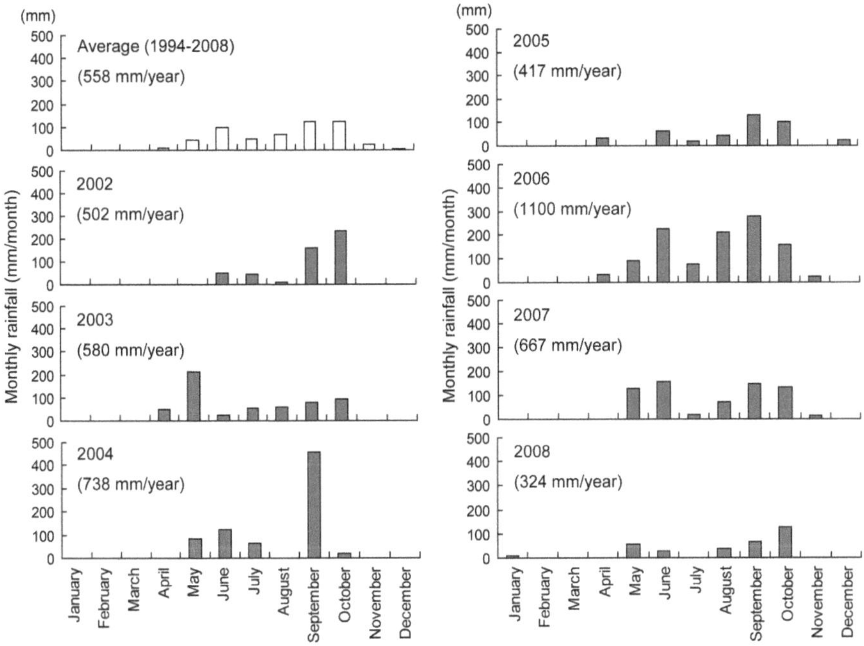

Fig. 6.3 Annual and monthly rainfall from 2002 to 2008 and the average from 1994 to 2008 in the survey site of Chaung Oo (Adapted from Matsuda 2013)

sated for by a good harvest of other crops in the same year, except in 2002. This suggested that the annual combined crop production, rather than that of any specific crop, was stable to some extent. On the basis of the ratio of sown area for each crop, an index of total annual crop production in the survey village was calculated (right-hand column in Table 6.1). The annual variation was more stable than that of the various individual crop yields. Even if farmers did not enjoy an extremely good harvest year, they could maintain around 60–70 % of the total production each year. The survey village suffered a very poor harvest in 2002 (due to very scarce rain throughout the year and continual rain during the time when the crops were flowering); however, according to the older villagers, such drastic failures in crop production were very rare and had happened only once several decades before.

The varying reasons for the poor harvest in each crop might account for the low frequency of total crop failures. Crop production was negatively affected not only by drought but also by other ecological factors, according to the local farmers. Rainfall conditions were the biggest factor, affecting the harvest directly and indirectly. Scarcity of rainfall in the growing period caused insufficient growth and poor harvests of pigeon peas, which have a relatively long growing period. In some cases, however, unexpected rainfall also caused poor harvests. For example, farmers might miss the appropriate time for sowing sesame due to heavy rains in early September, which would lead to a decrease in sesame production. Continual rain and cloudy weather for several days during the flowering time of the pigeon peas, around November, could often cause serious pest injury. Unexpected rainfall during

Table 6.1 Annual change in major crop yields and production in the survey village of Chaung Oo (Adapted from Matsuda 2013)

	Yield index[a] of major crops				
Year	Pigeon pea	Cotton	Sesame	Pulses	Sum of production index[b]
2002	0.07	0.11	0.52	0.16	0.13
2003	0.39	1.00	1.00	0.37	0.70
2004	0.67	0.93	0.54	0.68	0.72
2005	0.35	0.90	0.67	0.50	0.59
2006	0.81	0.50	0.39	0.97	0.70
2007	1.00	0.77	0.84	1.00	0.92
2008	0.51	0.62	0.76	0.84	0.62

[a]Yield index is the ratio of yield in each year to the maximum yield during the 5 years
[b]Production index is the product of the yield index and the estimated ratio of the sown area

sensitive periods for specific crops and scarcity of rainfall were two reasons for the frequent poor yields for specific crops.

All this suggests that the system of growing multiple crops might have functioned as a buffer against limited and uncertain rainfall. In the survey village, since a farm household grew on average more than three kinds of crops annually, this process could be performed at the household level. This finding supports the description in the gazetteer mentioned above. Egashira and Aye Aye Than (2006) and Ando et al. (2011) reported various cropping systems composed of multiple upland crops in the central dry zone. This might imply that a similar system could be found in cropping systems throughout the region. Hence a poor harvest of a single crop, even if it was frequent occurrence, might not be very serious for farmers.

Animal husbandry and paid labour as well as crop production afforded livelihoods to households in the survey village. Animal husbandry, of, for example, goats, sheep or cows, was widely found in the central dry zone. Roughly speaking, about half of household income was derived from crop production and the remaining half from animal husbandry (mainly goat rearing on fallow land) and paid labour (mainly agricultural labour) in the village. According to the interviews, the villagers had experienced extensive loss of young goats due to disease in some bad years. This would have a major negative impact on their livelihood, but it had never occurred in the same year as a very poor harvest. Diseases could be caused by excessive rain throughout a year, but abundant rain would not produce a total loss of crop harvest, according to the local people.

The neighbouring villages located near the Chindwin River have alluvial fields, and their crop production depends mainly on flood conditions, which are unrelated to the area's rainfall. Even if there were less opportunity for agricultural labour in the survey village, which is a rain-fed upland village, due to very scarce rainfall, the villagers could obtain paid agricultural work in the neighbouring villages, which were under different agro-ecological conditions. In fact, in 2002 when the survey village had the rare experience of suffering a poor harvest overall, income from animal husbandry and paid labour in other villages enabled the villagers to survive. Alluvial areas and areas with irrigation create diverse agro-ecological areas in the dry zone, which might serve as a safety net for people living in rain-fed upland areas.

3.3 A Strategy for Agriculture and Rural Development Considering the Historical Context

As discussed in the last subsection, a rain-fed farming village in the central dry zone might have cropping systems that put a priority on the annual stability of production in the semiarid climate. The cropping systems based on multiple crops could work as a shock absorber and prevent unstable rainfall from directly creating fluctuations in total production and income. Additionally, the whole farming system, including stock raising and paid labour in different agro-ecological areas, contributes to the stabilisation of people's livelihoods. Takaya (1985) pointed out that complex farming systems, consisting of mixed cropping and animal husbandry, had developed characteristically in the central dry zone. This might be a consequence of the historical development of area-specific systems following a local strategy towards stabilisation of livelihoods.

Compared with other regions with uncertain rainfall in Southeast Asia, this feature of the central dry zone in Myanmar seems to be unique. For example, rain-fed rice farming in northeast Thailand was a system largely dependent on a good harvest year, which occurred once every few years (Miyagawa et al. 1985; Fukui 1988). The Thai farmers said that a harvest in a good crop year could be equivalent to harvests sufficient for 3 years of living expense (Miyagawa 2000). The farmers had adapted to the environmental conditions by developing a cropping system that maximised the production in a particularly good harvest year. There was no technological adaptation to secure minimum yields even in bad harvest years, although farmers utilised scattered paddy fields to reduce the risk of flood and drought damage (Fukui 1988).

In contrast, the cropping systems of Myanmar's central dry zone, discussed here, are a kind of area-specific technological adaption to secure a minimum of crop production. Technological change with the aim of maximising productivity (which tends to reduce stability) would not be readily accepted here. In the survey area, intensive pig rearing was introduced and encouraged by an international agency for development assistance. However, it had not spread as expected, because it might be more vulnerable to price fluctuations because of the higher cost for feed than that required for goat grazing. (In addition, e.g. vaccination services for livestock might not be adequate there.) As for crop production, a modern, high-yielding variety of cotton was introduced using chemical fertilisers, but it too did not flourish. Although farmers preferred high yields in cotton, a major crop in the current system, it might be difficult to accept a general conversion of the existing system into one depending on a single specific crop.[4]

Considering the historical context of agriculture and rural development in the central dry zone, it is important to ensure the stability of agricultural production and rural livelihoods. The buffer function of the existing local farming systems, which are based on indigenous knowledge, need not be altered suddenly or drastically

[4] However, some characteristics of the new cotton variety, such as its early maturing and short plant type, were highly valued as suitable for intercropping with pigeon peas by farmers, rather than its potential for high yields. This was similar to the previous expansion of a high-yielding variety of rice in dry season cropping due to its photoperiod insensitivity at the beginning stage of the Green Revolution in Southeast Asia (Fukui 1997).

when modern (mostly intensive) agricultural technology is introduced or encouraged. It might be difficult to draw up a future plan for agricultural development in rural villages that have no 'normal year' under current ecological conditions. It may be desirable to propose multiple options by means of development assistance activities, from which local people would take the initiative in selecting and adopting only those congruent with the existing systems.

Appropriate cropping systems should be closely related to people's local economic environment and should be flexible. If the role of livelihood systems is generally strengthened by increasing the importance of other income sources, i.e. animal husbandry and paid labour, then the component of crop production could more readily accommodate intensive technology. There were some cases in which the increase in off-farm income caused changes in cropping systems. Indeed, in northeast Thailand since the late 1980s, as migrant workers from the area have injected cash into the economy, people have invested more in rice farming, which used to be extensively pursued (Miyagawa 2005).

4 Mountain Agriculture in Shan State

4.1 Socioeconomic Changes in the Mountainous Region[5]

This section introduces a case study of agricultural change in a mountain village in southern Shan State, a part of the mountainous zone of Myanmar. The mountainous zone almost coincides with the area of the states of various ethnic minorities (the non-Burma Proper region) – Chin State, Kachin State, Kaya State, Kayin State and Shan State. Shan State is located at the west end of the mountainous region of Mainland Southeast Asia, which includes southern China, Northern Vietnam, Laos and Northern Thailand.

The socioeconomic environment in the mountainous region has changed dramatically over the last few decades (Kono and Rambo 2004; Daniels 2007, 2008; Leisz et al. 2009; Merts et al. 2009). Since the mid-1980s, as the governments of the region have liberalised their economic policies, the market economy has become more common. China's rapid economic growth and improved economic infrastructure, especially in terms of transportation, propelled this change after the 1990s. The international community's concern for the conservation of the natural environment may have led to the adoption of a land use policy that encourages forest conservation and restricts shifting cultivation. Additionally, governments have intervened and tried to reduce the cultivation of opium poppies in the so-called Golden Triangle. Such socioeconomic transformations along with population growth might have induced the recent agricultural change from traditional shifting cultivation, which

[5] This section is largely adapted from Matsuda (2010).

was a sustainable system with a long-term fallow period, to continuous and commercial upland farming or short-fallow shifting cultivation.

The mountainous zone of Myanmar has experienced the transformation described above, and the people (who are mostly ethnic minorities) have been forced to adapt their livelihoods to the current socioeconomic environment. Although the government of Myanmar has attempted to develop an alternative agricultural system in the mountainous zone instead of shifting cultivation and poppy cultivation, there is no clear blueprint for this, as there is in other countries in the region.

4.2 Developing Irrigated Upland Farming Rather Than Terraced Paddy Fields

In the southern part of Taunggyi TS, southern Shan State (Fig. 6.1), paddy fields are prevalent in the lowland small basins. On the hillsides, on the other hand, people used to sustain shifting cultivation systems. At the time of present writing (Jan. 2015), they no longer practise shifting cultivation and instead grow annual crops on the rain-fed and irrigated uplands continuously, as well as perennial crops in gardens (rice terraces were rare on the hillsides). Field surveys were conducted in this area to investigate what kind of farming systems had been developed as an alternative to shifting cultivation. The answer will provide useful lessons regarding agriculture and rural development in the hillside villages facing livelihood changes in Myanmar.

The survey villages were about 40-min drive from Taunggyi City, the capital of the state. They were located at an altitude of 1,300–1,500 m, and they had approximately 1,500 mm of rainfall in the rainy season from May to October. Interviews were conducted with households in the villages about their farming systems and the historical changes they had undergone. According to the interviews, the population had doubled during the last half century. The local people had adapted their farming systems since the 1950s to maintain their livelihoods, and consequently subsistence rice production on upland fields as well as shifting cultivation had disappeared.[6]

In the 1950s, subsistence rice production was the main source of livelihood in the survey area, and upland rice was grown using shifting cultivation systems. At that time, the people grew rice in the first year after slashing and burning, followed by groundnut or other crops in the second year. After the 2-year cropping, they would allow the field to lie fallow for 3 years before the next cultivation. The duration of this fallow period may suggest that the cultivation system had already changed from the traditional one to short-fallow shifting cultivation, which was not sustainable. From the 1950s, they could not maintain a long enough fallow period in the survey area, probably because of population pressure.

[6] People in the survey villages had no experience of opium poppy cultivation.

Fig. 6.4 Garlic field irrigated using spring water in the summer season near Taunggyi (February 2008). The water conservation forest around the irrigated upland field has been maintained as a common forest by the villagers. A farmer is seen watering at the centre of this photo

The interviews also revealed that, since the 1960s, shifting cultivation had disappeared in the survey area, which might be earlier than in other countries in the region. Land that had been used in shifting cultivation systems had begun to be cultivated continuously since this period, and crop production had become more commercial. Cultivation of *thanatphet* (*Cordia dichotoma* Forst.) in gardens and summer cropping of wheat had increased and taken the place of shifting cultivation of upland rice. *Thanatphet* is a perennial crop, the leaf of which is processed and used to wrap cigars. Both *thanatphet* and wheat were grown as commercial crops, which were traded in the domestic markets through Taunggyi City. Many households currently engage in *thanatphet* cultivation and processing in the hillside villages, and most had started this in the 1960s and 1970s.

The most remarkable change in the area's agriculture during the 2000s was the intensification of farming technology in irrigated upland fields (Fig. 6.4). Farmers have grown garlic in the dry season using irrigation from spring water. This irrigated upland farming was carried on in the past when farmers mainly practised shifting cultivation, and garlic was one of a few commercial crops at that time. As the market price of garlic increased markedly from around 2000, the input of chemical fertilisers for garlic production also increased sharply. The farmers also began to use pesticides and insecticide, because diseases and insect damage began to occur from this period. Although production costs have gone up with technological intensification and the market price of garlic plateaued in the late 2000s, garlic farmers can still earn an adequate profit. According to the interviews in the survey village, the economic condition of the households that owned irrigated uplands and rode the boom in garlic cultivation had improved considerably and was better than those of other households.

This case study suggests that upland farming using irrigation could be a system with the potential for high productivity and profitability in the mountainous zone. Additionally, because irrigated farming generally offers more crop options than rain-fed farming, more varied cropping patterns are attainable. This means that irrigated upland farming has the flexibility to adapt to an unpredictable agricultural commodities market and that therefore it can ensure income stability. The public sector and international NGOs had, in fact, introduced modern irrigation systems into hillside villages in the mountainous region of Mainland Southeast Asia as part of development projects for income generation and opium reduction, for example, encouraging vegetable production using sprinkler irrigation in Northern Thailand (Badenoch 2006). However, the problem may sometimes arise that the benefits are unequally shared by the villagers, because the available natural resources (land and water) for irrigation are often very limited on the hillsides. Furthermore, an overdependence on agrochemicals can easily develop. Issues of equality and sustainability should be considered carefully when irrigated upland farming is promoted for rural development.

The upland irrigation farming found in the survey area was a consequence of site-specific development, which meant that the local people had not chosen to develop terraced paddy fields. Under certain conducive ecological conditions, for example, on land where spring water was available or in a valley where enough surface water could be caught, terraced paddy fields had often been developed in earlier periods in the mountainous region of Mainland Southeast Asia. However, if people prefer to engage in commercial agriculture in a market economy (rather than producing subsistence crops), irrigated upland farming may be one of the suitable options for agricultural land use. From the viewpoint of farming practice, if waterlogging is unnecessary, then fields with gently sloping ridges (rather than terraces) could offer the advantage of maximising the area for cropping and managing irrigation water efficiently.[7]

4.3 Distance from Central Government as a Context for the Region's Unique Development

In understanding the background of the development of irrigated upland farming, one must remember that this area has kept a distance from the institutions and policies of the Myanmar government. The Pao people, an ethnic minority, are dominant in the survey villages and the surrounding area, and the area has been under the control of the Pa-O National Organization (PNO), a political group of the ethnic

[7] Albano and Takeda (2012) reported the development of sloped fields for the commercial farming of vegetables after the 1980s in Ifugao in the Philippines.

minority, for a long time. The PNO had opposed the central government as an insurgent organisation until 1991, when it concluded a ceasefire agreement. After the agreement, the area was authorised as 'Special Region No. 6' and a degree of autonomy was granted to the PNO by the central government. The administration system of the central government has not yet been universally implemented. For example, the *Kwin* map, an official map of land plots used as a basis for managing agricultural land use in the country, covered only a very limited area of lowland in the area. This meant that a land register was not completed and that the people were outside the central government framework of institutions and agricultural policy, for example, planned cropping of selected major crops (rice was made a priority by the government) and their procurement by the government agency (abolished in 2003). Kurita et al. (2004) also suggested that enforcement of the centrally planned economy had been weakened in the periphery of the country as compared with the Burma Proper region.

The development and sustainability of irrigated upland farming in this area might have been indirectly promoted by the 'inadequacy' or 'malfunctioning' of the planned economic policy there over a long period. Because farmers in this area had for a long time been independent of the strict implementation of the central government's rice-oriented policies (unlike the Burma Proper region), they could realise appropriate land use to suit the market economy using their own initiative, even on fields where rice terraces could potentially be built.

The central government has strengthened after the 1990s its governance in the non-Burma Proper region and, since the 2000s, has tried to develop terraced paddy fields in the mountainous zone (Matsuda 2009). Since the colonial era, as Leach (1970) pointed out, government leaders have been eager to make terraces for rice cultivation to develop agriculture in the mountainous zone. Rice farming on terraced fields is a system that can generally achieve high productivity and sustainability in mountainous environments; however, it may not be the only way if people prefer rural development through the enhancement of commercial agriculture in a market economy rather than subsistence rice farming. Irrigated upland farming might be a possible option, because it is the result of local people's efforts to develop commercial agriculture in hillside villages over a long period. Although, of course, these cannot be applied to every case, the findings from this case study might encourage the central government to reconsider its inflexible development policy regarding mountain agriculture, which has insisted on rice production. Similar implications are also mentioned in Chap. 5.

4.4 Forest Management Through People's Local Initiatives

The management of forest land has also not been controlled by the central government in the Special Region. Although there were areas registered officially as 'reserved forest' by the government in the survey villages, the villagers did not recognise them. Forest land in the villages was not open access, but forest management was entrusted to the villagers who had a degree of autonomy. The forest land was divided into private forest, common forest, monastery forest and so on. Meetings of village representatives formulated rules for the use of the common forest, and the villagers have respected them.

This local system of forest management has been relevant to the development of irrigated upland farming in the area. To sustain adequate amounts of spring water for irrigating agricultural fields, a large-scale forest that would assist in water conservation is crucial. However, as the farming systems changed from shifting cultivation to continuous upland farming in the 1960s, the amount of forest land decreased rapidly owing to reclamation, which was a cause of concern to the villagers. At that time, the role of a water conservation forest and its importance was confirmed at meetings of village representatives, and they formulated rules to conserve the forest more consciously. Although, at that time, the economic importance of farming on the irrigated uplands would not have been as high as it was in the 2000s, this farming option has been sustained because of appropriate forest management by local people.

Myanmar has plentiful forest resources and has produced and exported high-quality timbers, for example, teak. As the basis of forestry development in Myanmar, two well-known systems of forest management, the *taungya* system and the Myanmar Selection System, have been implemented in the national forests (Takeda 1990; Bryant 1996). These were established in the colonial era and have been representative of forest management by the government agency. The *taungya* system is a reforestation method in which teak planting and shifting cultivation are combined. *Taungya* means 'shifting cultivation in hill terrain' in Myanmar. The government agency allocated forest plots to shifting cultivators who were expected to manage tree plantations and were allowed to practise intercropping. This method has been introduced to other countries as a successful means of agroforestry in the tropics. The Myanmar Selection System is a selective tree harvesting method. It aims to realise sustainable timber production, mainly in natural forests, with planned logging on the basis of logging plots determined year by year and criteria of diameter at breast height by tree species at harvest. After modifications, this system has now been implemented in Myanmar.

These might be considered typical examples of forest management implemented through the strong commitment of the central government. However, in areas outside the administration of the central government, such as the Special Region located mostly in the mountainous zone, it was found that the local community could sustain forest resources using their customary practices, as described here. Such community-based forest management is generally able to adapt to the circumstances of a particular region more easily than a standardised approach by the central government. In fact, there have been many cases in which local people were able to manage natural resources sustainably by themselves, and there have also been trials of forest management based on people's local initiatives in other countries (Feeny et al. 1990; Inoue 2003, 2004). Myanmar needs to maintain its natural resources effectively by establishing an institutional framework comprising local communities. Although the government instituted a 'Self-Administered Zone/Division' to replace the 'Special Region' in 2011, and continues in its attempts to strengthen its governance in the non-Burma Proper region in order to ensure national unity, the application of decentralised administration should be considered, especially for natural resource management.

5 Concluding Remarks

This chapter has examined the real situation of agriculture and rural livelihoods in Myanmar, mainly drawing on information from field surveys carried out in the 2000s. Section 2 revealed the intensification of rice farming in Myanmar, for which there were no reliable macro-statistics. It warned about the dangers of an overly extensive intensification of rice farming technology in Myanmar in the near future. However, Myanmar still has an advantage in terms of ecological sustainability and economic autonomy compared with other Asian countries. Myanmar should avoid excessive intensification of farming technology, for example, by encouraging environmentally friendly food-production technologies. These can mitigate negative impacts on the ecosystem and reduce vulnerability to unstable international markets in fertiliser and fossil fuels. Section 3 pointed out that indigenous knowledge in cropping systems and multiple income sources had stabilised people's livelihoods and ensured survival in the harsh natural environment of the central dry zone. This section insisted on how important it is that the development approach pay attention to the overall picture of existing livelihood systems. Section 4 described the post-shifting-cultivation farming systems and forest management in the unique economic and political conditions of the mountainous zone. These systems were established through people's local initiatives without significant commitment from central government. This section stressed the potential of local initiatives in site-specific agricultural development and forest management.

The findings obtained from the in-depth fieldwork have suggested the potential of Myanmar's agriculture and alternative strategies for sustainable rural development, in which indigenous knowledge should be taken into consideration. These ideas have been born out of studies on rural people's practices and experiences. Whereas not completely consistent with the central government's policy, they should be given careful attention in the formulation of policy. It is to be hoped that the government will try to understand and evaluate properly local livelihood systems and will offer options based on these for sustainable agrarian development in Myanmar.

References

Albano, A., & Takeda, S. (2012). Ifugao vegetable terraces: History and sustainability of vegetable farming in Tinoc, Ifugao, Philippines. *Research for Tropical Agriculture, 5*(extra issue 1), 103–104.

Ando, K., Lay Lay Khaing, Khin Oo, Khin Lay Swe. (2010). Farmers' cropping systems as adapted to the dry climate in Yamethin Township, Burma central plain. *Research for Tropical Agriculture 3*(extra issue 2), 129–130. (in Japanese).

Ando, K., Lay Lay Khaing, Khin Lay Swe. (2011). Cropping systems in abnormal weather in the dry zone of Myanmar's central plain. *Research for Tropical Agriculture 4*(extra issue 1), 85–86. (in Japanese).

Badenoch, N. A. (2006). Social networks in natural resource governance in a multi-ethnic watershed of Northern Thailand. Unpublished PhD thesis, Kyoto University.

Brookfield, H., Parsons, H., & Brookfield, M. (Eds.). (2003). *Agrodiversity: Learning from farmers across the world*. Tokyo: United Nations University Press.
Bryant, R. L. (1996). *The political ecology of forestry in Burma 1824–1994*. Honolulu: University of Hawaii Press.
CSO (Central Statistical Organization). (2006). *Myanmar agricultural statistics*. Yangon: CSO, Ministry of National Planning and Economic Development, the Government of the Union of Myanmar.
Daniels, C. (Ed.). (2007). *Kokkyo naki sanchimin: Tai bunkaken no seitaishi* [Hill people without borders: Ecological history in the Tai culture area]. Tokyo: Korosha. (in Japanese)
Daniels, C. (Ed.). (2008). *Monsuun azia no seitaishi 2: Chiiki no seitaishi* [Ecological history in monsoon Asia 2: Ecological history of the region]. Tokyo: Koubundou. (in Japanese)
Egashira, K., & Aye Aye Than. (2006). Cropping characteristics in Myanmar with some case studies in Shan State and Mandalay Division. *Journal of the Faculty of Agriculture, Kyushu University, 51*(2), 373–382.
FAO (Food and Agriculture Organization). (2009). FAOSTAT. http://faostat.fao.org/.
Feeny, D., Berkes, F., McCay, B. J., & Acheson, J. M. (1990). The tragedy of the commons: Twenty-two years later. *Human Ecology, 18*(1), 1–19.
Fujita, K., Mieno, F., & Okamoto, I. (Eds.). (2009). *The economic transition in Myanmar after 1988: Market economy versus state control*. Singapore: NUS Press and Kyoto University Press.
Fukui, H. (1988). *Donden mura: tohoku tai no nogyoseitai* [Don Daeng Village: Agroecology of Northeast Thailand]. Tokyo: Sobunsha. (in Japanese)
Fukui, H. (1997). Rice farming. In Center for Southeast Asia, Kyoto University (Ed.), *Jiten tonan azia* [Encyclopedia of southeast Asia: Landscape, ecology, and natural environment]. Tokyo: Kobundo. (in Japanese)
Hossain, M., & Singh, V. P. (2000). Fertilizer use in Asian agriculture: Implications for sustaining food security and the environment. *Nutrient Cycling in Agroecosystems, 57*(2), 155–169.
Inoue, M. (2003). Participation of local people in forest policy formulation. In K. Ikeya (Ed.), *Chikyu kankyo mondai no jinruigaku: Shizen shigen heno human inpakuto* [Anthropology of global environmental issues: Human impact on natural Resources]. Kyoto: Sekaishisosha. (in Japanese)
Inoue, M. (2004). *Komonzu no shiso wo motomete: Karimantan no mori de kangaeru* [Toward the idea of commons: From a field survey in the forest of Kalimantan]. Tokyo: Iwanami Shoten. (in Japanese)
IRRI (International Rice Research Institute). (2009). IRRI world rice statistics. http://www.irri.org/
Ito, T. (1979). Traditional technology of irrigation and the development of rice farming in Burma. *Shiroku Kagoshima University, 11*, 39–80 (in Japanese).
Kaida, Y. (1997). Landscape of the deltas: Introduction. In Center for Southeast Asia, Kyoto University (Ed.), *Jiten tonan azia* [Encyclopedia of Southeast Asia: Landscape, ecology, and natural environment]. Tokyo: Kobundo. (in Japanese)
Ko, J., Hall, C. A. S., & Lemus, L. G. L. (1998). Resource use rate and efficiency as indicators of regional sustainability: An examination of five countries. *Environmental Monitoring and Assessment, 51*(1–2), 571–593.
Kono, Y. (2009). Rice farming in semi-arid regions. In S. Haruyama, M. Fujimaki & H. Noma (Eds.), *Sekai chiri kouza 3 tonan azia* [World geography: Southeast Asia]. Tokyo: Asakura Shoten. (in Japanese)
Kono, Y., & Rambo, T. A. (2004). Some key issues relating to sustainable agro-resources management in the mountainous region of mainland Southeast Asia. *Southeast Asian Studies, 41*(4), 550–565.
Kurita, K., Okamoto, I., Kurosaki, T., & Fujita, K. (2004). Rice production-oriented policy and the rural economy in Myanmar: Income analysis on household survey data in eight villages. *Azia keizai (Monthly Journal of the Institute of Developing Economics), 45*(8), 2–37 (in Japanese).
Leach, E. R. (1970). *Political systems of highland Burma*. London: Athlone Press.

Leisz, S. J., Kono, Y., Fox, J., Yanagisawa, M., & Rambo, T. A. (2009). Land use changes in the uplands of Southeast Asia: Proximate and distant causes. *Southeast Asian Studies, 47*(3), 237–243.

Ma, W., Li, J., Ma, L., Wang, F., Sisák, I., Cushman, G., & Zhang, F. (2009). Nitrogen flow and use efficiency in the production and utilization of wheat, rice, and maize in China. *Agricultural Systems, 99*(1), 53–63.

MacLeod, C. J., & Moller, H. (2006). Intensification and diversification of New Zealand agriculture since 1960: An evaluation of current indicators of land use change. *Agriculture, Ecosystems and Environment, 115*, 201–218.

Matsuda, M. (2008). Stability of crop production under uncertain rainfall in the central dry zone of Myanmar. *Research for Tropical Agriculture, 1*(extra issue 2), 67–68 (in Japanese).

Matsuda, M. (2009). Dynamics of rice production development in Myanmar: Growth center, technological changes, and driving forces. *Tropical Agriculture and Development, 53*(1), 14–27.

Matsuda, M. (2010). Ecohistory in southern Shan State, Myanmar: The development process of commercial farming and indigenous irrigation systems. *Noko no gijutsu to bunka (Farming Technology and Culture), 27*, 109–134 (in Japanese).

Matsuda, M. (2011). Intensification level of rice farming in Myanmar: Implication for its sustainable development. *Environment, Development and Sustainability, 13*(1), 51–64.

Matsuda, M. (2012). Interaction between human and nature in Myanmar: Findings from recent field surveys and implications for agriculture and rural development. In K. Odaka & F. Mieno (Eds.), *Myanma keizai no atarashii hikari* [The new light of Myanmar's economy]. Tokyo: Keisoshobo. (in Japanese)

Matsuda, M. (2013). Upland farming systems coping with uncertain rainfall in the central dry zone of Myanmar: How stable is indigenous multiple cropping under semi-arid conditions? *Human Ecology, 45*, 927–936.

Merts, O., Padoch, C., Fox, J., Cramb, R. A., Leisz, S. J., Lam, N. T., & Vien, T. D. (2009). Swidden change in Southeast Asia: Understanding causes and consequences. *Human Ecology, 37*, 259–264.

Miyagawa, S. (2000). Rhythm of rice farming in rain-fed lowlands. In K. Tanaka (Ed.), *Shizen to musubu: no ni miru tayousei* [Linkages between humans and nature: Diversity in agriculture]. Kyoto: Showado. (in Japanese)

Miyagawa, S. (2005). Farming systems in Asia: Rain-fed lowlands in Thailand. In S. Miyagawa (Ed.), *Saibai shisutemu gaku* [Farming systems research]. Tokyo: Asakura Shoten. (in Japanese)

Miyagawa, S., Kuroda, T., Matsufuji, H., & Hattori, T. (1985). Don Daeng village in north-east Thailand: Typology of rice cultivation. *Southeast Asian Studies, 23*(3), 235–251 (in Japanese with English summary).

Miyata, T. (2008). Thai fragrant rice and north-east Thailand. *Toyo Bunka (Oriental Culture), 88*, 87–121 (in Japanese).

Nawata, E. (2008). Degradation of farm land and agriculture in Southeast Asia. In Y. Yamasue (Ed.), *Sakumotsu seisan no mirai wo hiraku* [Agriculture in the 21st century]. Kyoto: Kyoto University Press. (in Japanese)

Peng, S., Buresh, R. J., Huang, J., Yang, J., Zou, Y., Zhong, X., Wang, G., & Zhang, F. (2006). Strategies for overcoming low agronomic nitrogen use efficiency in irrigated rice systems in China. *Field Crops Research, 96*(1), 37–47.

Pimentel, D., Hurd, L. E., Bellotti, A. C., Forster, M. J., Oka, I. N., Sholes, O. D., & Whitman, R. J. (1973). Food production and the energy crisis. *Science, 182*, 443–449.

Saito, T. (1974). History of traditional weir irrigation systems in Burma: A case study of Kyaukse region. *Azia keizai (Monthly Journal of the Institute of Developing Economics), 15*(9), 21–39 (in Japanese).

Saito, T. (1987). Introduction and extension of high-yielding varieties of rice in Burma: Present situation and problems. In T. Takigawa (Ed.), *Revolution of farming technology and rural community*. Tokyo: Institute of Developing Economies (in Japanese).

Scoones, I., Devereux, S., & Haddad, L. (2005). Introduction: New directions for African agriculture. *IDS Bulletin, 36*(2), 1–16.
Scott, J. G., & Hardiman, J. P. (1900). *Gazetteer of Upper Burma and the Shan States. Part I (vol. 2)*. Rangoon: The Superintendent Government Printing.
Shimada, S. (2007). *Rural transition in modern Africa: Challenge of area study to read change*. Tokyo: Kokon Shoin (in Japanese).
Takahashi, A. (2000). *Myanmar's village economy in transition: Peasants' lives under the market-oriented economy*. Tokyo: University Tokyo Press (in Japanese).
Takaya, Y. (1985). *Nature and land use in Southeast Asia*. Tokyo: Keiso Shobo (in Japanese).
Takeda, S. (1990). Reforestation by the taungya system in the 1920s in Burma. *Bulletin of the Kyoto University Forests, 62*, 108–121 (in Japanese with English summary).
Tan, H., Zhou, L., & Xie, R. (2007). Farmland nutrient cycle and nutrient balance in various cropping systems for subtropical regions. *Tropics, 16*(2), 115–121.
Tanaka, K., & Matsuda, M. (2010). Changes in rice farming in the China border region of Myanmar. *Noko no gijutsu to bunka (Farming Technology and Culture), 27*, 86–108 (in Japanese).
Thawnghmung, A. M. (2004). *Behind the teak curtain: Authoritarianism, agricultural policies and political legitimacy in Rural Burma/Myanmar*. London: Kegan Paul.
Tilman, D., Cassman, K. G., Matson, P. A., Naylor, R., & Polasky, S. (2002). Agricultural sustainability and intensive production practices. *Nature, 418*, 671–677.
Tong, C., Hall, C. A. S., & Wang, H. (2003). Land use change in rice, wheat and maize production in China (1961–1998). *Agriculture, Ecosystems and Environment, 95*(2–3), 523–536.
Yanagisawa, M. (2000). Agroecological evaluation of the intensified cropping systems in the Red River Delta, Vietnam. Unpublished PhD thesis, Kyoto University.

Chapter 7
Post-colonial Industrialisation in Myanmar

Toshihiro Kudo and Konosuke Odaka

1 Introduction: Initial Conditions

Since 1948, the year that it gained political independence, Myanmar (then known as Burma in English) has aimed, in one way or another, economic development through industrialisation. Nevertheless, these efforts remained largely unfulfilled up until the end of the twentieth century. The present chapter will trace and analyse Myanmar's attempts towards industrialisation in the second half of the twentieth century as well as in the beginning part of the current century, providing a basis for understanding the prospects for successful industrialisation in the near future, as well as some of the potential challenges.

During the colonial period, Burma was renowned as the world's largest and most successful rice exporter under the system of global free trading, earning significant amounts of foreign exchange (mainly in British pounds and sterling).[1] This period, in fact, constituted the first phase of Burmese socioeconomic modernisation. Rice cultivation, designed mainly for exportation, took place in the lower delta area, which had been newly transformed by the British from a wild, animal-dominated,

The authors wish to express their appreciation to U Kyithu Shein for his skilful assistance in acting as an interpreter as well as in collecting pertinent information, both of which were essential in preparing this chapter. Please note, however, that the authors alone are responsible for the views expressed herein.

[1] Rupee was the domestic currency used by colonial Burma.

T. Kudo (✉)
National Graduate Institute for Policy Studies (GRIPS), Tokyo 106-8677, Japan
e-mail: t-kudo@grips.ac.jp

K. Odaka
Institute of Economic Research, Hitotsubashi University, Tokyo, Japan

Hosei University, Tokyo, Japan
e-mail: k-odaka@ier.hit-u.ac.jp

K. Odaka (ed.), *The Myanmar Economy*, DOI 10.1007/978-4-431-55735-7_7

and thinly inhabited deep forest into a rich, highly productive base for rice cultivation.

The rapid metamorphosis of the lower delta area was conducted in conjunction with active deforestation and a massive inland labour transfer from upper Burma. It occurred as a result of the active capital participation of British, Indian, and Chinese merchants, who not only came to dominate the economic transactions of the rice trade but also came to own much of the agricultural land of the area. In fact by 1947, as much as 80 % of the cultivated land of the area was owned by nonresidential landlords, most of whom were foreigners (Thakin Tin 1948: 1–11). While the rice trade greatly encouraged the commercialisation of the society, including the development of overseas and inland transport networks, commercial banks, and telecommunication devices, there was little industrialisation occurring in the colony.

2 Industrialisation Under Military and Semi-military Regimes

Facing the under-industrialised state of the economy shortly after the restoration of peace from the Second World War, the new post-colonial political leaders, led by U Nu, called for urgent economic rehabilitation. Immediately following political independence, the economic principle of *laissez faire* was thrown out of the window and replaced by a planned economic principle. However, the 1950s was the political age of parliamentary democracy, and the nation's pace towards socialism was glacial throughout the decade. Failed to be implemented was not only the Two Year Economic Plan of 1948 but also its de facto successor, the Eight Year Economic Plan (*Pyitawthar* Plan) of 1952, which courageously aimed at the establishment of a welfare state (Myat Thein 2004: 16–21).[2] A major cause of these failures was a shortage of much-needed funds and foreign exchange reserves, both of which slowed the pace of the nationalisation of major economic activities and of the establishment of public corporations.

As a result of these setbacks, there was a reorientation of the basic principles of economic policy, namely, an attempt at economic liberalisation, which was mandated in the new Four Year Plan (1961–1964) issued in 1961. The plan stated that inasmuch as

> the pattern of ownership of means of production and instruments of economic activity has considerably changed in the direction of socialisation, accompanied by efforts, not too successful, to transfer foreign-owned enterprises into the hands of nationals,

it was then appropriate

> to make full utilisation of private initiative and energy in the development of the economy, particularly in the field of industry .... The strengthening of the private sector will therefore rank as one of the most important objectives … (Ministry of National Planning 1961: 21)

[2]The Eight Year Plan was formed on the basis of a report submitted by an American consultant, KTAM (1953).

The plan represented political gradualism in transforming the nation into a modern, democratic, socioeconomic system. This attempt may be considered the first wave of post-independence, economic liberalisation.

The liberalisation process was forcibly interrupted, however, as a *coup d'état* by the National Army took place in 1962. The government was replaced by the Revolutionary Council of Burma (RCB), with leadership placed in the hands of General Ne Win. In the meantime, the military must have viewed the above-mentioned gradualism as being far off the royal road to socialism, as the reorientation towards liberalisation was perhaps considered totally unjustified in light of the original political ideals held by the members of the *Thakin* Party,[3] which had aimed at the total and final resolution of capitalistic exploitation, which exposed the lower classes of people to the exploitation by other dominant social classes.

As soon as peace was restored following the *coup d'état*, the new military administration announced that it would definitely proceed towards the establishment of genuine socialist institutions, a balanced nation, under the slogan of 'the Burmese way to socialism'. Thus, the first wave of liberalisation attempts ended as a short-lived attempt. It was replaced by a policy of strict nationalisation of private economic activities, starting with that of commercial banks in 1963.[4] Economic policy measures during the Ne Win administration were by no means successful in attaining higher per capital national income, especially in the latter half of the regime. The ex-military officers, who had been appointed as managers of newly nationalised enterprises, lacked professional expertise in business management. Furthermore, the central government had few monetary resources to boost the rate of capital formation, as the regime's policies opposed the introduction of foreign funds. New financial resources needed for economic growth had to be squeezed out of nowhere else but agriculture, the development of which was not moving along smoothly. This was mainly because the farmers had little incentive to actively improve their production efficiency under the strictly regulated cultivation plans and product prices. Living conditions, not only of the farmers but also of the entire nation, deteriorated.

In 1974, there was a second wave of economic liberalisation and reorientation of the national policy. The main changes comprised some loosening of the tight economic controls of the central government on the decision-making capacity of the nationalised enterprises. Most importantly, the regime announced it would now accept foreign funding through official development assistance (ODA).[5] However,

---

[3] The *Thakin* Party was organised in 1932, with its membership including Aung San, Takin Mya, Kyaw Nyein, Ba Swe, and Nu.

[4] Note, however, the collectivisation of agriculture was not introduced, and small-sized, family farming persisted. In this sense, agricultural farming has never been nationalised.

[5] During this phase of economic liberalisation, a sizable amount of ODA came from Japan. Japan had a reason to feel indebted to Burma, which was the first nation expressing forgiveness for Japanese aggression during the Pacific War. Partly for this reason, however, Japanese war reparations to Burma ended up being less than other Asian recipients. These circumstances seemingly led Japan to supply substantial quantities of capital goods in the early 1970s to support the Burmese import-substituting industrialisation projects.

these changes were not successful enough for the country to emerge from its low growth trap, especially after the mid-1980s, when ODA seemed to have resulted only in the accumulation of foreign debt. According to the official government statistics, GDP in real terms (expressed in 1985/1986 producers' prices) shifted from 21,745 million kyat in 1961/1962 to 55,989 million kyat in 1985/1986 and down to 53,647 million kyat in 1987/1988 (Myat Thein 2004: 246). The inevitable conclusion can only be that the second attempt at economic liberalisation was also ill fated.

The recession that began in 1985 continued on through the second half of the 1980s, leading to mounting dissatisfaction of common citizens. Such was the state of the society when an incidental street fight in Yangon in 1988 resulted in the collapse of the Ne Win administration.[6] It provided something of a mandate for the military junta, called the State Law and Order Restoration Council (SLORC for short),[7] which controlled the nation after 1988, to scrap the idea of Burmese socialism and to lean towards by then globally embraced market-economy principles. The termination of the principle of planned economy, indeed, was quite an important accomplishment of the civil, democratic movement of 1988.

Institutional transformation towards economic liberalisation was initiated right away under the new military junta. The ban against international economic transactions was gradually lifted, as new regulations on foreign direct investment were enacted in 1988, followed by the State-owned Economic Enterprises Law in 1989, which removed in principle the policy of nationalisation of industries – with the exception of designated 12 sectors where the state monopoly would still continue.[8] The latter law, however, contained a special clause that spelt out conditions that made it possible to establish private companies even in the state-monopolised areas mentioned above, either independently or in partnership with a state-owned enterprise. As a result, private concerns, both domestic and foreign, participated in some of the designated 12 areas (Table 7.1). One notable exception to this was in natural gas excavation, where concessions of the right to engage in mining were given to some private companies, allowing foreign direct investment to take place through product sharing contracts.

In the nonnatural resource sectors of the economy, too, there was also a swing towards liberalisation; the exportation of the so-called light manufacturing production (textile goods, for instance) increased. As a result, several business groups were

---

The capital equipment thus provided, however, could not be fully utilised, because many of the needed raw materials (iron ingots, etc.) and intermediate inputs (machine parts, etc.) had to be imported, while the required foreign exchange was inadequate. Moreover, the products of the state-owned enterprises (e.g. heavy-duty trucks, etc.) found few customers except for the government itself (e.g. the military forces). Consequently, those capital goods provided to the factories were often underutilised.

[6] It should be noted here that the year of 1989 marked the collapse of the Berlin Wall, followed by the reunion of East and West Germany in 1990 and collapse of the Soviet Union in 1991.

[7] Renamed as State Peace and Development Council (SPDC) in November 1997.

[8] The 12 government-controlled sectors were (1) teak logging (cutting and selling thereof), (2) forest planting and logging, (3) supply of mineral oil and of natural gas, (4) supply and export of gems, (5) fishing cultivation in designated research seashores, (6) postal and communication services, (7) air and land transportation, (8) insurance, (9) radio and TV broadcasting,(10) mining and exportation of its products, (11) electricity generation, and (12) arms production.

Table 7.1 Gross value added (GDP), cross-classified by industry and ownership, 1986, 1998, and 2007 (%)

	Fiscal 1986			Fiscal 1998			Fiscal 2007		
Industry	State owned	Cooperative owned	Privately owned	State owned	Cooperative owned	Privately owned	State owned	Cooperative owned	Privately owned
Agriculture	0.1	–	93.4	0.2	1.9	97.9	0.4	2.4	97.2
Livestock raising and fishery	1.3	2.6	96.2	0.3	1.1	98.6	0.1	0.7	99.2
Forestry	38.0	4.4	57.6	46.2	0.6	53.2	50.0	0.3	49.7
Energy	–	–	–	99.9	0.1	0.0	76.3	9.3	14.4
Mining	89.8	2.2	8.0	10.8	1.0	88.2	2.9	0.2	96.9
Manufacturing	41.6	4.2	54.2	28.2	0.9	70.8	9.2	0.2	90.6
Electricity	100.0	0.0	0.0	99.9	0.1	0.0	79.5	0.3	20.2
Construction	88.3	1.0	10.8	45.8	0.2	54.0	60.1	0.0	39.9
Transportation	36.0	4.9	59.1	29.8	1.0	69.2	1.5	0.1	98.4
Communication	100.0	0.0	0.0	100.0	0.0	0.0	100.0	0.0	0.0
Finance	98.9	1.1	0.0	88.8	0.5	10.7	68.9	3.8	27.3
Social and government services	98.8	1.2	0.0	88.8	0.5	10.7	76.9	0.2	22.9
Rental and other services	9.0	3.2	87.8	3.9	2.9	93.3	0.4	0.4	99.1
Commerce	33.9	13.5	52.6	21.3	2.4	76.3	5.0	2.4	92.7
GDP	24.6	6.8	68.6	21.8	1.9	76.3	7.8	1.5	90.7

Sources: Ministry of National Planning and Economic Development, *Review of the financial, economic and social conditions*, various years, and Central Statistical Office (CSO), *Statistical yearbook*, various years

formed on the basis of accumulated profits during the construction rush, which had taken place through the Asian financial crisis of 1997. Some foreign funds also joined the new business groups.[9] Another notable case of progress in the privatisation of economic activities was banking, where, following the enactment of Financial Institutions of Myanmar Law in 1990, the share of private enterprises in the gross financial value added increased from zero in 1991 to 30 % in 1998, although it was down to 27 % in 2007, having only partially recovered from the after-effects of a bank run in February 2003 (cf. Table 7.1).[10]

The allegiance to market principles, however, proved again to be short-lived. The setback coincided with the time of the Asian financial crises that took place in 1997, hitting Thailand the most seriously. While little is affected by the flight of foreign capital, the Myanmar government nevertheless seemed to have lost interest, at least temporarily, in further economic liberalisation. Moreover, the United States imposed the sanctions on the Myanmar military government in the same year, due to its poor human rights records and delayed democratisation.

The nation could afford to bear the retardation of its liberalisation process, it seemed, because its foreign exchange earnings increased in around 2004/2005 due to the commencement of natural gas exports. This was accompanied by the increased cooperation of the Chinese government, which generously supplied desperately needed materials, technologies, and financial resources. The setbacks were finally reversed in 2008, when the apparent decision of General Than Shwe, chairman of the SPDC, to step down provided the opportunity for political changes including the adoption of a new Constitution. A general election was held in November 2010, bringing new congressmen and women into the political sphere. Following the election, a new government took power in March 2011, headed by President Thein Sein. With this, a fourth wave of economic liberalisation began, and the stage for modern economic growth (MEG), it seemed, had finally arrived.

3 Industrial Structure

It would be a useful exercise to observe shifts, if any, of overtime changes in industrial structure of the economy during the post-independence decades, by utilising official macro statistics.

The figures in Table 7.2 were obtained by dividing the total value of national gross domestic product (GDP) into three major components, namely, primary (agriculture, forestry, and fishery), secondary (manufacturing, transportation, communication, and construction), and tertiary (commerce and various services) sectors, and

[9] The trend towards privatisation in construction business was depressed for awhile after 1998, however, when gigantic public projects (such as the building of the new capitol, Naypyitaw) were initiated.

[10] Private commercial banks accounted for 66 % of the total bank deposits at the end of 2002.

Table 7.2 Components of GDP in real terms (%)

Year[a]	Agriculture, forestry & fishery	Non-agricultural goods[b]			Services & trade	GDP		Notes[c]
		Total	Of which accounted for by mfg. & processing	Of which accounted for by power		%	Kyat million	
1946	42.9	8.7	5.4	0.0	48.4	100.0	3,821	At 1961/1962 prices
1948	48.1	8.4	6.4	0.1	43.4	100.0	3,864	At 1961/1962 prices
1950	43.8	9.4	6.6	0.1	46.8	100.0	4,393	At 1961/1962 prices
1955	36.3	15.5	9.6	0.2	48.2	100.0	5,651	At 1961/1962 prices
1960	32.0	18.1	13.8	0.5	49.9	100.0	7,385	At 1961/1962 prices
1963	32.4	18.5	14.4	0.3	49.1	100.0	8,040	At 1961/1962 prices
1965			10.6			100.0	8,785	At 1969/1970 prices
1970			10.6			100.0	10,388	At 1969/1970 prices
1974	40.0	23.4	9.8		36.6	109.8	7,396	At 1969/1970 prices
1975			10.0			100.0	11,072	At 1969/1970 prices
1980	37.7	19.9	9.1	0.3	42.4	100.0	46,362	At 1985/1986 prices
1985	39.7	21.5	9.9	0.5	38.7	100.0	55,989	At 1985/1986 prices
1990	38.7	22.2	9.1	0.7	39.1	100.0	50,260	At 1985/1986 prices
1995	37.1	23.5	9.3	1.0	39.4	100.0	66,742	At 1985/1986 prices
2000	33.6	26.9	10.1	1.1	39.5	100.0	100,275	At 2000/2001 prices
2005	40.2	25.2	11.4	0.1	34.6	100.0	4,675,220	At 2000/2001 prices
2010	30.1	32.1	18.9	0.3	37.8	100.0	20,891,324	At 2005–2006 prices

Sources: The 1946–1963 original figures have been taken from Ministry of National Planning, The Revolutionary Government of the Union of Burma, *The national income of Burma 1964* (1965), which are somewhat different from those of Kyaw Myint, which were quoted by Myat Thein (2004: 42). The value figures for 1960, 1965, and 1975 are from Myat Thein (2004: 106), which were cited from *Report to the people*. The 1974 original data have been taken from Kudo (2001: 64), whose value for 'agriculture' is interpreted here as referring to the entire primary industry. The value figures for 1980 and 1985 are from CSO, *Statistical yearbook 2002*: 310, and those for 1990–2010 years from CSO, *Statistical yearbook 2011*, pp. 404–405

Notes: [a]'1980' means '1980–1981' and likewise for other years in this table

[b]Non-agricultural goods include mining, manufacturing and processing, electricity, and construction. Included in 'services and trade' are transportation and communication

[c]In expressing the figures in real terms, five different price bases have been employed. The dotted horizontal lines mark five separate 'phases' which have made use of respective different price bases. Because of this style of computation, comparisons of the figures between different five 'phases' should be made with care

observing the changes in their relative proportions in GDP (called 'GDP ratios' hereinafter) over time.[11]

Analysis of the data in Table 7.2 leads to the following three points based on the assumption, needless to say, that the government statistics can be generally considered accurate:

1. The relative share of GDP of service-related activities has continuously remained at the top, although its dominance has steadily eroded over time.
2. The secondary sector has continued to occupy the lowest status throughout the 1980s. Whereas the share indicates upward movements in manufacturing for the mid-1950s through to the beginning of the 1960s, this was mostly ascribable to sluggish growth during this period by the primary sector (namely, agriculture, forestry, and fishery), which was struggling to regain prewar production levels. Furthermore, it should be noted that the energy-generating sector always comprised only a very small portion in the secondary sector.
3. Thirdly, it is difficult not to notice and wonder at relatively high share of the tertiary sector throughout the period of observation. This seems to imply that service activities of various kinds provided the source of economic growth during the periods of socialism and the military junta. In view of this, one might argue that it would be important for the nation to sustain and strengthen its service-related industries including commercial businesses of exporting and sales promotion inside and outside the nation.

In the first half of the Ne Win's administration, when the country was placed under a planned economic policy orientation, the basic tone of its manufacturing policy was that of import substitution, whereby the establishment of relatively capital-intensive (the so-called) 'heavy' industries was promoted. However, the state-owned economic enterprises (SOEs), whose production efforts were placed under the strong control of the central government agency, were not quite successful in achieving their expected economic performance. The figures reported in Table 7.3 are consistent with the observation by Tin Maung Maung Than (2007: 25–32) that the economic performance of SOEs deteriorated during the socialist decades.

As already noted, a redirection of the basic policy stance was attempted after 1972, namely, the reintroduction of autonomous decision-making by the respective enterprises. At the same time, a highly inward-looking political philosophy was adopted, whereby international economic transactions were kept at a minimum. The timing of the policy shift coincided with the country's foreign exchange reserves

[11] The output figures reported by CSO (the Central Statistical Office) and those in the report of the state-owned sugar factories (cited by Kudo 2002: 107) roughly coincide. Judging from this fact, one may suspect that the manufacturing production statistics published by CSO consist mainly of those reported by the state enterprises and tend therefore to overreport the actual situation of the industry, as is often the case in planned economies.

On the other hand, it is likely that the CSO data are underreported in as much as, firstly, they do not take into account the production occurring in underground manufacturing, if any. Secondly, they probably do not cover the majority of privately owned manufacturing factories, especially those of medium- and small-scale ones, because no comprehensive statistical survey on manufacturing was ever undertaken in the twentieth century Myanmar. It is hoped that such over- and underreporting more or less cancels itself out.

Table 7.3 Performance of public corporations, 1946–1962 (overlapping 5-year averages) (kyat million)

Period	Operating profit and contribution to general government				Operating saving		Advances from general government and expenditure on capital formation						Operating surplus		
	(a) Operating profit	(b) Production subsidies	(c) Contribution to general government	(d) Direct taxes	(e) Operating saving (a+b−c−d)	(f) Cumulative operating saving (Σe)	(g) Advances from general government	(h) Expenditure on net capital formation	(i) Purchase of existing assets	(j) Advances repaid to general government	(k) Current advances to be repaid to general government (g−j)	(l) Cumulative advances to be repaid to general government* (Σ(g−j))	(m) Net surplus (e+g−h−i−j)	(n) Gross surplus 1 (f−l)	(o) Gross surplus 2 (f−l+c+d)
1946–1950	215	20	150	0	86	236	153	40	0	97	56	234	102	1	151
1948–1952	334	24	217	0	140	475	51	65	0	42	9	263	85	213	430
1951–1955	389	6	239	114	41	684	123	204	1	63	60	353	−104	331	685
1953–1957	283	2	171	171	−57	629	173	236	1	41	133	596	−162	34	376
1956–1960	229	1	99	120	11	612	189	187	0	42	147	1,070	−29	−458	−239
1958–1962	270	4	69	139	65	716	172	230	0	107	65	1,212	−99	−496	−287
Average	284	9	150	91	52	548	154	167	0	80	74	628	−42	−81	160

Source: Ministry of National Planning, The Revolutionary Government of the Union of Burma, *The national income of Burma 1964*, p. 20

Notes: Fiscal year 1946 means years 1946–1947 and likewise for other years. Averages are based on annual data and do not necessarily agree with the values computed from 5-year averages. Cumulative figures (*) have been computed by assuming no interest charge

hitting all-time lows, which may have constituted an economic rationale for the government to adopt its policy of international isolationism.

Additional computational data analysis has also been attempted with respect to the country's employment of the labour force, yielding results ('employment ratios'), which are similar looking as those reported in Table 7.2 above. However, the labour requirement to yield one kyat (measured in real terms) varies from one sector to another, due to differences in engineering characteristics as well as in the rates of utilisation of production equipment of the respective sectors. Dividing the GDP ratios by the corresponding employment ratios yields the relative value-added labour productivity of each macro sector as compared with national averages (all in real terms). They represent, in other words, indicators (indices) of the sector's labour productivity, as compared with national averages.[12] Specifically, by writing the gross value added in the sector i as Yi (in real terms) and the corresponding employment in the same sector as Li, the relative value-added labour productivity of the sector i may be computed as the ratio of GDP proportions of the sector i divided by the employment proportions of the same sector, or

$$Yi / \Sigma Yi \div Li / \Sigma Li = Yi / Li \div \Sigma Yi / \Sigma Li.$$

The results of this computation are shown in Fig. 7.1, which indicates that the value of relative labour productivity was highest in the tertiary sector (services) throughout the period of observation, and lowest in the primary sector (agriculture), which required large inputs of labour services to yield a unit quantity of production. Again the secondary sector was placed in between the other two with an overall downward trend between 1963 and 1998. The above statistical observations lead one to conclude that industrialisation efforts during the period did not quite yield the expected results.

As a possible reason why the relative labour productivity of the tertiary sector indicated far superior values when compared with those of the other two sectors, one might argue that in the early decades of modern economic growth (MEG), the relative economic importance of commercial transactions was regarded quite highly compared with that of goods production.[13] On the other hand, whereas the productive efficiency of the goods-producing sectors normally increases over time, that of

[12] The weighted average of relative value-added labour productivities, with respective employment figures being used as weights, is equal to unity.

[13] The historical statistics of Japan in the years of 1906–1927, the first phase of its industrialisation, also indicate similarly high values of relative value-added labour productivity of the tertiary sector, as the result of identical computations shows (see Fig. 7.2).

There are two possible explanations for this result, one technical and the other historical. Firstly, since income figures of the tertiary sector were scarce, wage earnings of the secondary industries were used in estimating the value-added figures of the tertiary sector during the decades. However, there is good reason to believe that wages in the secondary sector were actually much higher than those in the tertiary sector. Secondly, in the early years of industrialisation, secondary and tertiary production activities were often carried out as side-employment activities of the primary sector, notably farming. Consequently, the tertiary employment figures must have been significantly underweighted (Saito and Settsu 2010). It may be possible that similar sorts of explanations are applicable to the tertiary-sector statistics of Myanmar.

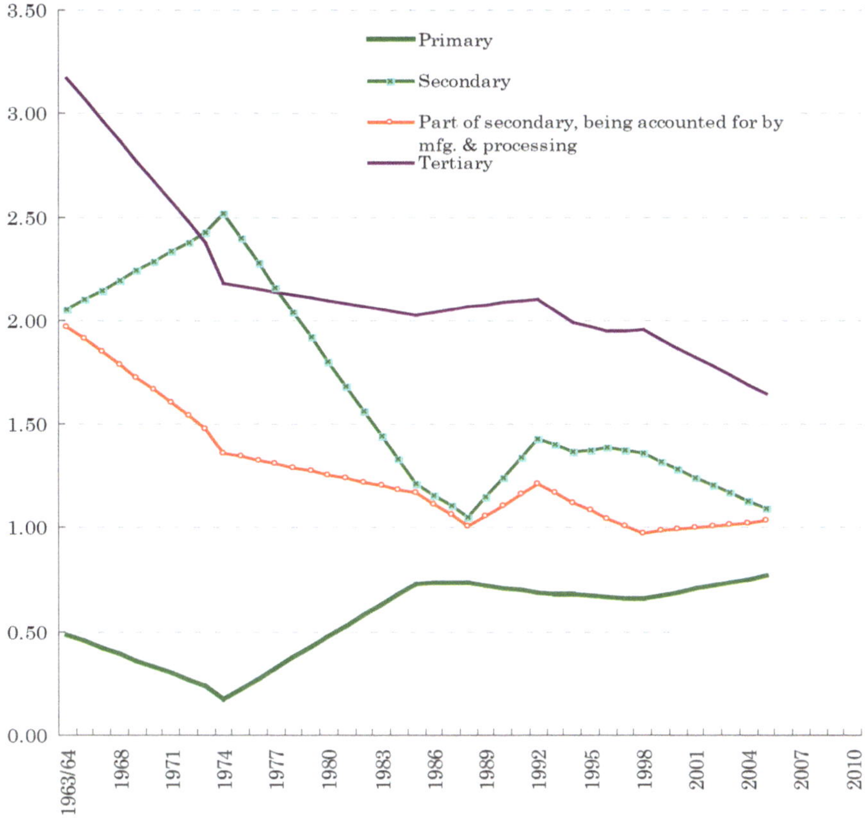

Fig. 7.1 Relative productivity $\left(Y_i / L_i \div \Sigma Y_i / \Sigma L_i\right)$ (*Sources*: GDP figures are the same as Table 7.2. *Sources* for employment figures have been taken from Kudo (2004: 138; 2010: 21) (originally from Ministry of National Planning and Economic Development, *Review of the financial, economic and social conditions*, and CSO, *Statistical yearbook*, various years). Notes: (1) '1967' means 1967–1968, and similarly for other years. The 1963 and 1964 GDP figures have been combined with 1964 and 1965 employment figures, respectively. Relative productivity figures for years 1966–1973, 1975–1984,1986–1987, 1989–1991, 1993, 1995, 1997, and 1999–2004 are interpolation. (2) The reason for the noticeable peak of the secondary industry observed on year 1974 is to be investigated. There may have been some inconsistencies in the classification of industries)

the service trades sector increases only slowly over time. Consequently, the productivity gaps between service-providing and goods-producing sectors should widen over time. Be that as it may be, inter-sector deviations in labour productivities are expected to decline over a long time period, provided that institutional barriers and/or technological constraints do not disrupt the redistribution (or social mobility) of the labour force from one sector to another.

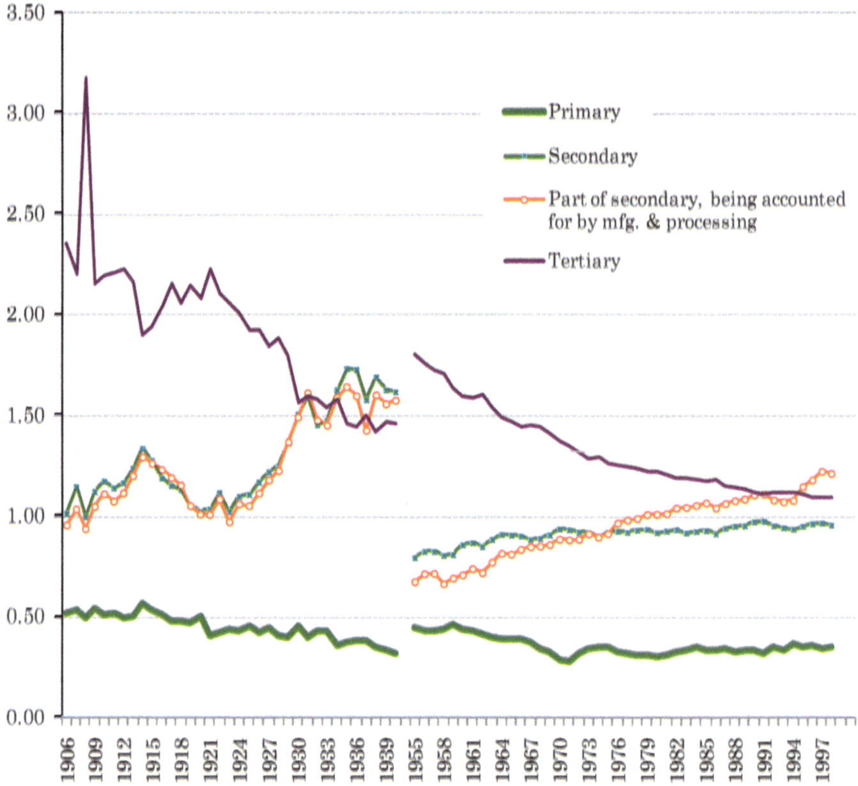

Fig. 7.2 Relative productivity $\left(Y_i / L_i \div \Sigma Y_i / \Sigma L_i\right)$, Japan: 1906–1940 and 1955–1998 (*Sources*: Pre-war GDP statistics from Ohkawa and Shinohara (1979: 278–80) supplemented by Ohkawa et al. (1974: 229–30), and pre-war employment from Umemura (1988: 204–15). Postwar GDP from long-run time series data on national income accounting reported by Economic and Social Research Institute, Cabinet Office, Government of Japan, and labour survey data reported by Statistical Survey Department, Statistics Bureau, Ministry of Internal Affairs and Communications, Government of Japan, available in *Japan statistical yearbook*, various years. Notes: Prewar GDP values are at 1934–1936, and postwar GDP at 1990 constant prices. The secondary sector includes electricity, gas and water-supply industries whereas the tertiary-sector transportation and communication industries in order to make them par with the Myanmar definitions (in Fig. 7.1))

4 State-Owned Economic Enterprises (SOEs)

In view of the pre-1988 history of industrialisation, it is highly important to observe the production records of state-owned manufacturing factories.

Immediately following the independence, the government characteristically attempted, as pointed out previously, to nationalise most of its manufacturing industries. The major objective of having state-owned (nationalised) economic enterprises (SOEs) during the period of 1948–1962 was to regain and retain managerial control of manufacturing production, on the basis of the Special Company Act of

1950, into the hands of Myanmar nationals. However, their economic performance was not commendable, especially at the very beginning. This was due in part to the lack of experience on the part of their employees and also due to frequent interference by politicians, although the situation gradually improved as time went on (Tin Win 2001: 77). Government statistics show that SOEs had not only positive profits (284 million kyats) during the period of 1946–1962, after having paid their due contributions (150 million kyats) and corporate taxes (91 million kyats) to the government, but also retained savings (52 million kyats) (see Table 7.3). The managerial supervision obviously honoured the commercial rules of the game.

Nonetheless, it so happened that huge borrowings from the government were needed by the SOEs in order for them to continue their efforts to improve their production capabilities by way of active capital formation. If one assumes that SOEs had annually paid back their debts thus incurred by using the accumulated savings, the overall budget for SOEs would have crossed the zero line by the second half of the 1950s.

During the subsequent Ne Win administration (1962–1988), attempts were made to do away with capitalist orientation of the companies, and the government policy was based on the principle of state control of manufacturing industries. Major private manufacturing corporations then operating were nationalised, and, at the same time, several new manufacturing SOEs were established. Some of the heavy industry corporations imported foreign-born technologies from the end of the 1960s to the early period of the 1970s.

For instance, Myanmar Automobile and Diesel Industries (MADI), a motor vehicle and diesel engine producer under the supervision of the then Ministry of Industry II, transplanted the basic production technology for producing heavy-duty trucks from Hino Motors and that of medium-sized utility vehicles from Mazda Motors (both Japanese corporations), retaining their production with no substantial model changes after the 1960s, the time at which the technologies were imported.

However, the production output of MADI remained very small. During the years between 1985 and 2006, for instance, the total number of vehicles it produced stayed roughly around the level of 1,000 units per year, with a maximum of 2,200 units (in 1985) and a minimum of 665 units (in 2006).[14] The size of the domestic market was mostly limited to public use, and the needed parts and components had to be produced internally.[15] The enterprise enjoyed highly favourable working conditions compared with the private sector, in terms, for example, of the presence of specially trained engineers and of relatively high stipends, which could hardly be justified in light of its low productive efficiency. On the other hand, an ever increasing number of second-hand, foreign-made vehicles were brought in (mostly from Japan) for the use of nonofficial transportation purposes, coming to form a separate

[14] Production figures are based on CSO, *Statistical yearbook*, in various years.

[15] The heavy industry-related products did not command the extensive national demand. Moreover, they required, if at all possible, the importation not only of raw materials but also of domestically unavailable machine parts and components. The direction of import-substituting policy that favoured the early choice of heavily capital-intensive industrialisation in the context of relatively labour-abundant Asian context placed an additional burden on macroeconomic management.

market completely independent of that for the vehicles made by the SOE, due mainly to quality and specification differences of the products.

By 2013, MADI, having been renamed as the No.(11) Heavy Industries Enterprise, was no longer in actual operation, but still maintained a large number of machine tools, which had been freshly imported in the 1960s and the 1970s, in relatively good working condition. Impressively huge, heavy-duty trucks were one of its products, a model of which was still in display in the middle of a large factory in the spring of 2013 (Fig. 7.3).

Among other establishments that relied on foreign-born technologies was a state-owned tyre maker, originally established with the technology imported from Czechoslovakia. The company, too, still kept its original production equipment that had been installed at the starting point of its operations (with some later additions from Taiwan, for instance) and remained in operating condition, though not in a fully fledged manner, in the summer of 2013. The top management of the company was very interested then in engaging in a joint venture with a foreign partner (as per policy direction of the central government).

By the same token, a large number of state-owned, operating manufacturing enterprises (SOEs) were established with foreign-made production equipment, which was largely maintained from that time with little replacement or renovation, partly because of the shortage of foreign exchange needed for the importation of essential materials and intermediary products, but more basically because of the philosophy that industrial production should proceed with no reliance on foreign nations: an idea unique to the socialist days when external trade was not favoured by the government.

In general, it seems probable that many of the production facilities at SOEs, especially those with capital-intensive technologies, must have been often underuti-

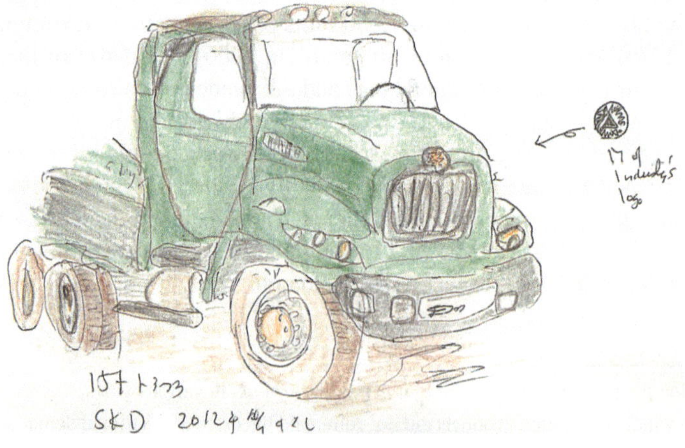

Fig. 7.3 A Chinese model heavy-duty truck, assembled at a state-owned enterprise

lised. This would have partly been because of the low demand for their products but also because of the shortage of imported, industrial raw materials and intermediate goods. They must also have suffered from serious internal difficulties, such as managerial problems arising from the lack of autonomous decision-making powers on the side of factory managers and insufficient work motivation on the part of the production workers. The majority of necessary machine parts and components were probably internally manufactured, as there existed few networks of parts and components suppliers – certainly the case for MADI. In other words, the benefit of the division of labour was not to (or could not) be made use of. For these and other reasons, the total revenues of the SOEs must have often failed to cover the total costs, both in the short run and longer run, leading to deficits that had to be met by extra subsidies from the government. In fact, deficits arising from state-owned enterprises formed an important reason for the fiscal deficit of the central government, especially in the 1980s (cf. Table 3.3 in Chap. 3 of the present volume).

Table 7.4 indicates that the absolute number of operating, state-owned enterprises continued to increase from 1980 to 2005, despite the fundamental principle of privatisation, which had been laid out in 1996 by then SLORC First Secretary Khin Nyunt. It should be noted, however, that the composition of industrial activities in state-controlled manufacturing provides a clear contrast to that of the private industries (as will be reported in Table 7.6 below), with the so-called 'heavy' industries such as chemical and metal fabrication dominated by SOEs, rather than those of the 'light' industries such as textiles and food processing.

The attempt to develop a domestic capital-intensive manufacturing industry (e.g. machine building industry) over 'light', labour-intensive industry at an early stage

Table 7.4 Public enterprises (SOEs) as classified by their industrial activities (%)

					Total	
Year	'Light' industries	Material suppliers	'Heavy' industries	Misc.	%	Actual number
1980	36.0	38.4	19.8	5.8	100.0	550
1985	37.7	36.2	19.1	7.0	100.0	597
1990	38.8	33.8	18.5	8.9	100.0	616
1995	35.0	29.8	18.2	16.9	100.0	708
2000	31.1	26.8	17.5	24.6	100.0	848
2005	30.6	21.3	33.9	14.1	100.0	947
2010	33.8	27.1	24.7	14.4	100.0	639

Source: 1980 and 1985 data from CSO, *Statistical yearbook 2002*, p. 153, and 1990–2010 data from CSO, *Statistical year book 2011*, p. 231; '1980' means '1980–1981' and likewise for other years in this table

Notes: (1) 'Light' industries include food and beverages, clothing, personal goods, household goods, and printing and publishing; material suppliers include construction materials, industrial materials, and mineral and petroleum products; and heavy industries include agricultural equipment, machinery and equipment, transport vehicles, and workshops and dockyards

(2) The figures probably cover only the state factories employing ten or more employees. According to the data cited by Myat Thein (2004: 258) as being provisional, the total number of SOEs in 1997/1998 was 1,600, of which small factories with less than ten employee counted 811

of industrialisation entailed the adoption of a vertical (i.e. top down, internal) division of tasks inside the factory (i.e., for the production of needed parts and components within the same factory) rather than that of horizontal division of tasks (i.e. using outside, specialised manufacturers). Production might therefore be likened to a small, isolated island in the middle of the ocean. Whereas being nicely equipped with modern production facilities, they could neither make both sides of their income statements meet nor transform themselves into self-sustaining, efficient private economic organisations right away. Many kinds of operational preparations are called for prior to their successful initiation as private concerns.

The speed and the manner with which the idea of socialism was thrown out of the window so quickly and replaced by the emphasis of liberalised market transactions were surprising given its long history. Nonetheless, transforming the institutional setup as well as the human and social behaviour to suit the changing ideological shift is no easy business and is, therefore, a time-consuming process. The most essential task of privatisation lies not in a simple change in asset ownership but in a substantial shift in institutional setups and human behaviour in relation to the managerial decision-making and in such a way that will conform to the rules and the customs of the market economy. Whereas the number of state-owned and operated enterprises began to decline in around the year 2005, it had not been made necessarily clear by then as to what extent privatisation had affected macroeconomic performance.

After the takeover of the socialist regime by the military rule of SLORC, the size of the deficit accruing to the activities of SOEs remained quite high, as shown in Table 7.5, indicating that it was not easy to resolve. The eventual goal of privatising many of the SOEs already constituted an important problem for the government to attain. There were calls for immediate, swift action, especially in light of the fundamental economic policy vision of the regime (SLORC) to introduce liberalisation of market transactions as early as possible.

Of special importance at the start of privatisation of SOEs is generally the acquisition of international competitive capacity in the secondary sector. As a matter of immediate, short- and medium-term strategy of development, serious consideration is necessary as to the choice of industry and of technologies, which should be placed in the context of appropriate time sequence (cf. Sen 1960/1968). The basic principle in making judgements on this issue would be the presence of the country's economic comparative advantage in terms of economic resources. This includes the basic materials for production as well as the factors of production and of the outlets for the products both in and out of the country. In the longer run, of utmost importance would be nurturing the growth potential of domestic industrial human resources, namely, production workers, middle management personnel, engineers, and entrepreneurs. Needless to say, the domestic presence of global corporations by way of foreign direct investment (FDI) will contribute to this cause.

Closely connected with the above-mentioned task is a serious and careful consideration needs to be given to the adoption of a protective industrial policy, commonly called the protection of infant industries. There are two important criteria in order to justify its adoption:

Table 7.5 Deficit of SOEs, 1989–1998

Year	SOEs' total income	SOEs' total expenditure	SOEs' total loss	Total deficit of the government budget	Ratio of SOEs' total loss to the government deficit (%)
1989/1990	26,812.8	29,977.5	−3,164.7	8,019.0	39.5
1990/1991	32,041.7	36,361.4	−4,319.7	11,204.0	38.6
1991/1992	36,399.0	40,110.8	−3,711.8	12,311.0	30.2
1992/1993	43,548.0	48,624.0	−5,076.0	12,096.0	42.0
1993/1994	52,044.5	60,723.8	−8,679.3	15,518.0	55.9
1994/1995	73,444.1	87,373.3	−13,929.2	29,648.0	47.0
1995/1996	88,182.9	101,853.6	−13,670.7	38,819.5	35.2
1996/1997	118,788.2	145,343.6	−26,555.4	54,469.8	48.8
1997/1998	213,192.2	257,663.4	−44,471.2	65,308.6	68.1

Source: Figures up to 1997–1998 taken from Tin Win (2001: 81)
Note: Original data are from the Ministry of National Planning and Economic Development, *Review of the financial, economic and social conditions*, various years

1. There is clear hope for the industry to attain international competitiveness of its products within the prescribed period (say, 5 years).
2. There is high likelihood that future gains from the presence of the industry concerned will exceed the cost of protecting the same.

International negotiations should start soon in this regard as to the extent of the coverage of the policy as well as the total time span during which the protection will be permitted. The governments of the neighbouring countries which happen to be in a more favourable condition in terms of economic competitiveness (for instance, Japan and Korea) should step forward in assisting such negotiations, on the basis of the argument that international cooperation in this manner with Myanmar is not only highly desirable but justified.

When considering the adoption of such industrial policies for domestic industries to guard against excessive competition from outside of the country, due attention is required, in the opinion of the present writers, for linking the protected industries with the growing industrial network of other domestic industries (i.e. in such a way that the domestic input-output (IO) table, if available, would become more and more densely filled with figures). During the process of economic catching up, economic dualism may arise: for instance, wide earnings differentials between super-modern industry equipped with advanced foreign technologies and indigenous industries still retaining traditional methods of production. However, this should not be a cause for concern as long as such signs of disequilibria are expected to become less serious over time.

5 Industrialisation in the Private Sector

The entry into the market by private enterprises became all the more evident in 2007. In fact, among the mining, manufacturing, transportation, and commercial industries, private ownership was the most important form of business organisation by then (see Table 7.1). In addition, the presence of private enterprises increased in the energy industry including electricity generation, which was permitted only to public concerns until 1998. Among the 13 areas listed in Table 7.1, the privatising trend was pervasive by 2007, with exceptions in only two notable fields: telecommunications, which was still dominated by the state, and construction, where a rush in public projects took place, including the opening of the new capitol in 2006.

In November 1990, the military junta enacted the Private Industry Law, which required all private enterprises with production facilities of three or more horsepower or ten or more employees to be registered at the Ministry of Industry I.[16] Table 7.6 below reports the result of the registration. According to the records, the largest share of manufacturing at the time was found in food processing, followed by construction materials, clothing and apparel, and mining and petroleum products. In addition, firms engaging in machine production and/or maintenance boasted a significant position in terms of their overall numbers.

The geographical allocation of manufacturing activities is also of high importance. As Table 7.7 indicates, the most highly industrialised area of the nation in the

Table 7.6 The number of private manufacturing factories, by type of products

Type of products	Fiscal 2004	Fiscal 2005	Fiscal 2006	Fiscal 2007
Food and drinks	26,896	27,337	27,601	28,137
Clothing and apparel	2,282	2,053	1,962	1,895
Construction materials	3,551	3,494	3,320	3,240
Living necessaries	1,071	1,023	1,015	1,054
Homeware	265	309	318	305
Printing and publishing	329	410	356	291
Industrial raw materials	1,183	991	1,011	947
Mining and petroleum products	1,832	1,668	1,786	1,665
Agricultural machinery	61	63	74	79
Machines and their components	338	280	254	300
Transportation machinery	138	141	156	238
Electric machinery	59	63	58	60
Others	3,430	5,492	5,510	5,552
Total	41,435	43,324	43,421	43,763

Source: Directorate of Industrial Supervision and Inspection (DISI), as cited by Kudo (2012: 275)

[16] Smaller firms were also requested to register with the government by the Promotion of Cottage Industries Law enacted in 1991, but registration was not compulsory.

Table 7.7 Geographical distribution of private manufacturing factories, 1997, 2000, and 2009

Regions and states	Annual distribution of private factories by region/state (%)			Estimated population in 2000 ('000)
	1997	2000	2009	
Mandalay	21.6	21.2	17.7	6,574
Yangon	15.5	14.2	14.0	5,560
Bago	12.3	13.2	10.9	5,099
Sagaing	11.6	11.0	10.8	5,488
Ayeyarwady	11.0	13.0	14.9	6,779
Magway	6.3	5.6	5.1	4,548
Shan	5.5	6.8	8.6	4,851
Mon	5.5	4.9	5.6	2,502
Tanintharyi	3.2	2.6	2.0	1,356
Rakhine	2.4	2.5	4.9	2,744
Kachin	2.4	2.2	2.3	1,272
Chin	1.1	1.1	1.2	480
Kayin	1.0	1.2	1.2	1,489
Kayah	0.7	0.7	0.8	266
Total number	35,348	36,152	43,787	49,008

Source: Directorate of Industrial Supervision and Inspection (DISI) as cited by Kudo (2004: 149; 2012: 282)

late 1990s was Mandalay, followed by Yangon, Bago, Sagaing, and Ayeyarwady with these five accounting for 70 % of the total number of manufacturing factories in 1997. Moreover, it is noteworthy that three out of the five districts, Mandalay, Yangon, and Bago, showed relatively dense shares of production facilities, as the number of factories per 10,000 residents exceeded 8. Whereas food and beverage processing accounted for the majority of manufacturing activities in all districts, a higher degree of product diversity was observed in Mandalay and Yangon, with substantial numbers of textile, metal fabricating, and machine processing factories. In particular, industrial zones in Mandalay, established in the early 1990s, have been noted for their machine fabricating workshops with spare parts production and a reputation for a high maintenance record of over 70 % of motor vehicles in the country. The Mandalay area has been also noted for its historical concentration of textile production, accounting for more than 60 % of the total number of textile-related enterprises.[17] Yangon, on the other hand, has been characterised by its overwhelmingly wide variety of manufacturing outputs, ranging from chemical, non-metallic, paper, plastics, and publishing to rubber products.[18]

[17] These two characteristics may be in a large part ascribable to the establishment in these cities of industrial zones, initiated by the central government.

[18] An analysis has been presented, showing that a two-polar growth strategy, with proper consideration given to border development, is likely to yield better performed (i.e. more efficient) and more balanced (i.e. more equitable) economic development than a single-polar or multipolar growth strategies (Kudo and Kumagai 2012). The "two polar" here refers specifically to Mandalay and Yangon.

In March 2000, the overwhelming majority of manufacturing was defined to be 'small' based on either the number of employees (less than ten) or the total horsepower of production facilities (less than three); in fact, 83 % of the total number of factories fell into this category. Nonetheless, it should also be noted that their share went down to 37 % when one looks at the distribution of total output value (Table 7.8).

We close this section with a brief note on entrepreneurial characteristics.

There were several classes of entrepreneurs who were already on the stage of active economic development of the nation, by the end of the twentieth century:

1. Ex-entrepreneurs from the pre-independence days, either of
   (1a) Myanmarese origin or
   (1b) Chinese or Indian origin
2. Self made entrepreneurs, either
   (2a) Those who had accumulated sufficient capital domestically or
   (2b) Those who had migrated abroad and returned with sufficient savings
3. Organisation-dependent entrepreneurs, who happened to be in a position to take advantage of vested interests, either related to
   (3a) The military or
   (3b) The government bureaucracy
4. Ceasefire-dependent entrepreneurs, who were once in a position to take advantage of
   (4a) Trading in the special zones that had been granted to a minority region in return for a cease-fire agreement or
   (4b) Financial transactions (for instance, by underground border traders) for fund-raising purposes to support anti-regime, political actions

A typical example of Chinese-origin entrepreneurs may be found in the case of the Pun brothers, who were born in Yangon but were forced to leave the country during the days of Burmese socialism (1965), when expatriates were under strong negative pressure from the government. Having received educational training in the USA and elsewhere, they started a new business with Hong Kong as its base. When signs of Burmese economic liberalisation appeared in the late 1980s, however, they chose to return to their home country and, in 1991, established a Myanmarese corporation.[19] Since then, they have actively engaged in commercial transactions of a high variety, ranging from finance, real estate, foreign trading, and manufacturing to even infrastructure building.

During the decades of the military junta, the government, in the hope of acquiring as much foreign exchange reserves as possible, encouraged Myanmar's citizens to work outside the country, by partially liberalising the passport control rules. As a

[19] Surge Pun Association (SPA).

Table 7.8 Private factories, cross-classified by size and geographical location (as of March 2000)

Regions and states	Number of factories				Number of employees				Output value ('000 kyats)				Horse power				Paid-up capital ('000 kyats)			
	Big	Medium	Small	Total	Big	Medium	Small	Total	Big	Medium	Small	Total	Big	Medium	Small	Total	Big	Medium	Small	Total
Mandalay	378	1,191	6,086	7,655	5,360	8,063	25,317	38,740	1,232	1,155	2,069	4,456	27,363	32,728	73,153	133,244	839	846	1,400	3,085
Yangon	678	996	3,443	5,117	26,028	9,282	14,081	49,391	5,912	1,733	2,307	9,952	67,867	26,224	38,630	132,721	2,685	946	654	4,285
Bago	228	447	4,109	4,784	6,014	4,733	14,422	25,169	1,947	1,055	1,397	4,399	22,485	15,935	53,663	92,083	536	250	575	1,361
Sagaing	115	327	3,544	3,986	1,657	2,736	11,730	16,123	1,051	883	992	2,926	6,973	11,088	40,826	58,887	105	173	496	774
Ayeyarwady	161	599	3,930	4,690	3,524	6,642	16,230	26,396	1,208	2,767	2,319	6,294	11,740	23,181	53,565	88,486	114	162	472	748
Magway	18	142	1,860	2,020	178	1,065	5,914	7,157	41	239	670	950	1,061	4,512	17,781	23,354	18	60	167	245
Shan (south)	10	58	1,732	1,800	222	355	5,126	5,703	59	64	364	487	814	1,926	22,187	24,927	34	26	173	233
Mon	58	120	1,600	1,778	485	902	4,848	6,235	131	397	1,136	1,664	7,026	4,370	18,416	29,812	26	25	112	163
Tanintharyi	70	56	797	923	1,300	290	2,056	3,646	66	53	64	183	13,809	1,982	6,758	22,549	98	14	48	160
Rakhine	58	76	775	909	984	521	2,356	3,861	526	139	163	828	8,518	3,042	9,850	21,410	126	16	54	196
Kachin	9	71	701	781	99	470	2,215	2,784	11	171	147	329	642	2,688	10,711	14,041	5	17	49	71
Shan (north)	15	43	589	647	333	263	1,743	2,339	89	47	159	295	1,221	1,428	7,545	10,194	51	19	59	129
Chin	–	2	399	401	–	12	1,097	1,109	–	–	52	52	–	57	3,391	3,448	–	–	16	16
Kayin	20	16	387	423	249	96	1,188	1,533	78	42	159	279	2,460	548	5,100	8,108	17	2	23	42
Kayah	3	26	209	238	39	130	798	967	4	37	75	116	332	876	2,493	3,701	2	6	29	37
Total	1,821	4,170	30,161	36,152	46,472	35,560	109,121	191,153	12,355	8,782	12,073	33,210	172,311	130,585	364,069	666,965	4,656	2,562	4,327	11,545

Source: Directorate of Industrial Supervision and Inspection (DISI), as cited by Kudo (2004: 152)

result of this policy change, quite a few citizens went abroad, especially to Thailand, and sent home the earnings from their labour. In addition, a number of illegal migrant workers crossed the national border (especially into Thailand and Malaysia) in order to gain opportunities to work (cf. Yamada 2012). The outmigration of the Myanmar citizens, one might say, has served as a valuable means for the country to earn foreign exchange in lieu of inflows of foreign capital.

Some entrepreneurs have taken the risk of associating themselves closely with select politicians in the hope of gaining opportunities to grow rich in their businesses. For instance, certain groups of industrialists were associated with the trading of arms and weapons. Such business transactions may have helped monopolistic power grow in the market. Those who came to enjoy such a powerful position may have had great advantage over ordinary private merchants in obtaining special government permissions and getting involved in certain public projects, for instance. A typical example of such a case is found among those who were associated with big holding companies,[20] which had great advantages over ordinary private concerns in getting government concessions and/or necessary official registration. Another example of politically related business opportunities may be found in the areas where peace treaties were successfully established between an ethnic minority group and the National Army. The government might have given former combatants, previously engaged in illegal trading, funds to start an entirely new business instead. Some such groups, occasionally joined by foreign funds and experts, grew to develop new types of highly profitable businesses.[21]

6 Small-Scale Machine Shops Observed in Mandalay and Yangon

In order to gain an overview of the current economic condition of small- and medium-scale enterprises (SMEs) in contemporary Myanmar, field visits were made by one of the authors in Mandalay and Yangon. Thirty-two relatively small- to medium-scale companies were visited in spring 2013. Most of these were producers of machine-related or metal-fabricated products, and they operated, at the time of the visits, in the government-established industrial estates either in Mandalay or in Yangon. On each visit, after having visited and observed the production site, a quick question-and-answer (Q&A) session was conducted.

The companies were chosen by a staff member in the local government and with advice from the leader of a local business association. The following observations, therefore, are not based on any claims of representativeness. Nevertheless, information obtained through these factory visits may have some value, as such information

[20] For example, Union of Myanmar Economic Holdings Limited (UMEHL) or Myanmar Economic Corporation (MEC).

[21] For instance, growing buckwheat (*soba* in Japanese), from which distilled hard liquor (*shōchū* in Japanese) is made for sale in both domestic and overseas markets.

tends to be highly limited. Moreover, the results of the survey may help transmit the atmosphere of manufacturing workshops in the early twenty-first century urban districts in Myanmar.

The factory visits focused on machinery production and related metal fabrication as, in the authors' view, machine building capacity is intimately related to a well-performing industrialisation process, not only because it helps create better machinery performance and is essential in maintaining existing productive equipment in good working condition but it also can stimulate fresh, new ways of thinking, possibly encouraging future innovation. A list of the companies visited is provided in Appendix Table 7.10.

The information obtained from the visit reveals that many of the factories visited had purchased productive equipment originally made in China or in Taiwan (often in second-hand markets). The equipment was utilised with necessary adjustments according to the companies' own engineering know-how, in ways that suited the demands of domestic customers. During the period of economic sanctions, the importation of machinery was almost impossible with the exception of imports from China. However, the local managers had no need to worry about competing against foreign-made machines (except perhaps from China), as the domestic manufacturers were automatically protected from international competition.

Among the machinery products from the surveyed SMEs were:

1. Agricultural (farming) tools.
2. Chinese-designed agricultural tractors, whose body plates and simple machine parts were domestically produced, whereas sophisticated machine products including engines were imported (see Fig. 7.4); the tractors were used for farming as well as transporting agricultural produce.
3. Copper-made statues of Buddha.
4. Large-sized hand-made cooking pans, manufactured using traditional methods of iron moulding.
5. Large-sized oil tanks for transporting liquid petroleum, made of steel plates that had been manufactured from scrapped iron and steel, and comprising an essential part of heavy-duty fuel trucks.
6. Plastic-made construction materials.
7. Propellers for small-sized boats, manufactured using processes such as moulding, welding, machine-tooling, etc.
8. Rolling bars for drying natural rubber sheets.
9. Whipping machines for commercial cooking purposes, made with the use of second-hand differential gears taken out of discarded automobiles.

Also visited were manufacturers of:

10. Agricultural fertiliser, which utilises used water purchased cheaply from nearby local brewers.
11. Traditional cookies and cakes produced in large quantities, using automated processes and assembly lines.

Fig. 7.4 A farming truck (*trargyi*) of Chinese design

12. A printing company that had installed a second-hand large colour printer made in Japan.
13. Traditional apparel (*longyi* in Burmese) for men and women.

Information gathered on the basis of interviews at these local factories is summarised in Table 7.9.

It should be noted that quite a few of the companies were established on or after the collapse of socialist regime and that enterprises established prior to this were limited to the manufacturing of traditional products such as textile goods and foods, made with indigenous technologies. The size of their operations in terms of the number of employees was limited, though not minimal (average 48, median 15), with most of them family-run businesses that were not legally incorporated. Some of them were members of local industrial associations. Daily wages seemed to be around 5,000 kyats, paid either on a daily basis (time rate) or linked with output (piece rate).

In some limited cases, state-owned land had been leased for a length of 30 years at a low rent, reflecting active administrative attempts to encourage the industrialisation of local communities. By the same token, one corporation was established in response, in part, to the government's call to promote the use of domestically made machinery in farming or in mining operations.[22] It is possible, however, that the information on this industrial promotion policy by the public authorities was not circulated widely enough, benefitting only those who happened to be in a position

[22] One enterprise had exchanged an agreement with a state-owned, mining company to supply some of its machine products.

Table 7.9 Characteristics of enterprises surveyed, 2013

Production process	Frequency
Lathe processing	11
Moulding	7
Forging	5
Machine assembly	4
Biscuit and cake making	3
Metal stamping	2
Plastic engineering	2
Chemical	1
Cloth making	1
Food making	1
Metal painting	1
Printing	1
Rubber product making	1
Welding	1
Average year of inauguration (number of responses)	1989(27)
Median year of inauguration (number of responses)	1990(27)
Average number of employees (number of responses)	61(27)
Median number of employees (number of responses)	15(27)
Number of enterprises surveyed	32

Source: Chap. 7 Appendix Table
Note: The number of production processes exceeds the number of enterprises surveyed because some enterprises are engaged in plural number of processes

to be connected with it. If this was indeed the case, it would be highly desirable for the government to establish an information channel so that public policies of this nature could be more widely disseminated.

An impression shared by the visitors to these factories was that quite a few of these SMEs were either established or widely activated after 1988, when the central government came to encourage the establishment of private enterprises. One such public initiative was the creation of industrial estates, where quite a few private factories assembled and utilised the common production facilities, such as energy sources, the supply of industrial water, and so on.

On the other hand, only a very limited number of companies made use of organised financial services (bank loans). In most cases, funding to initiate the establishment of manufacturing activities came from the owners' private sources, through monetary savings and/or borrowings from relatives and/or close friends. Obviously, institution building as well as related innovations in financial services will be highly beneficial in realising potential business initiatives for industrialisation. The provision of such financial services requires, however, not only advance information regarding profitability but also judicious judgement as to the risks involved in industrial ventures, both of which would become available only through time-consuming training and experience, with possible government assistance.

Of the enterprises that were visited, machine or machine-related products were primarily being supplied for use mainly in farming cultivation, food processing, mining operations, railroad maintenance, textile manufacturing, wood fabrication, and construction. The need for the products must have existed amply in the local area where these enterprises operated. In the beginning period of their operations, however, they probably engaged in made-to-order production (cf. Fig. 7.5).

Fig. 7.5 Machining at small enterprises in Mandalay (Spring 2013)

It was clear that a stable energy supply constituted one of the major tasks for most of these companies. Some companies were prepared for sudden blackouts, during the day and night, and had equipped themselves with self-generation facilities to provide electricity. However, this would squeeze into their profits, since buying electricity from the public corporation is much less expensive.

Quite a few raw materials utilised by these companies were imported. This is consistent with statistical observation that macro importation increases with the progress of industrialisation. Some of the machine-producing firms were making machines that served the same purposes with the same kind of products imported from China, which were much cheaper but not so durable as their own products. For this reason, the management staff of these firms had confidence that their products were sufficiently competitive with the comparable merchandise imported from China.

Technical ingenuity was displayed on various occasions. For instance, 7 out of 21 machine factories were making use of machine tools that had been self-designed and manufactured by their own hands, indicating the presence of some engineering maturity. However, this must have been possible partly because competition with the foreign-made machines had been precluded. There were also such cases as (1) where a producer of food mixers for commercial use made use of differential gears taken out of discarded old passenger vehicles, switching a vertical movement into a horizontal one, and (2) where the owner of a profitable printing company/publisher was making good use of a large, advanced Japanese-made colour printer for commercial use, which had been purchased second hand through a web-based auction service. All these incidents suggest that these management people were highly motivated to equip themselves with a competitive edge in such a way that would eventually enable them to be the suppliers of highly competitive products in the worldwide market.

The results of the visit and survey also indicated that there were some instances where producers' associations had been organised in order to share technological and other industry-related information.

7 Concluding Remarks: Has Industrialisation Come of Age?

A noticeable characteristic of the effects of industrialisation during the days of the SLORC/SPDC regimes, when market liberalisation was initiated, was to import both raw materials and production equipment and to start engaging in the production of exportable goods, especially textile products. An example of such a joint venture was a company that manufactured ready-made suits for gentlemen to be exported to Japan, using production equipment brought in from China and textile materials imported from Japan. In this company, the machinery was managed by Chinese engineers, while the labour-intensive production process was undertaken by male and female production workers, who worked in a production line according to the physical sequence of the manufacturing process. The line began with the cutting off of the woollen-cum-nylon textile materials according to the prescribed design and ended with the combining and manufacturing of the final product by using specialised equipment (especially sewing machines). Because of frequent blackouts of electricity, however, the company found it necessary to equip itself with its own electricity generator. This made the operation more costly, and the manager complained about the situation. At the time of the interview conducted in summer 2009, transporting the final product to the export gate was causing problems; moreover, the government bureaucracy required cumbersome paper work in order to obtain a permission for exportation without paying extra export duties – another source of headache even in these days.

Other, newly established enterprises of different kinds have also appeared in the early 2000s. There was, for example, a manufacturer of bottled health drinks using home-grown herbs. After processing at their factory, the manufacturers sold their products not only domestically but also exported them. Another noticeable example was a privately owned producer of tyres for vehicles that made use of rubber sheets. These were refined and semimanufactured from domestically grown natural rubber, then purchased and collected from local wholesalers of the same, and brought into the tyre factory in Yangon. The company was originally established by borrowing its production technology from a state-owned tyre maker, after sending a group of production engineers for on-site training.[23]

One of the authors also encountered a producer of natural rubber soles and shopping bags for ladies. It operated two factories as of the summer 2013, employing about 300 workers in total, including 155 former state-owned factory workers, who formed a production line in the order of machine processing. At a strong request of the government, the company had consented to the acquisition of a state-owned factory, which was converted together with its land and the employees into a second production site. The company also managed its own rubber plantation, as it wanted to use natural rubber of high quality, so that it could guarantee with confidence the quality of its final products.

From brief descriptions such as those provided above, it can be seen that, since the day of the government's decision to adopt the principles of market liberalisation, a definite, autonomous motion towards domestic industrialisation has clearly set in, with the support and participation of the international community including FDI. The production activities were mobilised, and manufacturing transactions have become more intensive since the 2000s, especially for natural resource-related goods such as food and drinks, textile goods, rubber products, and wooden products. Accompanying this, the demand for machinery manufacturing as well as parts and components has increased, providing the increasing number of relatively small-scale factories with opportunities to be engaged in production and sales. Naturally, these activities have resulted in increases in employment in the selected sectors of the economy. It is likely that these newly arising productive activities are closely

---

[23] The authors are indebted to Professor Shigeru Matsushima for this information.

related to, and been prompted by, reactivated consumer demand, but less directly with the demand from the activities of state-owned enterprises (SOEs).

Based on visits to select SMEs in Mandalay and Yangon, it could be concluded that Myanmar appears to have large numbers of well-motivated production personnel. At the same time, business leadership appears to be provided by entrepreneurs who are highly enterprising to make best use of newly arisen business opportunities. However, it seems natural at the same time that the country's workforce in the private sector has long missed opportunities to receive (or to be aware of) sufficient training necessary to acquire working knowledge and expertise in production control, quality control, and human resource management. This results in a lack and/or shortage of standardised of merchandise, know-how related to large-scale production, environmental safety, the sanitation and hygiene of the production environment, and so on. The network of (sometimes multilayered) market transactions of intermediate merchandise (e.g. machine parts and components) and/or business services remained underdeveloped in the 2010s. Most of the industrial enterprises were not yet quite prepared by then to meet and survive the challenges of international competition.

There is a lot of room for improvements in the current industrialisation outlook, ranging from physical to social areas, and the need to introduce new policy measures is also substantial. As time will be required to introduce and accomplish the measures for improvement, some protection of private sectors may be called for (and justified), provided that there are sufficient prospects, for the industries concerned, to attain a sufficient competitive edge within a prescribed timespan.

Urgent improvement is required in the monetary and fiscal areas, especially in expansion and deepening of the financial sector. If, for instance, the nation is equipped with the resources necessary to make judgements and decisions regarding appropriate economic policy directions (in addition to the drawing of a road map or a vision for social and economic progress), the nation will benefit from well-planned future industrialisation. There is an urgent need for the presence and training of specialised, experienced personnel in funds management, who are equipped with the knowledge and experience not only of financial resources but also of practical needs at production sites.

While Myanmar economy has been, and still is, a natural resource-rich, primary-sector-dominated one, it is possible to find some signs of movement towards industrialisation throughout all stages of its premodern and modern historical records. True, they were not always highly successful ones, and the proportion of economic contribution by the secondary sector in the total value added (GDP) has stayed at a low level throughout the second half of the twentieth century. In the 2010s, however, a bright new prospect for the nation's industrialisation has emerged. It is strongly hoped that the nation will trod a unique, new path of industrialisation, by mobilising the outcomes not only of modern science and technologies but also of human intelligence based in part on updated contributions from human and social studies.

Appendix

Table 7.10 Small- and medium-scale enterprises surveyed in 2013

	Date of visit	Enterprise ID	Merchandise produced and/or nature of production activities	Year of inauguration	Number of employees	Notable characteristics
1.	29iv2013	MRI	Forging and stamping for the manufacturing of steel balls for use at cement factories, machine elements for use by stone crushers and mining machines, dynamos and water pumps for home use, hammer harvesters (with Chinese-made engines), etc.	2005	142	(1) Inaugurated with support from the government
						(2) Domestic iron scraps collected and used as raw material
						(3) In line with the government policy to encourage domestic production of machine parts for domestic use
						(4) Chinese-made production equipment
						(5) Electricity supply limited to 5 h/day (demand for electricity beyond the capacity of self-generating electric power station)
						(6) Small-scale production of a variety of machine goods; quality much better, but far more costly, than comparable Chinese merchandise
						(7) Dividend paid only once since inauguration
2.	29iv2013	GBM	Stamping, painting and assembly of farming machines and equipment	1991; specialised in manufacturing in 1998	300 at Mandalay plant (1,000> in total)	(1) Engaged mostly in foreign trading up to 1997; moved to the industrial estate when felt sure of the sufficient demand for the products (1998)
						(2) Estate land and factory buildings self-financed
						(3) Needed fund for equipment etc. financed from a commercial bank at subsidised interest rate of 7.9 % as against city rate of 13 % per annum, as per policy direction of the Ministry of Agriculture and Irrigation
						(4) Chinese-design products transformed to suit domestic needs
						(5) Output volume adjusted to forecast demand; 40 % of the product price payable at the time of purchase, followed by 30 % each at every 6 months period
						(6) Began BOT (build, operate, and transfer) operation in 2012, whereby the government finances land, building and production equipment
						(7) 66 % of employees have continued working for longer than a decade

3.	29iv2013	U O. H. & Sons	Casting and lathe processing for the manufacturing of pumps for mines and residential houses	1970s	20 lathe operators and 10 casting facility operators	(1) Electricity supplied 5 h/day, balance being self-generated
						(2) Owns 2 factories (one for each of the two operations)
						(3) At the time of inauguration borrowed 4 million kyats from a commercial bank
						(4) Has used accumulated profits since 2007 on the purchase of production equipment
						(5) Minimum wage at 80,000 kyats/m
						(6) Has 20 regular customer companies and 7 associate companies
						(7) Approximately 100 enterprises compete in lathe processing business
4.	29iv2013	U A. T. O.	Lathe processing for the manufacturing of fuel pumps and oil containers for tank lorries	1998	15	(1) Raw materials imported from Thailand via trading companies in Yangon
						(2) At the time of inauguration borrowed 1 million kyats from chairman of the enterprise then employed
						(3) No debt outstanding with commercial banks; willing to apply for bank loans at interest rate of 8 % or less per year
						(4) Training requirement: 1 year for welding, 3 years for lathe operation
						(5) Uncle serving as technical advisor
						(6) There is industrial association
5.	29iv2013	O	Lathe processing for die making	Family business	?	(1) Products (dies) are used for making biscuits, video, soap, mosquito coils, etc.
						(2) Not engaged in subcontracting
						(3) Customer information in Yangon provided by father in law
						(4) Orders also come from producers' association
						(5) 100 bankruptcies in the same business in the past 1 year

(continued)

Table 7.10 (continued)

	Date of visit	Enterprise ID	Merchandise produced and/or nature of production activities	Year of inauguration	Number of employees	Notable characteristics
6.	29iv2013	U T. A.	(1) Assembling pumps for drawing up underground water and (2) making automobile parts to be assembled on second-hand 1 t trucks	1993	30 for pumps and 10 for vehicle parts	(1) Pump parts are internally manufactured from imported materials and assembled together
						(2) Manufactured truck parts include body heads, rear bodies, rear frames, etc., which are assembled on about 10 commercial vehicles per month
						(3) Assembly is all done manually
						(4) Many female workers are employed in the pump factory
7.	29iv2013	ZNP	Stone crushers (lathe processing)	Specialised since 1986	12 (grew from 5 to 6 when inaugurated)	(1) Loans extended once by a commercial bank and twice by producers' association (at the annual interest rates of 17 %, 36 %, and 24 %, respectively) when moved into the industrial estate (1988)
						(2) Products more expensive but more durable than comparable Chinese merchandise
						(3) Lathes made inside the industrial estate being used
8.	30iv2013	HB	Oil tanks used for tank lorries, farming and other machines (welding)	1990	20 (grew from 3 when inaugurated)	(1) Established immediately after graduation from technical school
						(2) Own-made lathes being used
						(3) Starting fund financed by parents (could not borrow at the interest rate higher than 8 %/year)
						(4) Installation of products to be done at customer's site
9.	30iv2013	K	Pumps for industrial use, stone crushers, etc. (lathe processing)	1990	15 (grew from 5 when inaugurated)	(1) Inaugurated by a parent
						(2) 30 million kyats financed by a bank at the time of inauguration: the maximum amount of loan possible, constituting 20 % of needed fund
						(3) Machine parts are largely designed and manufactured internally
						(4) Payment for merchandise normally 2 months after the delivery

10.	30iv2013	KN and Sons	Iron parts used for electric or railroad poles (casting)	1993	8 (down from 16 when inaugurated)	(1) Deliver high-quality (and more expensive) products mainly to government-related projects
						(2) No record of bank loans; however, necessary to borrow a rolling fund of about 5 million kyats at 36 % annual interest rate, as government's payment takes long after delivery; micro-finance is possible but application procedure too cumbersome
						(3) Employment decreased due to ex-employees' establishment of a new business
						(4) Materials imported mainly from Thailand
11.	30iv2013	ST	Food processing machines for the production of oil from peanuts, rape-blossoms, sun flowers, soy beans, etc. (forging and lathe processing)	1993	15 (down from 20 when inaugurated)	(1) Working capital made available by the Myanmar Economic Bank
						(2) Customers all over the country; 50 % payable at the time of ordering, the balance at the time of delivery
						(3) Machine products are designed internally
						(4) Materials imported from Thailand, India, and China
						(5) All the machine parts manufactured internally
						(6) Electricity blackout is a serious problem (even though self-generator being installed)
						(7) Plural number of manufacturers of the same products
12.	30iv2013	U P. G. and Sons	Drills (forging and lathe processing)	1985	Forging 4, lathe processing 7 (grew from 5 when inaugurated)	(1) Spot ordering
						(2) Own-made lathes being used
						(3) Drill making since 2000; quite a few competitors
						(4) Own products more expensive but of higher quality than comparable merchandise from China
						(5) Daily wage of skilled workers at 5,000 kyats/day, paid daily
13.	30iv2013	SSM	Iron-made baskets for use at alluvium gold mining	1982	6	(1) Materials provided by the government
						(2) Payments due 2 months after delivery, during which time need to survive with own funds
						(3) Earning at 10 % of sales value, approximately
						(4) Workers' wage 4,000 kyats/day inclusive of lunch

(continued)

Table 7.10 (continued)

	Date of visit	Enterprise ID	Merchandise produced and/or nature of production activities	Year of inauguration	Number of employees	Notable characteristics
14.	30iv2013	U Y. Z.	External frames of pumps for alluvium gold mining and for sugarcane squeezing (casting)	2006	?	(1) Succeeded the business initiated by father
						(2) Short-hour supply of electricity is a problem
						(3) 3–4 local customers; demand coming down
						(2) Workers' wage 5,000–6,000 kyats/day inclusive of lunch
15.	30iv2013	U T. A.	Water drawing machines for farming	?	?	(1) Working capital borrowed occasionally from relatives
						(2) Product more durable than those imported from China
						(3) Second son is a college graduate (majored in biology)
16.	30iv2013	TW Manufacturing	Jade processors, brick making machines, water drawing machines, and solar panels (casting and lathe processing)	1982	15	(1) Sufficient inauguration funds provided by family; no borrowings needed
						(2) Most materials imported (e.g. bearings from Japan, shafts from Thailand, etc.)
						(3) Lathes in part made internally (e.g. assembly)
						(4) Some workers graduates of engineering schools
						(5) Manager's stipend at 300 thousand kyats/m
17.	30iv2013	Ab M	Food mixers, etc. (lathe processing)	1981	6 (grew from 3 when inaugurated)	(1) Own-made lathes being used
						(2) Making use of second-hand differential gears taken out of discarded automobiles; full of ideas, wishing to be a manufacturer of motor vehicle parts and components
						(3) 15 out of 20 Mandalay biscuit makers are regular customers
						(4) Two sons went to colleges in order to go into professional fields (e.g. medicine) instead of succeeding this business

18.	30iv2013	U M. M.	Lathe assembly	1993	10 (grew from 3 when inaugurated)	(1) Casting operation done by two, small outside firms
						(2) Borrowed 2.5 million kyats in 1993 at annual interest of 17 %: too expensive to repeat
						(3) 1–3 products/m; expensive but of high quality
						(4) Gross profit at 15 % of sales
						(5) Net savings reinvested except for temple donation on New Year's Day at 900 thousand kyats
19.	30iv2013	YAP	Big cooking pans of 700–9,000 kyats each (aluminium casting)	1980	?	(1) Never borrowed from commercial banks
						(2) Labour intensive work in traditional style; sand moulding
						(3) Merchandise cheaper than comparable merchandise imported from China
						(4) There are 15 competitors
						(5) Skill formation by way of on-the-job training (OJT)
20.	30iv2013	TPW	Buddha statute made of copper (casting)	?	7–8	(1) Moved to this industrial estate in 2001; formerly produced inside a village
						(2) Copper and tin cheaply supplied by the government up to 2005
						(3) Takes 1–3 months to complete a product
21.	30iv2013	B biscuits	Biscuits	?	145 (grew from 35 when inaugurated)	(1) Production equipment from China; on-site instructions provided by Chinese engineers
						(2) Powdered milk imported from New Zealand; wheat flour domestically made
						(3) Female workers 110, male workers 35
						(4) Belt conveyor being partly utilised
						(5) A new plant being constructed in anticipation of the start of merchandise exportation
						(6) No borrowings from commercial banks ever attempted
						(7) Female employees retire when a new-born baby arrives, but may resume working when their children are old enough
						(8) Workers wage at 2,800–3,000 kyats/d, based on group piece rate

(continued)

Table 7.10 (continued)

	Date of visit	Enterprise ID	Merchandise produced and/or nature of production activities	Year of inauguration	Number of employees	Notable characteristics
22.	30iv2013	TPM	Agricultural fertilisers (chemical processing)	2001	Approximately 50	(1) Used to be engaged in delivering vehicles; business started at the request of local authorities to deal properly with disposed industrial water
						(2) Land offered by the central government free of charge
						(3) Making use of waste water from the nearby brewery
						(4) Inauguration expenses paid out of own funds; a bank loan used for the first time in 2012
						(5) Ingredients adjusted skilfully in conforming to the climatic characteristics of the region
						(6) 100,000 t output annually
						(7) Many competitors in the market
23.	30iv2013	HT	Colour printing	1988	70	(1) Imported papers are often used (previously recycled papers were also used)
						(2) Purchased land cheaply in 1992
						(3) Large, second-hand, automatic, Japanese-made colour printer is being used commercially, having been purchased at auction
						(4) Machine trouble, if any, is due mostly to the lowering of electric ampere
24.	1v2013	MMK	Traditional style cakes and biscuits	1974	Approximately 150 (grew from 40 when inaugurated)	(1) Commercial bank loan of 40 million kyats extended when moved into the industrial estate in 2002 at the annual interest rate of 17 %
						(2) Food materials purchased with the exception of edible oil and butter, both of which are internally made
						(3) Products, quality being of high importance, need to be consumed soon after purchase; sold only in Mandalay
						(4) Employees are made aware of the need to take utmost care on the quality of products

25.	1v2013	U G	*Longyi* (traditional skirts for men and women)	1963	35	(1) Cotton of long fibre imported from India (in part from China), silk from China; dyes purchased in the market
						(2) Domestic cotton unsuitable due to its fibre length
						(3) Machine weaving subcontracted to women in farm households; product quality carefully checked when delivered
						(4) Piece rate wages
26.	1v2013	TN	Dried mangoes	1993	10	(1) Used to run a coffee farm; purchased the land 20 years ago
						(2) Mango selection machine designed by a domestic engineer, and manufactured in Yangon
27.	3v2013	SK	Iron-made parts and components for railroad, farm machines, etc. (forging and lathe processing)	1982	10	(1) Engaged in machine repairing since around 1982; moved in to the industrial estate in 1990; a business turning point in 1992 when received order from the Ministry of Railroad
						(2) Also receives orders from public corporations engaged in electric power supply and the promotion of farm mechanisation
						(2) Raw materials purchased in domestic market
						(3) Own-made forging machine being used
28.	3v2013	KME Engineering	One stop repair and maintenance service of production equipment (lathe processing and other engineering operations)	2003	40 (grew from 4 when inaugurated)	(1) Owner/manager graduate of Yangon Inst of Technology; studied 1 year in Korea and worked 5 years in Malaysia
						(2) Net gains mostly reinvested; commercial bank loans not practical
						(2) Provides consulting service on production improvements
						(3) Under technological agreement with a US company
29.	3v2013	FPMP	Propellers for vessels made of steel or copper (casting, forging, and assembly)	2002/2003	7	(1) Moved to this industrial estate in 2012
						(2) Totally self-financed (with the exception of urgently needed 5–7 million kyats from parents)
						(2) Products to be connected with second-hand, Japanese-made truck engines
						(3) Large-sized products are order made with 50 % down payment
						(5) Provides designing support if requested
						(4) Training for production skills requires 7 years
						(6) Hopes to run a dockyard someday

(continued)

Table 7.10 (continued)

	Date of visit	Enterprise ID	Merchandise produced and/or nature of production activities	Year of inauguration	Number of employees	Notable characteristics
30.	3v2013	P Plastic	Plastic engineering (moulding and casting for the manufacturing of construction materials)	1985	Approx. 2,000 in whole land, of which production staff 9 % (grew from 3 when inaugurated)	(1) Started with paid-in capital of 10 thousand kyats, which grew by 2013 to 100 thousand kyats
						(2) Production employees comprise about 9 % of the total size of employment
						(3) Materials and production equipment all imported
						(4) Plastic engineering seems to be a highly profitable business
31.	3v2013	S Electrical	Plastic engineering	?	?	(1) Raw materials imported from Japan and Korea
						(2) In principle, the same mould is used for 3 days (not longer than 2 months)
32.	2&9ix2013	R Company	Sandals, shoes, etc. made of natural rubber	1995/1996	300 in Yangon (grew from 150 in 1998)	(1) Family business; father used to be engaged in sales of sandals and slippers
						(2) Land leased in 1998/1999 from the Ministry of Industry (for 30 years)
						(3)) In close contact with a section chief at the Ministry of Industry
						(4) Runs its own rubber estates to make use of smoked rubber sheets of good enough quality
						(5) Agreed to merge with a state-owned factory in a local town (together with its 150 employees)
						(6) Production equipment made in China
						(7) Products also exported to Japan
						(8) Piece-rate wages equivalent to U.S.$80/m (with the addition of $10–20 bonus/m)

References

KTAM (Knappen Tippetts Abett McCarthy Engineers). (1953). *Economic and engineering development of Burma, comprehensive report prepared for the government of the Union of Burma* (2 Vols.). Aylesbury/London: Haze/Watson & Viney, August 1953.

Kudo, T. (2001). Transformation and structural changes in the 1990s. In T. Kudo (Ed.), *Industrial development in Myanmar, prospects and challenges*. Chiba City: Institute of Developing Economies, Japan External Trade Organization.

Kudo, T. (Ed.). (2002). *Industrial development in Myanmar (2), prospects and challenges*. Chiba City: Institute of Developing Economies, Japan External Trade Organization.

Kudo, T. (2004). Myanmar ni okeru minkan kigyō no seisei to tokuchō, seizōgyō o chūshin to shite [The growth and characteristics of private enterprises in Myanmar, with focus on manufacturing industry]. In K. Fujita (Ed.), *Shijō keizai ikōka no Myanmar, sono hattenn katei oyobi genjō* [Myanmar economy in transition to a market economy, its development process and present condition]. Tokyo: Institute of Developing Economies. ch. 4.

Kudo, T. (2012). Explanatory note on data sources 4: Myanmar. In I. Kuroiwa, (Ed.), *Economic integration and the location of industries, the case of less developed East Asian countries*. New York: Palgrave Macmillan.

Kudo, T., & Kumagai, S. (2012). *Two-polar growth strategy in Myanmar: Seeking "high" and "balanced" development* (Institute of Developing Economies (IDE) Discussion Papers No. 371). Chiba City: IDE, Japan External Trade Organization.

Ministry of National Planning. (1961). *Second four-year plan for the Union of Burma: 1961–62 to 1964–65*. Rangoon: Superintendent, Government Printing and Stationary, Union of Burma.

Ministry of National Planning, The Revolutionary Government of the Union of Burma. (1965). *The national income of Burma 1964*. Rangoon: Central Press.

Myat Thein. (2004). *Economic development of Myanmar*. Singapore: Institute of Southeast Asian Studies.

Ohkawa, K., & Shinohara, M. (Eds.). (1979). *Patterns of Japanese economic development, a quantitative appraisal*. New Haven: Yale University Press.

Saito, O., & Settsu, T. (2010). Unveiling historical occupational structures and its implications for sectoral labour productivity analysis in Japan's economic growth. In *Research unit for statistical and empirical analysis in social sciences*. Tokyo: Institute of Economic Research, Hitotsubashi University.

Sen, A. K. (1960/1968). *Choice of techniques: An aspect of the theory of planned economic development*. Oxford: Blackwell.

Thakin Tin. (1948). The speech of the Honourable Thakin Tin, Minister for agriculture and forests, on the introduction of the Land Nationalization Bill, 1948, at the Sixth Session of the Parliament on the 11th October 1948. In Ministry of Agriculture and Forests (Ed.), *The Land Nationalization Act, 1948*. Rangoon: Superintendent, Government Printing and Stationary, Union of Burma.

Tin Maung Maung Than. (2007). *State dominance in Myanmar: The political economy of industrialization*. Singapore: Institute of Southeast Asian Studies.

Tin Win. (2001). Economic reforms and business organization: Property rights approach. In T. Kudo (Ed.), *Industrial development in Myanmar: Prospects and challenges*. Chiba: Institute of Developing Economies, Japan External Trade Organization, ch. 2.

Umemura, M. (1988). *Rōdōryoku; chōki keizai tōkei, suikei to bunseki* (Labour force; estimates of long-term economic statistics of Japan since 1868) (Vol. 2). Tokyo: Tōyō Keizai Shimpōsha.

Yamada, M. (2012). Myanmar jin imin no mondai – ekkyō suru jinteki shigen no yukue – [On the migration of Myanmar people, the future of human resources which cross over the national borders]. In T. Kudo (Ed.), *Myanmar seiji no jitsuzō – gunsei 23nen no kōzai to shin seiken no yukue* [The reality of Myanmar politics, evaluating the 23 years of military junta and the future prospects of the newly-born regime]. Chiba City: Institute of Developing Economies, Japan External Trade Organization. ch. 8.

Chapter 8
Economic Relations Between Myanmar and China

Atsuko Mizuno

1 Introduction

As the relationship between China and Myanmar became closer under the military regime, Myanmar deepened its economic dependence on China: economic cooperation played an important role in the economic growth of the country; the volume of trade increased gradually and China became Myanmar's largest trading partner in 2011; foreign direct investment (FDI) from China improved notably after 2004 and made it the largest investor in Myanmar in 2010. Although economic ties with China contributed to the stability of Myanmar, they were also seen as a factor that hindered the country's reforms under military rule.

After a new government was installed in 2011, its rapidly improving relations with the USA and other developed countries enabled Myanmar to broaden and to restore balance in its external economic relations. Myanmar's economic dependence on China is likely to be affected and mitigated by this development, though not very soon. Nevertheless, the bilateral economic relations will continue to have a strategic impact.

Based on such issues regarding the economic structure of Myanmar, this chapter studies the economic relations between China and Myanmar, those from the establishment of bilateral diplomatic relations in 1950 until the early years of the post-military periods as well as historical changes in, and the strategy of, diplomacy, Chinese foreign aid and economic development. The main principle underpinning Chinese foreign aid was 'equality and mutual benefit' to support the 'self-reliance' of the recipient country. However, over time, China shifted its economic development strategy from 'self-reliance' to 'reform and opening-up' in 1978 and later to international expansion. Regarding the supposed self-reliance of the recipient

A. Mizuno (✉)
Department of International Economy and Business, Faculty of Economics,
Kyushu University, Fukuoka 812-8581, Japan
e-mail: amizuno@econ.kyushu-u.ac.jp

K. Odaka (ed.), *The Myanmar Economy*, DOI 10.1007/978-4-431-55735-7_8

country, the consistency of the development strategy between China as the donor and the recipient countries gradually appears to have become an issue. This chapter will examine the expansion of Chinese economic assistance to Myanmar and will also consider the effects of economic development strategy both on China as the donor and Myanmar as the recipient.

Economic interest was an integral part of the bilateral relationship, though not a singular, objective explanation for it. For instance, Myanmar's geopolitical importance was also a motivation for Chinese assistance. Because of this, neighbouring countries also took steps towards closer relations with Myanmar in order to counterbalance Myanmar's dependence on China and to secure their influence in the country.

Furthermore, alongside the political and economic reforms in Myanmar after 2011, public opinion progressively became a possible determining factor in its political economy. Simultaneously, the USA and the EU lifted economic sanctions and the developed world began to provide a significant amount of ODA to support reforms and the progress of Myanmar's development. This chapter will discuss these issues involving the economic relation between China and Myanmar in the post-military period, aiming to provide meaningful suggestions not only for the future of relations between Myanmar and China but also for Myanmar's future economic development.

2 Economic Relations with China Until the End of the 'Burmese Way to Socialism'

2.1 The U Nu Period

Burma was the first non-communist country to recognise the People's Republic of China in 1949. The two countries established diplomatic relations in 1950. But their bilateral ties were not tight in the beginning. In the early Cold War period, U Nu's attitude towards the two blocs led by the USA and the Soviet Union was an independent course, and Beijing did not attach much importance to Burma, which did not ally itself with any power (Steinberg and Fan 2012: 10–27).

The bilateral relations became closer after the symbolic exchange of visits between Zhou Enlai and U Nu in 1954. In the early 1950s, in order to recover against the USA's containment and encirclement, China gradually adjusted its policy towards neutral countries to unite all countries that wished to maintain peace with China and to create a safe buffer zone between China and the West. During the same period, Burma's foreign policy of neutrality and non-alignment was gradually formulated (ibid: 29–33). Both China and Burma played important roles at the Bandung Conference in 1955, the most immediate antecedent to the creation of the non-aligned movement.

In 1960, China and Burma signed both a treaty of friendship and mutual non-aggression and a boundary agreement, which were the first treaties signed by China with a non-aligned Asian country. A year later, in 1961, the two countries signed an agreement on economic and technical cooperation. With this agreement, China pledged to provide Burma with concessional interest-free loan amounting to £300 million. This was an epochal event at the time, as the amount was larger than what had been given by the Soviet Union and Eastern European countries. It was the third-largest grant ever given to Burma, after those of Japan and West Germany, the largest and second-largest donors, respectively. The grant conditions were favourable: as much as, or more than, those imposed by Western countries (Matsumoto 1975: 69).

2.2 *In the Era of 'the Burmese Way to Socialism'*

In 1962, 'the Burmese Way to Socialism' was adopted by Ne Win as an effort to create self-reliance based on strong nationalism as well as closed-door and non-aligned policies. It was radically different from the socialism of the three socialist countries in Indochina allied to China or the Soviet Union. The Burmese non-alignment policy kept its relations with China neither too tight nor too tense. As the Sino-Soviet polemic gradually escalated with respect to the socialist countries of Indochina, it was crucial for China to maintain its friendship with Burma, even though Ne Win's strict nationalisation damaged the Chinese community in the country. The administration of Chinese aid was slack, while the government of Burma restricted its acceptance of foreign aid in an effort to eliminate foreign influence.

At that time, China provided foreign aid as a component part of its foreign policy to consolidate friendly relations with other developing countries regardless of profit. China granted aid without imposing burdens on the recipient countries based on the 'Eight Principles of China's Foreign Economic and Technical Aid', as laid out by Prime Minister Zhou Enlai during his 1964 visit to 14 countries in Asia and Africa. Among the main contents of these principles are equality and mutual benefit, respect for sovereignty, reducing the economic obligations of the recipient countries, self-reliance and independent development. Having experienced the disadvantages of depending on foreign aid after such aid was withdrawn by the Soviet Union in 1960, China deliberately chose the self-reliance of developing countries and the equality and mutual benefit of both the donor and the recipient as the key principles of its foreign aid (Jin 2004). During the Cultural Revolution (1966–1977), China provided economic assistance to neighbouring socialist countries in Asia as well as to countries in Africa as a means to expand its friendly relations (Tamachi 2005).

However, when anti-Chinese riots occurred in Rangoon (present Yangon) in June 1967 because of the Cultural Revolution, the government of China criticised Ne Win's regime and terminated its economic aid. Furthermore, China strongly supported the Communist Party of Burma (CPB), which was fighting alongside ethnic groups in the border regions of Burma to overthrow Ne Win's government. This antagonism made the Burmese regime suspicious of, and vigilant about, China. The anti-Chinese movement occurred not only in Burma but also in some other Asian countries and isolated China increasingly on the world stage because of its Cultural Revolution. Consequently, China adjusted its 'world revolution' to a more practical policy line. As relations with Burma had been the previous good model of China's external relations, the renormalisation of bilateral relations was significant for China (Steinberg and Fan 2012: 128). The government of Burma also needed to restore relations with China to combat the CPB's growing power, because it was already dealing with a wide range of armed ethnic opposition groups.

In 1970, China and Myanmar agreed to reinstate their ambassadors and a true normalisation of relations occurred after the end of the Cultural Revolution. However, the relative importance of Burma's relations with China declined in inverse proportion to active diplomacy through a neutral/non-aligned foreign policy after power was transferred to a 'civilian' government led by the Burma Socialist Programme Party (BSPP) in 1974. While China restarted the flow of aid towards Burma simultaneously with the normalisation of relations (Matsumoto 1975: 72–74), the Cultural Revolution hampered China's ability to provide foreign aid to developing countries in the mid-1970s. China radically altered its policies on foreign aid without regard for cost and efficiency, thus, reducing amounts[1] (Tamachi 2005; Jin 2004). Meanwhile, Burma revised its restricted attitude to official development assistance (ODA) and began to accept more starting in the mid-1970s in order to rebuild its ailing economy. In the same period, the developed world provided more ODA to developing countries. The major donors to Burma were Japan and other developed countries, as well as multinational organisations.

In the 1980s, economic ties between Burma and China were insignificant. Burma restricted foreign trade and did not permit border trade which involved cross-border smuggling. During the last years of socialism (fiscal years 1983–1987), trade with China amounted to an average of only 98.9 million kyats in exports and 136.6 million kyats in imports. China's share of overall Burmese trade was only 3.4 % of imports and 3.0 % of exports (Ministry of National Planning and Finance, Burma 1987; Ministry of National Planning and Finance, Myanmar 1990). On the other hand, China was anxious about the decline in its relations with Burma and other previous recipients of its aid packages, to which many developed countries provided more ODA. Also, Chinese economic 'reform and opening-up' attracted Burmese attention and interest. Economic issues drew more and more attention when the two summit leaders held talks in the 1980s (Steinberg and Fan 2012: 147).

3 Close Economic Relations Between the Myanmar Military Regime and China

3.1 The Significance of Economic Support from China

China was the first country in the world to recognise Myanmar's military regime, the State Law and Order Restoration Council (SLORC; later re-established as the State Peace and Development Council, SPDC, in 1997) which opposed the democratic movement and took power in September 1988. China held fast to its

[1]The total amount of Chinese aid, which had reached its highest-ever level (US $1.1 billion) in 1970, was gradually reduced between 1976 and 1983 to a per annum average of only US $150 million (Lin 1996).

policy of non-intervention in Myanmar's domestic affairs and strengthened its relationship with the country. Although Myanmar had profound suspicions of China, which had supported the ethnic anti-government armed forces, it was crucial for Myanmar to promote friendship with China that respected the regime's stability and did not condemn its human rights abuses.

In January 1989, Myanmar first opened border trade with China, before its other neighbouring countries. The bond between the two nations tightened with a 12-day visit to China in October 1989 by a 24-member military team. Full-scale arms imports from China began in 1990.[2] However, the result of the May 1990 elections prompted Western countries to criticise and push the SLORC to transfer power immediately to the opposition National League for Democracy (NLD)[3]; the government of China invited Saw Maung, the Chairman of the SLORC, to Beijing in August 1991. During this visit, the two sides signed their first agreement on economic and technical cooperation since the founding of the SLORC. This agreement pledged to provide an RMB 50 million (US $9.8 million) interest-free loan (Ministry of Foreign Affairs, Myanmar 1991). Although the amount was by no means large, it must have given the isolated military regime a sense of confidence and of security.

In 1992, the first FDI from China was permitted. As Western economic sanctions tightened, notably after the USA banned all new US investments in Myanmar in 1997, Myanmar's economy gradually deepened its dependence on China, which played a certain role in Myanmar's economy. Consequently, China's assistance to Myanmar was sometimes regarded as a factor that hindered the efforts of the international community which limited its ODA and imposed economic sanctions as a measure to encourage democratic reforms. However, maintaining close relations with China might have been the only option for the Myanmar military junta, since its connections with the developed world were limited.

3.2 *China's Economic Policy of Reform and Opening-Up and Its Re-expansion of Foreign Assistance*

From China's perspective, economic interests counted a great deal in its policy towards Myanmar. By way of background, China gradually increased its provision of foreign aid from 1983 onwards, being anxious about the decline in its relations with previous recipient countries, in conjunction with its domestic and foreign economic development strategies, based on the principle of equality and mutual benefit. The

[2] Myanmar had previously imported weapons mainly from Western countries, but after they simultaneously imposed an arms embargo, Myanmar came to depend on China for almost all its imported weapons.

[3] The purpose of the 1990 election is a matter of some dispute. The NLD, the USA and other Western countries regarded the election as a national election with the purpose of transferring power and criticised the SLORC for ignoring the results. From the opposing standpoint, the election which Ne Win had promised to convene was a constituent assembly charged with the writing of a new constitutions and the power should be transferred when a constitutionally formed government was established (Aung-Thwin M., and Aung-Thwin M. 2012: 266–267).

steady economic growth of China brought about by its ‘reform and opening-up’ policy strengthened its capacity to provide foreign assistance (Ma 2007).

In 1995, China conducted an overall reform of its foreign aid framework that aimed to integrate foreign trade, capital flow and international economic cooperation[4] and to boost the country’s economic growth by making use of internal and foreign funds, resources and markets. In addition, the development strategy called the ‘three alongs’ (along the sea, along the river and along the border) began in 1992, while the Great Western Development Strategy, adopted in the late 1990s, provided an impetus to combine the development of border areas with assistance for neighbouring countries. Furthermore, the ‘go abroad’ policy, which encouraged outbound direct investment (ODI) by Chinese firms, was also combined with China’s foreign assistance from the beginning of the 2000s. China expanded strategic aid with the promotion of its exports through trade and investment (Jin 2004: 124). China’s foreign assistance strategy has been characterised by its aim of espousing economic development both for China itself and for the recipient countries (Kobayashi 2007).

For instance, in many cases of old-fashioned foreign assistance projects such as the construction of facilities for import substitution industries and infrastructure, Chinese enterprises contracted these projects, and this type of foreign assistance grew by supporting the expansion of Chinese enterprises abroad. The expansion of economic cooperation with neighbouring countries contributed to the development of inland Western China, which had been left behind in terms of economic development. Regarding assistance for the development of natural resources such as oil and natural gas and the construction of special economic zones, which expanded after the beginning of the 2000s, they seem to have been motivated by the following objectives, respectively: to secure oil and natural resources, for which there was a rising demand in light of economic development, and to support ODI by Chinese firms.

Whereas Chinese foreign aid has been combined with economic cooperation, it has had no standards equivalent to those of the OECD’s Development Assistance Committee (DAC), such as the requirement of a grant element of at least 25 %. According to a white paper on China’s foreign aid (State Council, China 2011), the amount of foreign aid provided in 2009 was RMB13.3 billion (US$1.9 billion), equivalent to only 0.4 % of its gross national product. At the same time, economic cooperation with developing countries[5] amounted to US$41 billion in the same year (National Bureau of Statistics of China 2010, *China Statistical Yearbook*). Furthermore, some ODI projects, notably those by state-owned enterprises, have been secured by official bilateral agreements and directed or even guaranteed by the Chinese government. Such ODI seems to have been characterised as official assistance.

---

[4] According to the China Statistical Yearbook, foreign economic cooperation consists of contracted projects, labour service cooperation and design and consultation services with foreign countries that have been approved by the Department of Commerce of China at various levels. Foreign aid projects are also included.

[5] In order to focus on the element of aid for economic cooperation, this excludes amounts for countries having a GDP per capita higher than that of China in 2009 (World Bank, World Development Indicators).

In addition, foreign assistance by China, which is not a member of the traditional international donor community but an emerging donor, has unique characteristics. First, China does not impose any political conditions on recipient countries except for endorsing the One-China policy, which acknowledges China's position that Taiwan is part of its territory. The Chinese government has distributed aid without conditionality to countries to which the developed world does not provide aid due to certain domestic affairs such as: the legitimacy of, and governance by, the regime ruling the recipient country, unaccounted-for expenditures of grants and violations of human rights. Secondly, China does not necessarily abide by the practice of requiring environmental and social conditions in the recipient countries, as in international standards.

Thus, China provided economic assistance to Myanmar by combining economic cooperation, trade and investment, without imposing any political conditions. In addition, China's extensive, indeed overpowering, assistance to the geopolitically significant country has been motivated not only by economic exploitation but also by securing Myanmar's internal stability as well as strategic access through Myanmar to the Bay of Bengal (Steinberg and Fan 2012: 308–313).

3.3 *Expansion of Chinese Economic Cooperation with Myanmar*

Chinese economic cooperation with Myanmar increased after the mid-1990s (Fig. 8.1). Myanmar became a significant recipient of Chinese assistance; it was in the top rank for the distribution of Chinese foreign economic cooperation during the 2000s. In contrast, the provision of ODA to Myanmar has been at quite a low level since it drastically declined at the end of the 1980s, because the developed world halted the flow of ODA to Myanmar except for emergency and humanitarian aid,

Fig. 8.1 Trends in ODA recieved by and turnover of China's economic cooperation with, Myanmar (*Sources*: *China Statistical Yearbook* (National Bureau of Statistics of China 2010) and *World Development Indicators* (WB))

Table 8.1 High-level visits between Myanmar and China (2000–2013)

	From Myanmar to China	From China to Myanmar
2000	Maung Aye, Vice-Chairman (June)	Hu Jintao, Vice-President (July)
2001		Tian Fengshan, Minister for Land Resources (July)
		Jiang Zemin, President (December)
2003	Than Shwe, Chairman (January)	Li Lanqing Vice-Premier (January)
	Win Aung, Foreign Minister (January)	
	Maung Aye, Vice-Chairman (August)	
2004	Khin Nyunt, Prime Minister (July)	Wu Yi, Vice-Premier (March)
2005	Soe Win, Prime Minister (July, October)	Li Zhaoxing, Foreign Minister (July)
2006	Soe Win, Prime Minister (February, October)	
2007	General Thura Shwe Maun (January)	Tang Jiaxuan, State Councillor (February)
	Thein Sein, Acting Prime Minister (June)	
2008	Thein Sein, Prime Minister (August, October)	Yang Jiechi, Foreign Minister (February)
2009	Thein Sein, Prime Minister (April)	Li Changchun, member of the Standing Committee of the Political Bureau of the CPC Central Committee (March)
	Maung Aye, Vice-Chairman (June)	Xi Jingpin, Vice-President (December)
2010	Tin Aung Myint Oo, First Secretary (July)	Wen Jiabao, Premier (June)
	Than Shwe, Chairman (September)	
2011	Thein Sein, President (May)	Jia Qinglin, Chairman of CPPCC (April)
	Wunna Maung Lwin, Foreign Minister (October)	
2012	U Shwe Mann, Speaker of Pyithu Hluttaw (Lower House) (February)	Wang Gang, Vice-Chairman of CPPCC (May)
	Thein Sein (September)	Meng Jianzhu, State Councillor and Minister of Public Security (July)
	General Soe Win, Deputy Commander-in- Chief (November)	Wu Bangguo, Chairman of the Standing Committee of the National People's Congress (September)
	Aye Myint Kyu, Culture Minister (November)	
2013	Thein Sein, President (April)	Yang Jiechi, Chinese State Councillor (July)
		Liu Yandong, Vice Premier (December)

Source: *The New Light of Myanmar*, *Xinhua*, website of the Ministry of Foreign Affairs, China (December 2013)

due to concerns regarding the suppression of human rights under the military rule (Mizuno 2008). China's economic cooperation soared dramatically after 2007. However, it has been difficult to gain a clear grasp of China's economic cooperation with Myanmar because little information on the details has been publicly released. Instead, the main economic cooperation projects will be surveyed here using agreements signed during a series of high-level bilateral visits since 2000[6] (Table 8.1). In many cases, Chinese economic cooperation projects were composed after an agreement was signed during a high-level official visit.

In July 2001, China and Myanmar signed a MOU concerning cooperation in geological and mineral resources and agreed to encourage cooperation between institutions and companies for the exploration and development of these resources. This added momentum to China's cooperation in these sectors. In December 2001, President Jiang Zemin paid the first visit to Myanmar by a Chinese head of state. During this visit, the two nations signed an investment promotion and protection agreement, and a series of loans was pledged for specific projects, including hydropower plants. In January 2003, during the visit to China by SPDC Chairman Than Shwe, the government of China announced the provision of a US$50 million grant and the extension of a new concessional loan of US$200 million. This was the highest-ever recorded assistance by a large-scale Chinese concessional loan, as well as the extension of a credit line to Myanmar.

In August of that year, Vice-President Maung Aye visited Beijing and signed an MOU on the construction of the Yeywa hydropower plants in Myanmar with a concessional loan granted by China in the amount of US$200 million. At that time, Western countries had imposed economic sanctions on Myanmar due to the Depayin massacres in May 2003 during which the regime placed Aung San Suu Kyi in custody and under house arrest for the third time. In the following year, the visit to Myanmar by Vice-Premier Wu Yi in March resulted in a further strengthening of economic and trade ties, with Beijing agreeing to provide a new preferential loan and extra funding for a range of infrastructure and agriculture projects. A total of 21 agreements and MOUs were signed by the two sides, including a grant of assistance for the construction of an international convention centre in Nay Pyi Taw. During the visit of Prime Minister Khin Nyunt to China in July 2003, a total of 12 agreements and MOUs were signed, such as an interest-free loan and an agreement on economic and technical cooperation.

Prime Minister Soe Win, the successor to Khin Nyunt, visited China four times: in July and October 2005 and in February and October 2006. Along with these visits, the two countries agreed to pursue comprehensive economic cooperation in addition to economic assistance in fields including energy, railways and special trade zones. Chinese committed a grant of RMB 70 million (US$ 8.5 million) and a low-interest concessional loan of US$ 200 million for these projects.

In June 2010, which marked the 60th anniversary of the establishment of diplomatic relations between the two countries, Premier Wen Jiabao paid an official visit to Myanmar. During this visit, the construction of the Myanmar-China oil and natural gas pipeline project was formally launched by the prime ministers of both countries, and the Myanmar International Convention Centre in Nay Pyi Taw, which had been built with Chinese grant assistance, was formally handed over. In September of the same year, SPDC Chairman Than Shwe visited China and agreed to a series

[6] Unless otherwise noted, the contents of this section hereinafter mainly based on the feature articles on the high-level bilateral visits in the *New Light of Myanmar (NLM)*, which is a state-owned and the only English newspaper published by Ministry of Information.

of projects, including hydropower plants, copper mines, arterial roads to border areas in China, wharfs in Yangon port, an automobile factory and a paper mill.

On the swearing-in of the new government in March 2011, Jia Qinglin, Chairman of the National Committee of the Chinese People's Political Consultative Conference (CPPCC), paid an official visit to Myanmar at the beginning of April. In May 2011, President Thein Sein visited China in his first state visit since being sworn in as president. In a joint statement issued at the end of the talks between the presidents of the two countries, the relationship between the two nations was referred to as a 'comprehensive strategic partnership'. The two sides also agreed to further enhance coordination and cooperation and signed a series of economic agreements in such areas as energy, transport and agriculture.

Since the Myitsone dam project was suspended in September 2011 as explained later, visits by high-level officials from China seemed to have stagnated. However, Wang Gang, Vice-Chairman of the National Committee of the CPPCC, and Meng Jianzhu, State Councillor and Minister of Public Security, paid official visits to Myanmar in May and July 2012, respectively. In September 2012, an official delegation led by Wu Bangguo, the first Chairman of the Standing Committee of the National People's Congress (NPC), visited Myanmar, the first time since the establishment of diplomatic relations. He had a discussion with President Thein Sein on how the visit could contribute to friendship and cooperation between the two countries and the continuation of long-lasting ties promoting the comprehensive strategic partnership from the Pauk-Phaw level. During the visit, the two nations signed nine economic and trade cooperation documents and two agreements on loans for the Thahtay and Baluchaung hydropower projects.[7]

3.4 *Trade with China*

Following the opening of the border to trade in 1989, the volume of trade between the two nations began to increase (Fig. 8.2). In the late 1990s, Myanmar's imports from China stopped rising and its exports declined. Consequently, China's share in Myanmar's total trade dropped from 23.0 % in 1995 to 13.8 % in 1999. In the 2000s, both exports and imports increased again. In the late 2000s, the trade volume with China soared even more and China became Myanmar's largest trading partner in 2011. However, its expansion of exports exceeded that of imports, resulting in Myanmar's trade deficit with China surging year after year. In 2013, the trade volume reached US$10.6 billion with a share of 34.6 %. Myanmar ran a large trade deficit of US$5.3 billion with China, its largest import partner with a share of 39.8 % and the second-largest export partner with a share of 24.5 %, after Thailand.

[7] The president's office in Myanmar stated that the 'Visit of the PRC delegation to Myanmar contributes to the continued maintenance of long-lasting friendly ties fostered by the leaders of two countries', http://www.president-office.gov.mm/en/briefitng-room/news/2012/09/15/id-681, accessed on 30 September 2012.

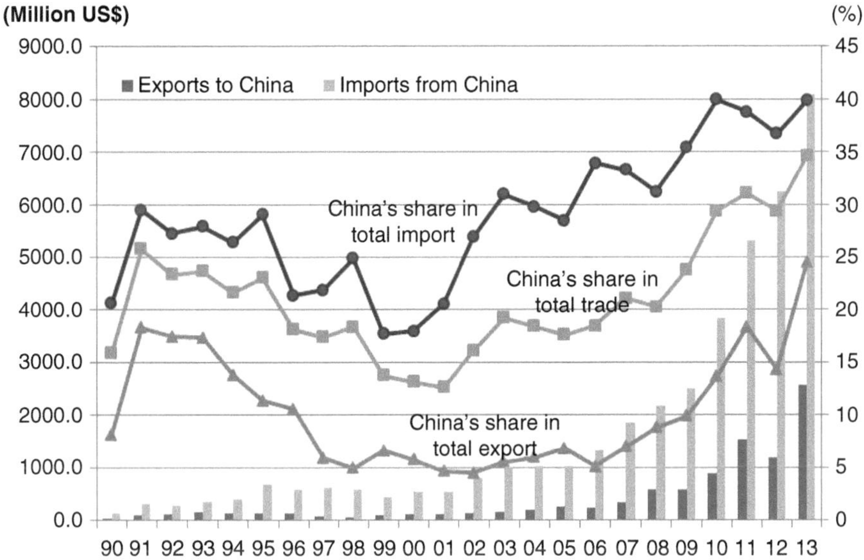

Fig. 8.2 Trends in Myanmar's trade with, and trade dependence on, China (*Source*: IMF *Direction of Trade Statistics*)

By contrast, Myanmar was not such a significant trading partner for China, with a share of 0.18 % in 2011 (*China Statistical Yearbook* 2012), but was the largest trading partner of the Yunnan Province, which shared a long border with Myanmar, accounting for 10.8 % of its total trade (imports, 6.8 %; exports, 15.3 %) in 2012.[8]

Figure 8.3 shows the major commodities of trade between China and Myanmar in 2012 by sections of 'the Harmonized Commodity Description and Coding System (HS)', as reported by the UN Comtrade statistics. China exported mainly manufactured products: Sec. XVI (machinery and electrical equipment), accounting for 28 %, was the main product, followed by Sec. XVII (vehicles, 19 %) and Sec. XV (base metals and articles thereof, 18 %), which ranked second and third, respectively. In contrast, China imported mainly primary products from Myanmar such as Sec. IX (wood and articles thereof, 28 %), Sec. XIV (precious stones and articles thereof, 23 %), Sec. V (mineral products, 22 %) and Sec. II (vegetable products, 9 %). Myanmar obviously deepened its dependence on vertical trade with China. This fact suggests that the close economic ties with China failed to have a substantial impact on Myanmar's broad-based economic and industrial development (Kudo 2006). As mentioned below, oil, gas and mining exploration, as well as electricity development, progressed in Myanmar, in cooperation with China, from the mid-2000s. Once these projects reach the production stage, expanding exports of natural resources and energy to China will reduce Myanmar's trade deficit with China and simultaneously strengthen further its vertical trade structure.

[8] Kunming Customs District website, http://kunming.customs.gov.cn/publish/portal174/tab61642/module168591/info424618.htm, accessed on 20 December 2013.

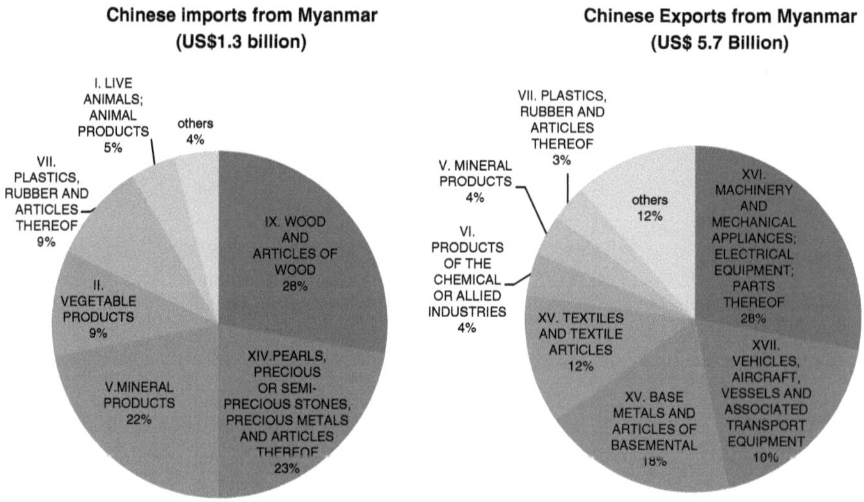

Fig. 8.3 Bilateral trade structure between Myanmar and China by HS section (2012) (*Source*: UN Comtrade)

3.5 Foreign Direct Investment from China

From 1992, when the first Chinese FDI project was permitted, up until 2003, only 13 Chinese projects have been engaged in FDI in Myanmar,[9] amounting in total to US$380 million (CSO 1995–2005, *Statistical yearbook*). The factors behind the sluggish inflow of Chinese FDI to Myanmar up until the mid-2000s include the following: (1) Chinese ODI itself began to expand after 2000 and (2) the SPDC's foreign economic policy tightened, especially after the late 1990s. Chinese firms did not make inroads into Myanmar, where tightened economic policies discouraged firms, especially export-oriented manufacturers, from investing.

However, it should be noted that many Chinese mainland companies had ties with Myanmar Chinese entrepreneurs, which were revitalised outside the jurisdiction of the law on FDI since the transition to a market economy was launched. For instance, the Myanmar Chinese Chamber of Commerce (MCCOC),[10] re-embarked on its business activities and also enhanced economic exchange with overseas associations of Myanmar Chinese and sent delegations to various places in mainland China (MCCOC 2009). For mainland and overseas Chinese companies, the accessibility of Myanmar Chinese enterprises was instrumental in extending their

[9]FDI consisted of what was permitted by the Myanmar Investment Committee under the Foreign Investment Law.

[10]The CCCM was organised by Myanmar Chinese entrepreneurs in 1909, which had been proscribed during the era of the Burmese Way to Socialism, although social welfare for the Chinese community had been their main activity during the era of 'Burmese Way to Socialism'.

business in Myanmar in cooperation with them as domestic companies.[11] They were seen involved in the garment industry, in small-scale processing on commission and in service sectors such as real estate, retail, hotels and construction. According to the CCCM, the number of members exceeded 600 by the end of 2011, and cooperation with mainland Chinese companies particularly increased since 2006.[12]

FDI from China to Myanmar improved after the mid-2000s and China became the largest investor in 2010. Meanwhile, FDI from developed countries had been sluggish due to the economic sanctions imposed by Western countries. Although FDI from China decreased after fiscal 2011, China had the largest shares of one-third of accumulated FDI to Myanmar up until fiscal 2013 (Figs. 8.4 and 8.5).

China's Ministry of Commerce and Ministry of Foreign Affairs recommended manufacturing (electronics and machinery; vehicles and parts; paper and paper products; chemical materials and products; processing of wood, bamboo, and rattan; agricultural equipment) and construction as Myanmar industries for targets of Chinese ODI, as well the natural resources sector (such as oil, natural gas, jewels, tungsten, nickel and copper), agriculture (crops), forestry and fisheries (Ministry of Commerce and Ministry of Foreign Affairs, China 2004). Among these sectors, China mainly

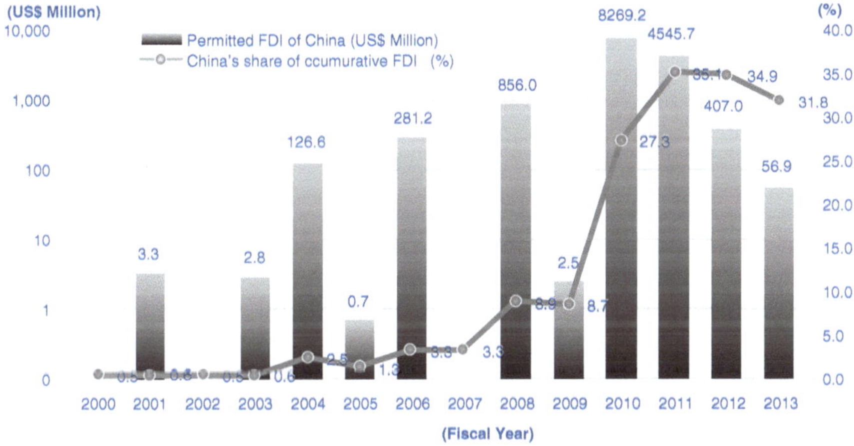

Fig. 8.4 Flow of permitted FDI from China to Myanmar (From fiscal year 2000 to 2013) (*Source*: CSO 1995–2012, 2010–2014)

[11] According to Chinese statistics, FDI to Myanmar reached US$1.9 billion through 37 companies up to the third quarter of 2002 (website of the Ministry of Foreign Affairs (in Chinese) accessed on 6 July, 2008), which exceeds the amount according to Myanmar's statistics.

[12] The information was available during author served as a researcher/advisor for the embassy of Japan in Myanmar from 2008 to 2012. Unless otherwise noted the same shall apply hereinafter in this chapter.

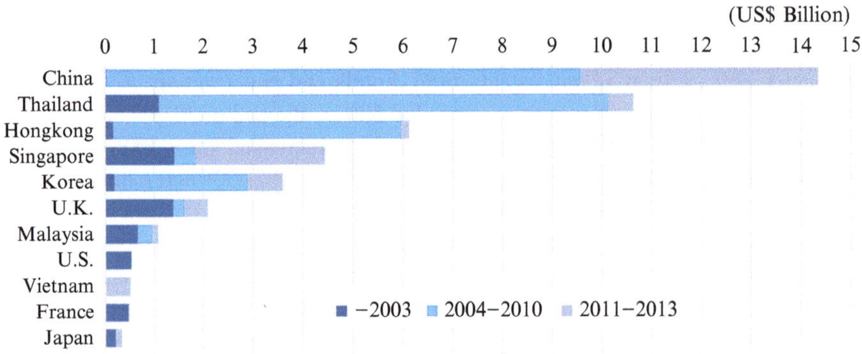

Fig. 8.5 Cumulative FDI by country of origin (From fiscal year 1989 to 2013) (*Source*: CSO 1995–2012, 2010–2014)

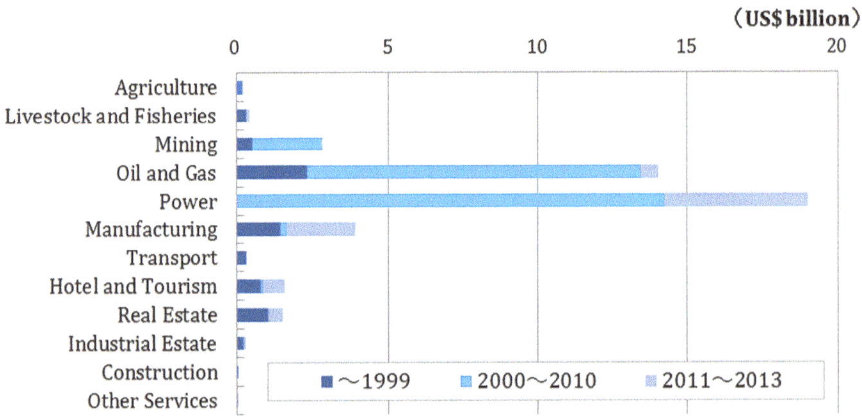

Fig. 8.6 Cumulative FDI by sector (From fiscal year 1989 to 2013) (*Source*: CSO 1995–2012, 2010–2014)

invested in the power sector, the oil and gas sector and the mining sector. Chinese FDI in the mining, oil and gas and power sector is often combined with its economic cooperation because of their significance for China's natural resources strategy. In contrast, the FDI in the manufacturing industry remained quite low. Figure 8.6 shows that the structure of FDI broken down by sector was lopsided. Along with the growth in FDI from China, Myanmar came to lean on energy development.

4 Economic Relations with China in Selected Sectors

Since the socialist period, Chinese economic cooperation was disbursed mainly for infrastructure projects such as roads, railways, airports, telecommunications, dams, water transport, hydropower plants and import substitution industry facilities for state-owned enterprises. Notably after the mid-2000s, hydropower plants and the natural resources and energy sector were mainly promoted, paralleling the intentions of the government of Myanmar.

4.1 Assistance for State-Owned Enterprises and Their Reforms

A number of plants and factories of state-owned enterprises (SOEs) were improved, with both technical and financial support from China. As Kudo and Odaka discuss in Chap. 7 of this volume, SOEs increased even after the start of the transition to a market economy. Although the number of SOEs was far smaller than that of private enterprises, their ratio in capital-intensive and technical-intensive industries were relatively high.[13] In addition, SOEs were operated at a loss, which accounted for two-thirds of the national deficit. China's economic cooperation contributed to the production capacity of these SOEs, especially in import substitution industries that targeted the domestic market. It can be said that this Chinese support resulted in a delay in government reforms regarding SOEs.

However, since the mid-2000s, the main projects supported by Chinese economic cooperation gradually shifted from SOEs in old-fashioned import substitution industries to hydropower and energy development. In addition, some cases appeared in Chinese enterprises and SOEs establishing joint enterprises, not under official assistance rules but operating under commercial terms as the state embarked on a campaign to privatise state-owned enterprises and properties in late 2009.[14]

4.2 Construction of Infrastructure Towards the Border with China

Infrastructure development in Myanmar provided a geopolitically important transportation line from the border area of China to the Bay of Bengal and promoted the development of this part of China's border region. The long border shared by Yunnan and Myanmar was open to economic growth and mutual economic interdependence. For instance, increasing bilateral trade, most of which was conducted via this border, made Myanmar the largest trade partner of the Yunnan Province. For landlocked inland Yunnan, it was crucial to construct or upgrade transportation networks stretching to the border both in China and Myanmar. Consequently, the Yunnan Province has been keenly involved in economic cooperation.

[13] In fiscal 2007, there were 917 public industrial enterprises, of which 'transport vehicle's was the largest (169; 18.4 %) followed by 'construction materials' (125; 13.6 %) and 'workshop and dockyard' (112; 12.2 %). In contrast, of the 43,763 private factories, 'food and beverage' was the largest (28,137; 62.3 %), followed by 'construction materials' (3,240; 7.4 %) and 'garment and apparel' (1,895; 4.3 %) (CSO 2009, *Selected monthly economic indicators*).

[14] The number of public industrial enterprises decreased to 639 in fiscal 2011.

Massive infrastructure development projects were carried out with Chinese assistance or as build-operate-transfer (BOT) projects by Chinese companies, specifically including: trunk roads from the border area of Yunnan to central Myanmar and water transportation on the Ayeyarwady River, such as the ports of Myitchina and Bhamo and dredging downstream of these ports. Also a rail transport corridor extension project between Kunming via Myanmar's border town of Muse and Kyaukphyu, a port city in western Rakhine State, was adapted to be jointly built by the China Railway Group Limited and the Myanmar Union Ministry of Rail Transportation.[15]

Because the Chinese inclination was to provide assistance in the context of economic benefits for China itself, infrastructure development assistance from China tended to favour geopolitically important areas and massive infrastructure. Thus, infrastructure development in cooperation with China tended to lack consideration for balancing national land development, and it was not expected that such infrastructure development would satisfy the needs of local community lives (Shimada 2008). Furthermore, civil society and academic observers expressed concerns about the impact of Chinese economic activity in Myanmar; examples are the impact on the environment and human rights (in terms of forced relocation and forced labour) of logging (e.g. Global Witness 2003) and of massive infrastructure development in border areas, such as the construction of dams and pipelines.

For ethnic communities in the border areas, such infrastructure developments in cooperation with China were threats to their societies. One example of this was the estimated 15,000 residents being displaced due to the construction of the Myitsone dam (KDNG 2009). A series of bombings also occurred in April 2010 at the project site, which was located in an area sacred to the Kachin people and it was suspected that some of those who were opposed to the construction were involved. As economic cooperation increased and political ties with China were tightened, it became more crucial for the military regime of Myanmar to maintain peace and stability on its side of the border; hence, it had to satisfy a diplomatic request to directly contribute to promote the interests of both countries. Simultaneously, the transformation of ethnic armed forces into the Border Guard Force (BGF)[16] after 2008 was crucial for Myanmar to achieve the transition to democracy in accordance with the state constitution.

4.3 Hydropower Plants

A number of power plants, mainly hydropower, were built to deal with a severe shortage of electricity under the military regime (Table 8.2). China was involved in almost all these projects, although the extent of China's involvements in some

[15] In April 2011, the China Railway Group Limited and the Myanmar Union Ministry of Rail Transportation signed an MOU to jointly build a rail line (*Xinhua*, 27 April, 2011).

[16] Prescribes that all the armed forces in the union shall be under the command of the Defense Services.

Table 8.2 Growth in hydroelectric power plants (From 1988 to 31 December 2010)

		As of the end of 2010		
Capacity	1988	In operation	Under construction	Total
Under 1 MW	70	3,225	n.a.	3,295
1–10 MW	2	16	3	19
10–500 MW	2	15	44	59
Over 500 MW	0	2	15	17
Total	74	3,258	62	3,320

Source: Ministry of Information, Myanmar (2011)

projects was unclear. Many huge hydropower projects (over 500 MW) with significant impacts on the electricity situation in Myanmar involved China (Table 8.3).

One reason for China's involvement in power plant construction in Myanmar was to ensure its own energy security by drawing off the bulk of the generated power. For example, Shweli I dam, completed in 2009, was China's first BOT hydropower plant project in a neighbouring country, and 85 % of its electricity was estimated to be allocated for export to China.[17] Similarly, most of the electricity from the series of hydropower plants in the upper stream of the Ayeyarwady River in Kachin State to be built by China Power Investment Corporation (CPI) at a total estimated cost of US$20 billion, including the Myitsone hydropower plant, was also to be allocated for export to China.

However, such electricity allocation for export to China stirred anti-Chinese sentiment. The Myitsone project drew not only local but also national criticism. In compliance with widespread public protest against the construction, President Thein Sein announced in a statement dated 29 September 2011 that the government of Myanmar would suspend its work at least until 2015.

4.4 *Mining Sector*

China's permitted FDI for the mining sector on a product sharing basis, such as copper, nickel, lead and zinc, amounted to US$1.8 billion, which accounted for 75 % of the overall total allowed FDI for this sector. Table 8.4 shows the major mining projects by Chinese companies

The largest mining project China cooperated in Myanmar was the Tagaung Taung nickel mine located in Thabeikkyin township in the Mandalay Region, having an estimated 700,000 tonnes of nickel resources. In July 2004, the China Nonferrous Metal Mining (Group) Co., Ltd. (CNMC), which is managed by the state-owned Assets Supervision and Administration Commission, signed an explo-

[17] Website of China Huaneng Group, the largest share folder of Yunnan united Resource & Engineering Co., Ltd. http://www.chng.com.cn/eng/n75871/n75965/n112742/index.html. Accessed 23 May 2010.

Table 8.3 Massive hydroelectric power plants (over 500 MW) with Chinese involvement

Region/state	Hydroelectric power plants/capacity	Particulars
Mandalay Region	Yeywa/790 MW	CITC, Sinohydro, CNEEC, CHMC. China provided a US$200 million concessional loan. Completed in February 2010
Shan State	Shweli (1)/600 MW	Yunnan United Power Development Co., Ltd. Through the JV/BOT project. Completed in May 2009; 85 % of the generated power is estimated to be allocated for export to China
	Shweli(2)/640 MW	Huaneng Lancang River Hydropower Co., Ltd. and Asia World Company Ltd. through the JV/BOT system; MOA was signed in November 2010
	Tasaung (Upper Thanlwin [Mongton])/7,100 MW	China Three Gorges Corporation; the MOU was signed in November 2010
	Upper Thanlwin Kunglon/1,400 MW	Farsighted Investment Group Co. Ltd. (Hanergy Group) and Gold Water Resources Ltd; the MOU was signed in April 2007
	Naung Pha/1,200 MW	China Hydropower Engineering Consulting Group (HydroChina). The agreement was signed in December 2010
Kachin State	Myitsone/6,000 MW	China Power Investment. Construction began in 2007 and was suspended in 2011
	Chibwe/2,800 MW	China Power Investment. Construction began in 2007
	Khanuglanpu/2,700 MW	
	Laiza/1,900 MW	
	Lakin/1,400 MW	
	Pashe/1,600 MW	
	Phizaw/2,000 MW	
Karen State	Hatgyi/1,360 MW	Sinohydro. MOU was signed in August 2008. Almost all generated power is allocated for export to Thailand
Kayar State	Ywathit/600 MW	China Datang Corporation. MOU signed in January 2010
Yakhaine State	Laymyo/600 MW	China Datang Corporation. MOA signed January 2011

Source: Ministry of Information, Myanmar (2011), *New Light of Myanmar, Myanmar Times, Xinhua* and other materials

Table 8.4 Major mining projects by Chinese companies

Date	Particulars
July 2004	The China Nonferrous Metal Mining Co. (CNMC) signed an agreement to conduct exploration of the Tagaung nickel deposit. China EXIM Bank and the China Development Bank provided funding for this US$80 million project
May 2005	Yunnan Machinery and Equipment Import and Export Company Limited (YMEC) was awarded the mining and operation rights to reclaim lead and zinc from the tailings at Namtu. YMEC invested US$5 million
August 2005	Kingbao (Jinbao) Mining Co. signed agreements to conduct exploration and feasibility studies to explore the Mwetaung nickel deposit
July 2008	The production-sharing contract was signed between the CNMC and the No. 3 Myanmar Mining Enterprise for production at the Tagaung nickel mine
June 2010	The Monywa Copper Mine Project Cooperation Contract was signed between China North Industries (NORINCO) and the Union of Myanmar Economic Holdings Limited (MEH), during Premier Wen Jiabao's visit to Myanmar
April 2011	A production-sharing contract for Sabetaung, Sabetaung South and Kyisintaung copper mine was signed between Wan Bao (a subsidiary of NORINCO) and the Union of Myanmar Economic Holdings

Source: *The New Light of Myanmar*, *Xinhua* and other materials

ration agreement and a feasibility agreement with No. 3 Mining Enterprise of Myanmar. The production sharing contract (PSC) of the project was signed in July 2008. According to the CNMC, total investment in the project exceeds US$800 million, with an estimated annual output of 85,000 tonnes of ferronickel after completion. This is also the largest project China has invested in with a neighbouring country. Taiyuan Iron and Steel (Group) Co., Ltd. (TISCO), the largest stainless steel manufacturer in China, joined the project in 2010, and operation commenced in March 2011 (*The New Light of Myanmar* (*NLM*) 30 March, 2011).

The largest copper project was the Monywa copper mine comprising the Sabeitaung, Kyayzintaung and Latpadaungtaung projects in the northwestern Sagaing Region. These projects were undertaken through a joint venture between the military-owned Myanmar Economic Holding Ltd. (MEH) and two Chinese firms, Wanbao Mining Ltd. and Yangtze Copper Ltd., subsidiaries of NORINCO (China North Industries Corporation).[18] It was scheduled to enter into operation in June 2013. However, in mid-2012, protests against the planned expansion of the Latpadaungtaung project occurred and the project was suspended. As a result, riot police using tear bombs and water cannons moved into the protest camps on November 29, 2012. The 'Investigation Commission' chaired by Aung San Suu Kyi was formed in accord with President Office's Order No. 95/2012, dated 1 December.

The report of the Investigation Commission, released in March 2013, supported the continuation of the project; however, it concluded that the compensation to local

[18] The total investment of $1.07 billion was approved by the Myanmar government in March 2010. The PSC was signed in April 2011 during the visit of Jia Qinglin, the Chairman of the 11th National Committee of the Chinese People's Political Consultative Conference, to Myanmar.

farmers was 'improper' and 'lacked transparency' and that the mine 'lacked environmental protection measures'. In responding, MEH, Wanbao and the government revised the contract and a new contract was approved in July 2013 which stipulated the profit sharing of the project as follows: the government, 51 %; Wanbao, 30 % and MEH, 19 %. Wanbao and MEH decreased 21 points and 26 points from their original profit shares of 51 % and 45 %, respectively. Although the new contract also stipulated that the project allocates $1 million for corporate social responsibility and $2 million for environmental preservation annually and that it increases the amount of compensation to local farmers, the protests did not cease soon. For instance, in November 2013, nine policemen and five protestors were injured in clashes between 150 protestors and police with antiriot shotguns and rubber bullets (*NLM,* 17 November 2013). This incident showed that some local villagers continued to feel that the project threatened their livelihoods.

4.5 Development of the Oil and Gas Sector

Soon after Myanmar and China agreed to encourage cooperation for the exploration and development of geological and mineral resources in 2001, the China National Petroleum Corporation (CNPC) acquired a stake in Myanmar oil and gas onshore blocks in November 2001. The involvement of Chinese companies such as the CNPC, the China Petroleum and Chemical Corporation (Sinopec), the China National Offshore Oil Co. (CNOOC) and the North Petrochemical Corporation Limited (NPCC) in onshore and offshore oil and national gas projects occurred notably after 2004 (Table 8.5).

Since some Western oil companies had withdrawn their investment in Myanmar after the USA banned new investment by US companies in 1997, Chinese involvement contributed to energy development in Myanmar and its presence in energy development gradually increased. One of the emblematic events of the two countries' bilateral relations was the signing of a PSC between the CNPC and Myanmar in January 2007. This came only 3 days after China vetoed a draft UN Security Council Resolution calling on Myanmar's government 'to cease military attacks against civilians in ethnic minority regions and begin a substantive political dialogue that would lead to a genuine democratic transition'. Myanmar might not have implemented its natural resource development without China's cooperation.

In 2008, the CNPC signed a 30-year hydrocarbon purchase and sale agreement for the Shwe gas fields, which are operated by a Shwe consortium, including Daewoo and Myanmar Oil and Gas Enterprise (MOGE). In 2009, an agreement was signed to build the Myanmar-China oil and gas pipeline from the coastal township of Kyaukphyu to the Yunnan province through the border town of Ruili, which planned to deliver gas from Shwe fields and oil from the Middle East and Africa to China. The gas pipeline, whose construction was completed in May 2013, started to deliver gas in late July 2013. However, it was not clear when the operation of the

Table 8.5 Development of oil and gas by Chinese companies

Date	Particulars
November 2001	The CNPC signed an agreement to acquire 70 % interest in three production-sharing contracts for onshore blocks (IOR-3, RFS-2 and 3)
December 2001	The CNPC entered into a 20-year contract of improving oil recovery on block IOR-4
September 2004	Sinopec signed an exploration contract for onshore block PSC-D
October 2004–January 2005	The CNOOC, Golden Aaron Pte., Ltd. (the present China Focus Development) and the China Huanqiu Contracting and Engineering Co. (HQCEC) signed a series of exploration and production-sharing contracts for three onshore blocks (PSC-C1, PSC-C2, PSC-M) and two offshore blocks (A-4, M-10)
January 2007	The CNPC signed exploration and production-sharing contracts for three promising offshore blocks (AD-1, AD-6, AD-8)
December 2008	The CNPC signed an agreement for the Shwe gas fields (A-1,3), which are operated by a Shwe consortium including Daewoo and MOGE, amounting to 6.5 tcf to China over 30 years
July 2010	The NPCC signed a contract for the shared exploration and production of inland oil and gas on onshore block PSC-F (Ngahlaingdwin area) on a joint-venture basis
April 2013	The CNPC signed a transfer contract, which divides co-equity with Sinopec, to jointly develop onshore block PSC-D

Source: *The New Light of Myanmar*, *Xinhua* and other materials

parallel crude oil pipeline would begin, because the construction of an oil refinery was delayed in China (*Myanmar Times*, 17 November 2013), while the construction on the Myanmar side was almost complete as of the end of 2013.

The pipelines were expected to produce revenue through transit fees and royalties for Myanmar. Additionally, expanding exports of natural resources and energy to China would reduce Myanmar's trade deficit with China. For China, being involved in the oil and gas sector in Myanmar enabled it to meet its increasing domestic demand for energy.[19] China succeeded in building this energy artery because of its strengthened relationship with Myanmar.

Since the USA and the EU moved to ease economic sanctions, many of the larger US and European energy companies, which had previously been prevented from pursuing opportunities, were enabled to compete for projects in the resource-rich country.[20] The international tender for 18 onshore blocks by the Ministry of Energy

[19] CNPC President Jiang Jiemin said that this pipeline project would establish a new land route for the supply of oil and national gas and would diversify China's energy imports and stressed that this project would also add to energy security and contribute to the Great Western Development Strategy (*Xinhua Yunnan*, 10 September 2010).

[20] The USA suspended sanctions barring US investment in Myanmar in response to political reforms on 17 May 2013.

in January 2011,[21] followed by many tenders for a number of onshore and offshore blocks, gave momentum for the development of oil and gas.

However, the Myanmar economy, in which natural gas accounted for 28.5 % of exports in 2010 (CSO 2011, *Selected monthly economic indicators*), will become further dependent on natural resources. This may cause the 'Dutch disease' of negative impacts on export-oriented, labour-intensive manufacturing industries or the 'resource curse', whereby rich endowments of natural resources can introduce serious distortions to an economy, potentially resulting in sluggish further economic and political reforms and broad-based economic development for Myanmar.

4.6 Special Economic Zones

Special economic zone (SEZ) projects involving collaboration between China and Myanmar can be traced back to 'Notes on the Master Plan for Thanlyin-Kyauktan Industrial Zone', which was signed between the two countries during Prime Minister Khin Nyunt's visit to China in July 2004 (*NLM*, 26 July, 2004). At the time, this project was planned to be the largest industrial zone in Myanmar, aiming to attract investment mainly from China, and was to be completed in 2006 (*Myanmar Times*, 9–15 August 2004). Corresponding to the intentions of Khin Nyunt, the government of China assigned Shanghai's Pudong District for this project. The master plan for the Thilawa[22] Special Industrial Zone was formally handed over to Myanmar in December 2005. Since then, Myanmar has sat down to draft the Special Economic Zone Law, upon China's recommendation, for this project. Succeeding Prime Minister Soe Win visited China four times in 2006 to discuss the enactment of the SEZ law and the Thilawa project, as well as inspect Chinese export processing zones (EPZs).[23]

The establishment of the industrial zone, which had been agreed upon in 2004, seemed to be acceptable to the SPDC for two reasons. First, in China, EPZs took the lead in reforms and played an important role in the country's transition from a socialist planned economy to a (socialist) market economy by serving as a pilot projects for absorbing FDI. Second, their establishment and operation were carried

[21] Nine blocks were awarded for seven companies out of 18 set for the bidding (MOE Website, http://www.energy.gov.mm/index.php/en/about-moe/menu-moge, accessed on 10 December, 2013).

[22] Thilawa is located about 25 km south of Yangon along the Yangon River in Thanlyin and Kyauktan townships.

[23] Soe Win paid an official visit in February and Chinese Premier Wen Jiabao pledged to provide continued assistance to the Thilawa project (*NLM*, 21 February, 2006). Soe Win also visited the Shenzhen EPZ and inquired about the provisions of the SEZ law and the management system for the zone and expressed the view that the Thilawa project and the enactment of the SEZ law were significant for the two nations' relations (Jin 2006). In November 2006, Soe Win also inspected the Wuhan Economic and Technological Development Zone in the Hubei Province and discussed the establishment of special economic development zones with China (*NLM*, 6 November, 2006).

out under the strong leadership of the government. Shanghai's Pudong government, which was involved in Thilawa's master plan, mentioned that strong and speedy development under the leadership of the government was an appropriate model for an economic strategy to be applied to developing countries like Myanmar.[24] On the other hand, China was involved in the project with the aim of combining assistance for Myanmar by attracting FDI and promoting China's ODI itself. China's Ministry of Commerce requested that the Shanghai Pudong District design the Thilawa SEZ to set up favourable investment circumstances for Chinese companies (Jin 2006).

However, the Thilawa project was not implemented with Chinese assistance. The reason that the project stagnated was unclear but could be partly explained as follows: in the late 2000s, the SPDC did not attach much importance to promoting or attracting FDI. At the same time, China also gradually put more priority on hydropower plants, natural resources and the energy sector, instead of establishing industrial zones aiming to promote export-oriented manufacturing.

The SEZ Law was enacted on January 2011, 3 months before the new government came into being. The new government of Myanmar announced that it would develop Thilawa through the SEZ Law and invited local and foreign investment in the project in December 2011. Myanmar signed a memorandum for an overall project for the development of Thilawa as a joint operation with Japan during Thein Sein's visit to Japan in April 2012. The infrastructure development project in Thilawa was started in November 2013, using a 20 billion yen low-interest, long-term loan from Japan's ODA.[25] Consequently, most SEZ activity in Myanmar was centred on Thilawa which was supposed to be one-third completed by 2015.

In the meantime, China's involvement is mainly centred in Kyaukphyu, where a deep seaport and an oil port import terminal were constructed and operated by China; the Myanmar-China oil and gas pipelines is starting; and the railway will link with China's Yunnan. Kyaukphyu is a strategically important area for logistics, energy and security for China. The China International Trust and Investment Corporation (CITIC), which is a Chinese state-owned investment company, and Myanmar's Ministry of National Planning and Economic Development signed a supplementary contract under an MOU on the Kyaukphyu Economic and Technological Development Zone and related port and railroad development projects in February 2011 (*Xinhua*, 16 February, 2011). However, the project was dropped because the supplementary 6 months of the MOU had expired.[26] The Kyaukphyu SEZ Bid Evaluation and Awarding Committee (BEAC) which was formed on August 17, 2013, with a membership consisting of deputy union ministers, high-ranking ministry officials and other experts, invited expressions of interest from domestic and international firms

[24] Author's interview with Mr. Xianjun Tao, Chief of the Economic and Trade Bureau of Shanghai, Pudong New Area Industry and Trade Department, on 22 November 2007.

[25] Press Releases 'Signing of Exchange of Notes concerning Yen Loan to Myanmar' issued May 26, 2013 by the MOFA, Japan.

[26] The BEAC website http://kpsez.org/en/about-us-2/, accessed on 23 December, 2013.

for the services to develop a comprehensive strategy for promoting the Kyaukphyu SEZ in September 2013[27] (*NLM*, September 8, 2013).

Although China seemed to have gradually lost its initial enthusiasm for the SEZ, especially with target for promoting manufacturing industry since the late 2000s, Chinese involvement with the SEZ projects in Myanmar was worthy of note because it could be regarded as assistance for reform and opening-up in Myanmar, of which SEZ projects are symbolic.

5 Economic Relations with Neighbouring Countries in the Era of the Military Junta, Counterbalancing China

The tightening of relations between Myanmar and China resulted in neighbouring countries taking steps towards closer relations with Myanmar in order to counterbalance Myanmar's dependence on China and to secure their influence because of its geopolitical importance. Relations with China and other neighbours were significant for the Myanmar junta, facing international isolation. In addition, improving relations with other neighbouring countries reduced the risk of the Myanmar junta having excessive dependence on China. For instance, the admission of Myanmar to ASEAN was opposed by the USA and Europe; however, Myanmar formally became a member of ASEAN in 1997. Its successful entry to ASEAN served a dual purpose: improving the country's international image, so as to legitimise military rule in the face of international isolation, and counterbalancing China's influence in the region, both in Myanmar and ASEAN (Gao 2007).

The expansion of Chinese influence in Myanmar was of particular concern to India, as it gave China the potential to deploy its sea power in the Bay of Bengal. India has endeavoured to expand its influence in Myanmar in order to moderate China's control and to protect its national interests and also those of Myanmar's. Although the Indian government had signalled its commitment to pro-democracy groups from when the SLORC came into power until 1993, India reviewed its policy towards Myanmar to achieve its strategic objectives (Thant Myint 2011: 268–270). Border trade between India and Myanmar was opened in 1995, and India invited Myanmar to join the Bay of Bengal Initiative for Multi-Sectoral Technical and Economic Cooperation (BIMSTEC) in 1997 (Gurmeet 2010). Relations were cemented through a series of high-level visits, which took place on both sides starting in 2000, beginning with the visit of Senior General Maung Aye, Vice-Chairman of the SPDC, in January and November 2000 and another visit in 2008. Chairman Than Shwe paid state visits to India in 2004, 2008, and 2010. From the Indian side, President Dr. A.P.J. Abdul Kalam paid a state visit in March 2006, which was the first visit by an Indian head of state to Myanmar since Prime Minister Rajiv Gandhi's

[27] A total of 31, including 5 Chinese firms, submitted their EOIs by September 25. The BEAC has screened their detailed proposals, submitted up to 19 November 2013, and will announce the winner.

visit in 1987. After the swearing-in of the new government, President Thein Sein, accompanied by ten ministers, including the Minister for Border Affairs and Myanmar Industrial Development, the Minister for Foreign Affairs and the Minister for Agriculture and Irrigation and other senior officials, visited India in their first state visit in October 2011.

Along with these high-level visits, India has increasingly provided development aid to Myanmar since 2000 (Yhome 2009). India provided lines of credit amounting to nearly US$300 million by 2011 for the development of sectors such as railways, transport, power transmission lines and oil refineries. During Thein Sein's visit in 2011, the Indian side announced the extension of a new concessional facility of a US$500 million line of credit to Myanmar. The two sides reiterated their commitment to cooperate in the implementation of hydropower plants in the Chindwin River basin and also agreed to enhance bilateral cooperation in the oil and natural gas sector (*NLM*, 16 October, 2011).

The Kaladan Multi-Modal Transit Transport Project was a significant infrastructure development project which was signed in April 2008 and began in 2009 and which includes the reconstruction of Sittwe port and the dredging of the Kaladan River from Sittwe to Setpyipyin in Chin State. It also includes the construction of roads from Setpyipyin to India's border state, Mizoram. The estimated total investment granted by India is US$117.38 million (memo issued by the Myanmar Port Authority in January 2011). India is also providing grant assistance and is supporting road construction, namely, the Moreh-Mae Sot Road, which would connect India and Thailand via Myanmar, and the Ledo Road, from Ledo, India, to Muse, Myanmar (*NLM*, 16 October 2011). Moreover, India provided assistance for transportation development in Myanmar, connecting inland areas for the purpose of developing them, in the same way as China.

Similar features were also seen in hydropower projects in which India was involved, such as the Thahthay Chaung hydropower project (111 MW) in Rakhine State, for the construction of which India's EXIM bank signed a US$60 million line of credit with the MFTB in 2007, and two massive hydropower plants in the Chindwin River basin in Sakaing State. The latter were the Shwezaye hydropower project (880 MW), which was to be constructed by the National Hydroelectric Power Corporation, an Indian state-owned company, and Thamanti hydropower project (1,200 MW), from which some 80 % of the electricity generated was planned to be allocated to Manipur State in India. The government of India was working on a power import policy that aims to broaden the base of the country's energy security by securing hydropower resources in neighbouring countries, including Myanmar, and by drawing off the generated power to India in the late 2000s (Yhome 2009). India as well as China provided strategic assistance towards this geopolitically important country. Hence, the priorities of their assistance projects tended to be allocated to meet their own interests.

6 Some Issues Concerning Economic Relations Between China and Myanmar in the Post-military Period

Thein Sein's decision to suspend the construction of the Myitsone dam in September 2011 was welcomed and greeted with great surprise by Myanmar's people, not only because the decision was in compliance with public protest but also because the project was being conducted as a joint project with China, Myanmar's most important partner. On 10 October 2011, Foreign Minister Wunna Maung Lwin visited China as a special envoy of President Thein Sein and talked with Chinese Foreign Minister Yang Jiechi and Vice-President Xi Jinping. Both sides agreed to settle matters related to the suspended project and pledged to further enrich the comprehensive and strategic partnership between the two nations (*Xinhua*, 10 October, 2011). However, the decision to suspend the Myitsone dam project was often read as a sign that the new government of Myanmar was reconsidering its close relation with China. Interestingly, from mid-2011 onwards, Myanmar's relations with developed countries and multinational organisations improved.

Alongside political and economic reforms launched by the new government of Myanmar, public opinion started to gain influence in the political arena and Myanmar's benefits from the economic cooperation began to be evaluated more carefully. As improving relations with the developed world enabled Myanmar to broaden and improve its external economic relations, Myanmar's economic dependence on China is likely to be affected and mitigated by this development, though not very soon. The economic relations between the two countries appeared in a new light.

6.1 *Public Opinion Towards the Economic Relations with China*

China's strategic economic support for Myanmar became a cause of anti-Chinese sentiment among Myanmar people having misgivings that China's support for Myanmar intended to preserve the military regime and to gain strategic access to the Indian Ocean, while exploiting the country's natural resources. In addition, the widespread belief that corruption was rampant during the negotiation and implementation of the economic projects between China, the military regime and its cronies also became a cause of anti-Chinese sentiment along with anti-military sentiment. The military regime had brutally ignored public opinion by suppressing them for years. From China's perspective, public opinion in Myanmar did not constitute a critical challenge to China's interest as long as the regime backed Chinese projects (Sun 2012).

However, the suspension of the Myitsone hydropower dam project and the Latpadaungtaung copper mining project showed that public opinion became a determining factor in Myanmar economic politics. Alongside political and economic reforms launched by Thein Sein's administration, public opinion gained weight in the political arena and Myanmar's benefits from such projects began to be evaluated more carefully. The two hydropower projects in the Chindwin River basin, which involved India, also suspended any further action by an agreement between the two countries in July 2013, having taken into consideration questions raised with regard to the economic viability of the projects.[28] To prevent crippling its influence by losing in a 2015 general election, Thein Sein's administration seemed to recognise that it had to show the fruits of the political and economic reforms and adopt pro-democratic ideas and populism. For China, domestic politics and public sentiment seemed to cause uncertainties for their projects in Myanmar (Sun 2013). To implement these projects, it is crucial to improve relations with local communities and to contribute to Myanmar's broad-based economic development, benefitting a large portion of the population.

6.2 *Improving Myanmar's Relationship with the International Community*

Myanmar's junta considered that Western countries were interested in a regime change in Myanmar not simply for human rights concerns but perhaps more importantly because Myanmar was the weakest link in their 'containment' policy towards China and that the West, notably the USA, was attempting to turn Myanmar into their satellite state (Hla Min 2004: 88–89). Myanmar's junta mitigated its fear against the 'regime change' policy of the USA to a certain extent by maintaining close relations with China and, to a lesser degree, India and ASEAN (Steinberg and Fan 2012: 312).

In response to political reforms in Myanmar after 2011, developed countries took steps to improve relations with Myanmar. The USA and EU eased their sanctions on Myanmar; in addition, a large amount of bilateral and multinational ODA began to be provided to the least-developed country. Improving relations with the international community enabled Myanmar to broaden its external economic relations. It could bring significant changes in its economic relations with China and mitigate the excessive dependence on China.

The Obama administration rejected the idea that the USA outreach to Myanmar was partially motivated by the growing influence of China, as Hillary Rodham Clinton, the first US Secretary of State to visit Myanmar in 56 years, said on 1 December 2011: 'We welcome positive constructive relations between China and her neighbors. We think that it is in China's interest as well as in the neighbourhood's interest'.[29] On the Chinese side, regarding Clinton's visit to Myanmar, Foreign Ministry Spokesman Hong Lei declared that China is attempting to improve its relations with Western countries and that China insisted that relevant countries should lift sanctions on Myanmar and promote Myanmar's stability and development.

[28] *The New Indian Express*, 6th June 2013.

[29] Press Availability in Nay Pyi Taw, Burma, 1 December 2011, issued by the US Department of State.

As these diplomatic turns of phrase implied, in spite of some residual Cold War attitude, if a prosperous and stable Myanmar was in China's interests, improved relations between Myanmar and the USA, without being too close, would be supportive of, and quite appropriate for, China's position in Myanmar (Steinberg and Fan 2012: 358–359). Myanmar's improved relations with the international community did not necessarily negatively impact its relationship with China but introduced new issues for economic relations between Myanmar and China. For instance, economic assistance from China, which is not a member of donor community organisations such as the Development Assistance Committee, raised the following questions: how to coordinate with other donors in order to contribute to further reforms and economic development in Myanmar; what if each of the bilateral donors provided aid to Myanmar as a political or commercial tool as a competition among donors? As a matter of course, the competitive attitude of donors could lead to an impairment of the needs- and merit-based allocation of aid within the recipient country and its effectiveness.

7 Concluding Remarks

Along with close relations with China under the military regime, Myanmar eventually came to depend on vertical trade with China as its trade deficit increased. China's economic cooperation, with the strategic aim of meeting its own interests, was provided mainly to develop massive infrastructure near China's border in the hydropower, energy and mining sectors. Such assistance had supported the stability of the Myanmar junta but made little contribution to Myanmar's broad-based growth and industrial development and even resulted in hindering the country's reforms and in causing anti-Chinese sentiment.

As its improving relations with the international community enabled Myanmar to broaden and balance its external relations, the developed world began to provide a large amount of ODA to the least-developed country. Consequently, China's significant economic presence in the country seemed to be mitigating; however, the basic fact remained that China was its biggest economic partner with respect to sectors such as trade, economic cooperation and FDI.

It is feared that reduced economic ties with China, a big-power neighbour, will hinder Myanmar's economy and jeopardise bilateral relations. The country's economic development and stability are also in China's interests. It thus seems to be crucial for both Myanmar and China to maintain and to adjust their existing economic relations to further economic and political reforms in Myanmar in order to contribute to long-term economic development. However, if its assistance strategy remains unchanged, economic assistance provided by China as well as other neighbouring countries might fail to have a substantial impact on these reforms and development.

As China succeeded in industrialisation, using its open-door policy to achieve long-term economic growth, similar reforms are essential for Myanmar. It is also crucial for China to improve relations with local communities in Myanmar and to secure broad-based economic growth, since public opinion has gained weight in the political arena and Myanmar's benefits from economic cooperation are being evaluated more carefully. In addition, along with increased bilateral ODA flow on the part of developed countries to Myanmar, the economic assistance offered by China, which is not a member of the traditional donor community but rather an emerging donor, poses another issue: how to coordinate between China and other donors, despite residual Cold War attitudes, in order to promote economic development and contribute to the welfare of the people.

References

Aung-Thwin, M., & Aung-Thwin, M. (2012). *A history of Myanmar since ancient times: Traditions and transformations*. London: Reaktion.

Central Statistical Organization (CSO). (1995–2012). *Statistical yearbook*. Yangon/Nay Pyi Taw: CSO.

Central Statistical Organization (CSO). (2010–2014). *Selected monthly economic indicators*. Nay Pyi Taw: CSO.

Gao, X. (2007). *Towards resolution: China in the Myanmar issue.' silk road paper*. Washington, DC: Central Asia-Caucasus Institute and Silk Road Studies Program.

Global Witness. (2003). *A conflict of interests—The uncertain future of Burma's forests*. London: Global Witness.

Gurmeet, K. (2010). A strategic perspective on India-Myanmar relations. In L. Rieffel (Ed.), *Myanmar/Burma: Inside challenges, outside interests* (pp. 134–149). Washington, DC: Brookings Institution Press/The Konrad Adenauer Foundation.

Hla Min. (2004). *Political situation of the union of Myanmar and its role in the region*. Yangon: Department of International Affairs & Research, Ministry of Defence.

International Monetary Fund (IMF). *Direction of trade statistics*. http://elibrary-data.imf.org/QueryBuilder.aspx?key=19784661&s=322. Accessed June 2014.

Jin, Y. (2004). Sengo Chugoku Gaiko to Taigai enjo [China's Foreign Policy and Foreign Aid], Japan Center for International Finance, *Chugoku Sintaiseika niokeru Shomondai-Taichu Sien no Arikata nitsuite* [Problems regarding assistance for China under the new leadership] (pp. 115–131) (in Japanese).

Jin, S. (2006). *'zouchuqu' jianshe jingwai jiagongjidi – chengjie <zhongguo yuan miandian kaifaqu>koshi* ['Go Abroad' Construction of Overseas Processing Zones < China's Assistance to Myanmar for Planning of Development Zones> Report] shanghai: Shanghai Municipal Government (in Chinese).

Kachin Development Network Group (KDNG). (2009). *Resisting the flood resisting the flood*. Kachin Development Network Group. http://www.kdng.org/images/stories/publication/ResistingtheFlood_english.pdf. Accessed 23 May 2010.

Kobayashi, T. (2007). Chugoku no Enjo Seisaku- Taigai Enjo Kaikaku no Tenkai [China's foreign aid policy – Reforms of foreign aid mechanism]. *Journal of JBIC Institute, 35*, 109–147. (in Japanese).

Kudo, T. (2006). *Myanmar's economic relations with China: Can China support the Myanmar economy?* (Discussion Paper No. 66). Chiba: IDE-JRTRO.

Lin, T.-C. (1996). Beijing's foreign aid policy in the 1990s: Continuity and change. *Issues & Studies: A Journal of Chinese Studies and International Affairs, 32*(1), 32–56.

Ma, C. (2007). Henbou suru Chugoku no Taigai Enjo [Changing of China's foreign aid]. *Chinese Economy, 498*, 56–85. (in Japanese).

Matsumoto, S. (1975). *Chugoku no Tai Ajia Keizai Seisaku* [China's Economic Policy toward Asia]. Tokyo: Institute of Developing Economics (in Japanese).

Ministry of Commerce and Ministry of Foreign Affairs, China. (2004). *'duiwaitouziguobie changye daoxiang mulv* [Guide Catalogue of Countries and Industries for Investment Abroad]. Beijing: Ministry of Commerce and Ministry of Foreign Affairs. (in Chinese).

Ministry of Foreign Affairs, Myanmar. (1991). *thamain:asinalakyai:ma:tho tayou-myanma khyi'kyiyei:khayi* [The Historic China–Myanmar Goodwill Visit]. Yangon: Ministry of Foreign Affairs (in Myanmar).

Ministry of Information, Myanmar. (2011). *tamato aso:ya le'hte' nainganto hpwanhpyu:to:te'hmu hma'tan* [The State Development by the Tamadaw (Army) Government] (2010) (1988-31.12.2010)]. Nay Pyi Taw: Printing and Publishing Enterprise, Ministry of Information. (in Myanmar).

Ministry of National Planning and Finance, Burma. (1987). *1987–88 khuhni' atwe' pyi:thaunsu shohyali'thanmahta myanmanainganhto yi bandayaye:| si:pwaye:| luhmuye : ahkyeanemya: tinpyakye* [Report to the Pyithu Hluttaw, financial, economic and social conditions of the Socialist Republic of the Union of Burma, fiscal 1987–88]. Yangon: Ministry of National Planning and Finance (in Myanmar).

Ministry of National Planning and Finance, Myanmar. (1990). *pyi:thaunsu myanmanainganhto yi bandayaye:| si:pwaye:| luhmuye : ahkyeanemya: tinpyakye 1990–91khuhni'* [Financial, economic and social conditions of the Union of Myanmar, fiscal year 1990–91]. Yangon: Ministry of National Planning and Finance (in Myanmar).

Mizuno, A. (2008). Taigai Keizaienjo no Kakudai to Kadai [Expansion of Chinese Foreign Economic Assistance]". In S. Nobuaki (Ed.), *Chugoku no Kaikaku Kaihouo 30 nen no Meian* [Bright and dark sides of thirty years of Chinese reforms and openness] (pp. 72–83). Kyoto: Sekaishisosha. (in Japanese).

Myanmar Chinese Chamber of Commerce (MCCOC). (2009). *shiji huadam jinian tekan yijiulingjiu-erlinglingjiu* [The 100th Anniversary Commemorative Book 1909–2009]. Beijing: China Statistics Press (in Chinese).

National Bureau of Statistics of China. (2010). *zhongguo tongji nianjian* [China Statistical Yearbook]. Beijing: China Statistics Press (in Chinese and English).

Shimada, H. (2008). Infura no Genjyo to Myanmar Seifu no Taiou – Doro to Denryoku wo Taisho toshite [Present status Quo of infrastructure and response of the Government of Myanmar – Road and electricity]. In K. Toshihiro (Ed.), *Myanmar Keizai no Jitsuzo – Naze Gunsei ha Ikinokotta noka* [Real image of Myanmar economy: How did the military regime survive?] (pp. 97–87). Chiba: IDE-JETRO. (in Japanese).

State Council, China. (2011). *White paper on China's foreign aid*. Beijing: Information Office of the State Council.

Steinberg, D. L., & Fan, H. (2012). *Modern China-Myanmar relations: Dilemmas of mutual dependence*. Copenhagen: NIAS press.

Sun, Y. (2012). China's strategic misjudgement on Myanmar. *Journal of Current Southeast Asian Affairs, 1*(2012), 73–76.

Sun, Y.(2013). Chinese investment in Myanmar: What lies ahead? *Great powers and the Changing Myanmar* (Issue Brief 1). Stimson Center. http://www.stimson.org/images/uploads/Yun_Issue_Brief1.pdf. Accessed 13 May 2014.

Tamachi, N. (2005). *Chugoku no Taigai Enjo no Rekisiteki Kousatsu (jo, ge)* [Historical review of China's foreign aid (I, II)]. *Sekai Shuhou (World Affairs Weekly), 86*(9):26–31, *86*(10):30–34. (in Japanese).

Thant Myint, U. (2011). *Where China meets India: Burma and the new crossroads of Asia*. London: Faber and Faber.

United Nations (UN). UN Comtrade: United Nations Commodity Trade Statistics Database. http://comtrade.un.org/db/default.aspx. Accessed 13 May 2014.

World Bank (WB). World Data Bank World Development Indicators. http://databank.worldbank.org/data/views/variableSelection/selectvariables.aspx?source=world-development-indicators. Accessed 13 May 2014.

Yhome, K. (2009). *India-Myanmar relations (1998–2008)* (ORF Occasional Paper No.10). New Delhi: Observer Research Foundation.

Chapter 9
Summary and Conclusion: Capitalistic Development a là Myanmar

Konosuke Odaka

1 Introduction

A new light has emerged in the Myanmar economy. Whether or not the economy will succeed in taking off into sustained growth depends, in part, on how the economy's past legacies are either reformed or adapted to the new environment. It will also be determined by the nature and the content of a new road map for development that will be drawn and executed with support from both inside and outside of the country.

Myanmar commands a unique geophysical location that could act as an ideal hub for trade interactions in that part of Southeast Asia, which includes the areas northeast of India, southeast of China, northwest of Thailand and so on. The people of Myanmar – characteristically warm hearted, enduring, properly educated and industrious – are in a good position to achieve and benefit from the fruits of modern economic growth (MEG).

However, from the gaining of independence in 1948 up until the early twenty-first century, the nation was placed in a situation where it was unable to realise MEG. Particularly in the period since the middle of the 1960s, Myanmar (then called Burma) has isolated itself from international transactions under the 'Burmese Way to Socialism'. The seclusion continued under the post-1988 command-type military regimes, which were faced with international economic sanctions from the mid-1990s until the early 2010s.

In contrast, if Myanmar ever succeeds in taking advantage of the favourable conditions for economic growth that it possesses and receiving the positive outcomes of that growth, not only will its own citizens benefit from the improved

K. Odaka (✉)
Institute of Economic Research, Hitotsubashi University, Tokyo, Japan

Hosei University, Tokyo, Japan
e-mail: k-odaka@ier.hit-u.ac.jp

K. Odaka (ed.), *The Myanmar Economy*, DOI 10.1007/978-4-431-55735-7_9

standard of living but the neighbouring nations, and eventually the international community at large will gain improved socioeconomic welfare.

In order for Myanmar to make the abovementioned situation feasible, it is necessary for the nation to realise long-term market development while maintaining democratically ruled political stability. Myanmar first needs to lessen its excessive transaction costs – a basic impediment for modern economic growth – by renovating and/or establishing infrastructure.[1] At the same time, it must realise as many economic returns as possible by utilising its rich natural resources, followed in succession by environmentally friendly industrialisation.

With this high expectation in mind, the paragraphs below will summarise the major issues presented in the present volume, followed by a brief concluding comment.

2 Legacies of Burmese Economic History

A fundamental aim of the British colonial policy on Burma (now called Myanmar) was to make it function as an Asian rice supply centre for the British Empire. In exercising this policy intention, the British government took advantage of inter-tribe competition, skilfully utilising a 'divide and rule' principle. However, it seems that the well-organised, rational manner of the colonial ruling imbedded deeply rooted antiforeign sentiment in the minds of the seemingly obedient subordinates.

Anticolonial feeling, bound with liberal ideology such as Fabian socialism introduced from the West, prepared a long, latent way for Burmese socialism, which was adopted after the independence. Its policy stance, however, came to be characterised as grossly inward-looking.

In 1990, the Burmese National Army opted to ignore the voice of the populace that had clearly been expressed through the national election result. It did so on the basis of a strong desire to maintain national unity in the face of frequent civil strife among and against small ethnic groups, especially in the national border areas. It was only when the domestic civil strife came to be more or less stabilised that the army-controlled government revised its policy stance. In 2008, the government drew up a new constitution and established a parliamentary democracy, having finally held the long-promised, and by then overdue, general election. Beginning in 2012, the international economic sanctions were gradually lifted and the country finally came to the starting point for industrialisation.

[1] Infrastructure (or social overhead capital) is used here in a very wide sense. Public facilities, for example, can encompass things such as transportation and communication facilities, while institutional devices include legal and bank deposit insurance systems.

3 Old but Fresh Ideas for Promoting Economic Development

Under the British colonial rule of the early twentieth century, the Burma Delta successfully developed itself into a fertile, rice-cultivating area, which quickly became the major rice-exporting area of the world. A significant portion of its economic gains fell into the hands of rice merchants engaged in milling and trading in both the domestic and foreign markets. Most of these merchants were of British, Chinese or Indian origins. Additionally, the land, owned and cultivated by Burmese farmers, was used as collateral for the funds they needed to acquire in order to continue their production. Particularly after the Great Depression of 1929, the land was gradually accumulated by large landowners, leaving the majority of the cultivators in a poverty-stricken state.

This historical legacy became the core of the inward-looking ideology that constituted the post-independence economic policy of the then Burmese government, particularly during the period of the 'Burmese Way to Socialism'.

Professor Hla Myint, while recognising the circumstances that brought about the birth of the ideology, warned against it. The ideology would, in his opinion, deprive the country of the widely open opportunity to engage in foreign trade, which would help the country move successfully into economic prosperity. Instead, he highly recommended that the economic strategy should promote market development by encouraging agrarian growth and the exportation of its produce, which would act as a 'vent' for the surplus economic resources of the nation (in particular, labour). This would eventually lead to the accumulation of national wealth and an improved standard of living for the nation. Hla Myint argued, in addition, that institutional innovation would be essential for market development to proceed successfully.

Professor Hla Myint's major academic papers were written in the days when he was deeply involved in the early phase of Burmese economic policy-making. However, the actual process of events moved in a direction completely opposite to that which he would have approved of. At the time, Hla Myint forecast that the inward-looking strategy would end up in the bureaucratically controlled, misery-stricken failure of the economic policy.

In designing and implementing the basic road map for economic policy for present-day Myanmar, it is still worth giving serious attention to the early economic policy recommendations made by Professor Hla Myint.

4 Macroeconomic and Monetary Policies

Myanmar's macroeconomic performance up to the early 2000s lacked clear-cut consistency, which most probably suggests that the government had not prepared a solid, long-term macro-development plan. Short-term needs were quickly met with clear effects, for example, allowing foreign cash inflows to provide funds for highly demanded construction projects. However, fundamental structural renovation, such as restructuring the multiple foreign exchange regime, was left untouched.

On the other hand, the country's monetary policy was far from independent of the government's financial policy. The central government's financial deficits were often met by an increase in the high-powered money supply, leading to price hikes and negative real interest rates. In contrast, the financial development of the country remained being unfulfilled. During the final decades of the twentieth century, for instance, private commercial banks, which were under strict government regulatory controls, such as fixed interest rates, were afforded few appropriate investment opportunities due to the slow pace of the industrialisation process. In turn, the banks were often attracted by high-risk, bubble-causing operations, which eventually led to a bank run in 2003.

Despite the gloomy prospects of the macroeconomic and monetary conditions, frequently voiced predictions by overseas economists of a deadlock of the Myanmar economy were luckily avoided. This was largely due to the increased foreign exchange earnings resulting from the government's exportation of natural gas from around 2004, which took pressure off of its budget. Newly arisen after the bank run has been a fresh prospect for the growth of healthy commercial banking, which will perform its highly essential role of acting as financial intermediary. As of 2013, however, many tasks still remained which called for further restructuring of the economy. The Government of Myanmar's road map for medium- and long-term macroeconomic development needs to be kept continuously under the watchful eye of the wider public.

5 Foreign Exchange Rate Regime

For many years after 1974, Myanmar was under the multiple foreign exchange rate regime, whereby the official exchange rate was kept at a fixed rate (6 kyat to a US dollar). The use of the official rate was reserved for official needs such as the importation of intermediate and material goods for the operation of state-owned enterprises (SOEs). Up until around 2002, the international balance of payments was often in the red. When foreign exchange was in scarce supply, it was often rationed by the government and released to the public by special permission. Foreign exchange dealing was somewhat liberalised in 1988, and its unofficial market rate since then depreciated to as low as 1,400 kyat to a US dollar in 2001. In protest against the ruling government's refusal to honour the results of the national election of 1998, Western countries have since then laid economic sanctions against Myanmar. As a result of these sanctions, the country suffered a great loss in its export market, resulting in the accumulating deficits in its balance of payments.

The country's balance of current trade has however taken a favourable turn, in large part due to the exportation of natural gas initiated by the government with the financial cooperation of foreign corporations. This led to the nominal appreciation of the kyat against the US dollar.[2] However, the resulting new foreign exchange earnings had little effect on general price levels, as the earnings went mostly into the government account without increasing the money supply.

In 2012, the multiple exchange system was at long last unified into a single-rate regime. This was all the more welcome as the country was now moving quickly into international economic transactions. However, in the event that the current trade surplus becomes dominated by the sales of natural gas, plentiful inflows of foreign currencies may lead to excessive appreciation of the kyat – an unfavourable situation for exportation. The government is well advised to exercise careful policy handling so as to avoid the so-called Dutch disease.

6 Social Overhead Capital (SOC)

The shortage and/or lack of appropriate social overhead capital, both hard and soft in nature, is the most immediate barrier to the industrialisation of any economy. The supply of a sustainable source of energy (gas and electricity), transportation and communication devices, water and sewerage disposal systems is the first and foremost requirement for modern economic growth (MEG). In addition, the proper setting and operation of social institutions, such as a legal system, and good quality basic and higher education, is quite essential.

Physical social overhead capital was clearly undersupplied in twentieth century Myanmar. Among other problems, the disruption of electricity supply was a daily occurrence; the railroad system needed renewal and more frequent and systematic maintenance; and the sewerage systems were inadequate. An obvious reason for this undesirable state was the shortage of public funds. Whereas effort had been earnestly made, with moderate success, to fill the shortage of social overhead capital by mobilising private as well as foreign funds, it was clear that additional measures (such as a new principle of service charge) were called for.

7 Agrarian Development

Rural development is a prerequisite for successful industrialisation. However, after its independence, agriculture in Myanmar has long been kept underdeveloped due to the quantity-oriented, rice-first policy ('rice trauma') of the ruling regime. This policy was composed of (1) a compulsory production quota and (2) overly low output prices determined by the government. The rice policy, in part a legacy of the planned economy ideology, was rooted in a strong conviction that the maintenance of the minimum living standard was absolutely essential to suppressing the nation's

[2] The kyat exchange rate in real terms (viz nominal exchange rate divided by consumer price index or CPI) showed a clear downward trend since its peak of 2000.

spirit of insubordination. The policy, however, deprived the farmers of economic incentives for producing higher-quality rice more efficiently.

In the areas of non-rice production, the selection of crops was subject to official regulation, and highly profitable cash crops, such as cotton and sugar cane, were kept under the government's direct control.

While clear improvements, such as the introduction of new kinds of crops, retail trade, marketing and exportation, have been observed since the beginning of the twenty-first century, the government's agricultural policy still remained either highly quantity oriented and ignoring of price or excessively supply-oriented while neglecting demand factors. It should be mandatory for the government to abolish the 'rice trauma' and to honour market-driven price mechanisms so as to give the farmers a proper economic incentive for producing higher-quality, price-competitive rice.

At the same time, the government would be well advised to introduce a new institutional device in order to protect the cultivators from overly fluctuating international rice prices.[3] A renovation of the agrarian financial system would also be needed in order to prevent the farmers from being forced to resort to overly costly informal means of financing. In addition, the poverty-stricken conditions of a large number of landless agricultural labourers need to be improved quickly. This improvement could, for instance, be achieved by the landless becoming tenant farmers under the new Farmland Law of 2012.

8 Sustainable Farming

In the remote areas close to the national borders where government control has been neither very tight nor penetrating, farmers by their own initiative have chosen to replace traditional methods of shifting cultivation with cash crops, such as wheat and garlic. Although natural conditions (such as a highly unpredictable climate, widely varying rainfall and soil quality unfavourable to rice cultivation) are unfavourable, the farmers have managed to keep their income levels more or less stable. This can be attributed to their choosing appropriate crop portfolios, consisting of different kinds of crops with a variety of biological characteristics that make up for the severe environment.

The case studies vividly illustrate the feasibility of sustainable development by honouring the sovereign autonomy of private farmers, who would discover the best crop combinations by properly taking into consideration natural, geographical and market conditions in their farm management. The story may be extended to the possibility of rain-fed, organic rice being grown with minimum levels of chemical fertiliser.

[3] Thailand's experience of 'the rice premium' system may prove to be a good reference point here.

9 Industrialisation

During the Burmese socialist regime, the government kept an inward-looking stance in its economic policy, putting little emphasis on the country's commercial trade with the outside world. State-owned economic enterprises (SOEs), on the other hand, with their relatively high proportion of capital-intensive operations, almost continuously faced financial difficulties. As a result, these enterprises had to be supplemented by government subsidies. This was in itself a factor explaining the government's fiscal deficit. The situation changed little until the early twenty-first century despite the presence of three possible turning points of economic liberalisation: 1961, 1974 and 1988. The first two proved ineffective, while the third was disrupted by the Asian financial crisis of 1997.

Partly for these reasons, Myanmar's manufacturing sector stagnated during most of the second half of the twentieth century. As a result, large shares of manufacturing value outputs were dominated by food processing and textile industries, although some metal-processing activities took place in the Mandalay area.

Nonetheless, since the third economic liberalisation, a sizable number of private entrepreneurs either started up or extended their production activities with some success. These private manufacturing operations were almost exclusively run as family businesses with limited production facilities, whereas trained engineers and sophisticated capital equipment were mostly confined to SOEs. The situation was bound to change, however, in as much as the country is sufficiently equipped with highly motivated human resources: the most important condition for modern economic growth (MEG). In fact, the fourth wave of economic liberalisation arrived as the military junta stepped down in 2008. With the due completion of institutional building needed for market development under the democratic politico-economic set-up, the stage will be ready for full-fledged industrialisation with the sequential (sometimes overlapping) choices of manufacturing industries, being in accordance with the nation's economic comparative advantage.

10 Myanmar-China Economic Relations

When Myanmar's international political isolation was deepened in the late 1990s, it was natural that the country would enjoy/move towards closer relations with China. This was the case not only in the area of official economic assistance but also in commercial trade and foreign direct investment.

During the late twentieth century, the Chinese government concentrated its assistance to Myanmar on the operations of state-owned enterprises, with the consequence that the latter's import-substitution-style industrialisation was promoted. Conversely, in more recent years, a significant shift has been observed, namely, an increased emphasis on the strengthening of Myanmar's social overhead capital – a conspicuous example of which has been the construction of hydraulic power stations,[4] highways and oil and gas pipelines and the exploitation of Myanmar's natural resources.

The closer relationship between Myanmar and China has been influenced not only by their geographic closeness but also by the international political environment. It can be expected that the relationship will take a somewhat different shape in the future as Myanmar is now more closely tied to the international political community.

11 Concluding Remarks: Road Map for Economic Development

Immediately after the collapse of the Soviet Union (USSR) in December 1991, international consensus rapidly showed that a tamed form of capitalism would provide the best economic principle upon which to base economic policy. Under the system of capitalist economic development, industrialisation may be divided into three stages: (1) setting of the initial conditions of three production factors (i.e. capital goods, human resources and land), (2) the phase of market development and (3) that of modern industrialisation.

Initial conditions in stage (1) vary from one country to another, depending partly on the country's natural endowment, political setting and the degree of commercialisation at the terminal point of the nation's premodern age. The style and speed of the early industrialisation process (phase (2)) are affected by the initial conditions that form the characteristics of premodern commercialisation, for example, the extent of monetisation and the degree of mutual trust in interpersonal transactions.

During the phase (2) market development, assuming the country is politically stable, the most important areas for policy consideration are the building of social overhead capital of both physical and social in nature, the development of financial institutions and the building of education and training schemes. In addition, attention should be turned to the establishment of a legal system which is consistent with international standards. The systems of mobilising national savings, to be utilised for private capital formation, and of supplying managerial experts (i.e. business and civil administrators, engineers and entrepreneurs), are also highly essential. Because the gestation period for these systems and processes is often quite long, well-prepared, advanced planning is required.

During the phase of modern industrialisation (3), the choice of industry and technology should be in-line with the economic comparative advantage of the nation, with due attention being paid to the national resource endowment.[5] Concurrently,

[4] It may be noted in passing, however, that a significant portion of the electricity thus generated has been exported to China.

[5] One may argue, however, that Myanmar is in a position to come up with a unique development strategy by taking advantage of its economic 'backwardness'. One recalls here a somewhat similar argument set out by Gerschenkron (1962; first essay).

the role of the public industrial policy is to assist the private sector to overcome information asymmetry, to improve its productive efficiency and to protect against unforeseeable business risk.

Finally, when the economy is sufficiently developed to a point where it reaches the technological frontier, the economic policymakers may let the market take care of itself, intervening only when the latter fails to play its expected role. The policymakers may, for example, step in when external diseconomies are manifest, the risks are too large and/or information asymmetry is too great for the private sector to bear. In addition, it is appropriate for the government to play the role of a referee to ensure that market competition is conducted in a fair and just manner. Most surely, the country in question will then move into sustained economic growth, with due consideration for the betterment of the global environment.

Reference

Gerschenkron, A. (1962). *Economic backwardness in historical perspective: A book of essays.* Cambridge: Harvard University Press.

Index

K. Odaka (ed.), *The Myanmar Economy*, DOI 10.1007/978-4-431-55735-7

MIX
Papier aus verantwortungsvollen Quellen
Paper from responsible sources
FSC® C105338

If you have any concerns about our products,
you can contact us on
ProductSafety@springernature.com

In case Publisher is established outside the EU,
the EU authorized representative is:
Springer Nature Customer Service Center GmbH
Europaplatz 3, 69115 Heidelberg, Germany

Printed by Libri Plureos GmbH
in Hamburg, Germany